THE IDEOLOGICAL PATH TO

SUBMISSION

THE IDEOLOGICAL PATH

TO SUBMISSION

...and what we can do about it

BY HOWARD ROTBERG

mantua books

2017

Published by: Mantua Books Ltd.
Canada
mantuabooks.com
Email: administration@mantuabooks.com

Copyright© 2017 Howard Rotberg

Library and Archives Canada Cataloguing in Publication

Rotberg, Howard, 1951-, author

The ideological path to submission : ...and what we can do about it / Howard Rotberg.

ISBN 978–1–927618–06–6 (softcover)

1. Toleration. 2. Submissiveness. 3. Islamic fundamentalism. 4. Islamic renewal. I. Title.

HM1271.R675 2017   305.8   C2017-902231-8

Cover Art by David Strutt

We wish to acknowledge that some of the chapters in this book are adapted from essays previously published in Frontpage Magazine and Canada Free Press.

*This book is dedicated to Shirley
And to the hope that life in my grandchildren's world will be free of
the ideologies criticized in this book, and that freedom and justice
and human rights will prevail.*

Preliminary Praise for

THE IDEOLOGICAL PATH TO SUBMISSION
...and what we can do about it

"very apt treatment of the Islam problem"

- Daniel Pipes, Middle East Forum

"very impressive ... an approach or framework ... to explain the state of affairs in the West under siege by the totalitarian-minded folks on the left"

- Professor Salim Mansur, Western University

"could even change the direction of discussion about the largest matters"

- Professor Paul Merkley, Emeritus Professor of History, Carleton University

CONTENTS

For those readers who have not already read the book for which this work serves as a sequel, I am providing in this Preface some thoughts contained in my *Tolerism: The Ideology Revealed*. If the reader has already read *Tolerism*, he/she can probably skim through this preface; the following sets out the foundation of my thinking about this ideology which I have named tolerism. The purpose of this book, as a sequel, is to trace the path of current ideologies which have started with tolerist thoughts and now are moving along a path of ideologies, which include the following: inclusive diversity, denialism, multi-culturalism, masochism, undue respect and compassion, empathy, and Islamophilia, which all pave the way for a **submission** of the free world to an ideology called Islamism which is based on Islam and has captured a large part of the leadership of the religion of Islam. To the extent that the West refuses to drive a wedge between ordinary Muslim immigrants to the West and the Islamist political and religious and terrorist leaders, is the extent to which we shall fall into submission.

Some of us feel that the mere toleration of any Muslim immigration is premature until some serious reform is undertaken in some of the problematic verses of the Koran and Hadith. Others prefer not to think about the problem, instead sweeping it under the carpet of multiculturalism and cultural relativism. And others, including myself, argue that along with immigration pauses, we must encourage a re-education of Muslims so that they will find some way to make their religion compatible with liberal democracy and some way to rebel against a leadership, which for too long has been allowed by regular Muslims and western intellectuals alike, to espouse radical concepts. The Islamist challenge to our values might not be a problem to a West that is strong, proud and free, but in the case of a culturally weakened West, with ideologies discussed in this book, we have a problem, that we must stop tolerating and denying in a mass deception that is mind-boggling.

To all those who will say that Islam itself is the problem, I cannot disagree with you. That is why this book canvasses the ideological confusion of the West when faced with this problem. But beyond identifying the problem, we have to work on a solution. The West must seize the initiative from the Islamists and their supporters and direct ourselves to the defeat of the Islamists and their western supporters and the tolerists. We must end western complicity with the Islamists and we must be unafraid to tell our Muslim citizens and immigrants that we in the West expect something very different from them than what exists in their home countries. Winning votes at election time by appeasing local Islamist leadership is suicidal.

Says Muslim Professor of Political Science at Canada's Western University, Salim Mansur, in his book, *Islam's Predicament: Perspectives of a Dissident Muslim*:

> In the face of Muslim extremism and terror that went global with 9/11, there remains the urgent need for Muslims to confront and repudiate those who have perverted their faith, or hijacked it, and made of Islam an ideology of bigotry and war (jihad).
>
> Muslims, Arabs and non-Arabs alike, will not make progress as people and countries unless they subject their history to a critical examination. Their religion, Islam, has been conditioned by their history much more so than the other way around. Subjecting their history to critical examining will open the necessary space for Muslims to progress and reconcile themselves with the requirements of the modern world by separating religion from politics, and by making faith a personal matter between man and God. This is a long, unavoidable and necessary historical process of Muslim reform of their society and of the reformation of Islam.

But western elites, in the name of tolerance, should not be standing in the way of this reformation by supporting, tacitly or otherwise, the Islamists. We must object to their attempts to control and radicalize all Muslims in the West as they do in their home countries. We must clearly and unequivocally stand with the reformers, to the extent of being intolerant of the Islamists. We must stand for the rights of women, gays, children, intellectuals, minorities, and others who are daily abused by the Islamists.

The time for pursuing intellectual arguments on how Islam is the gun powder for the Islamist rifles is past. We now need to pursue strategies of ensuring that our Muslim citizens or prospective immigrants have cleansed the gun powder from their religion. It is their choice, and if they will not do it, we have no obligations to them. That should not become an incendiary discussion when we put it in the proper context. However, we must understand that our leaders, too, have been a problem. This book attempts to put the problems in an ideological perspective, because without understanding the ideologies, we cannot counter them.

We shall later discuss the relationship of Islamism to Islam and we shall study the various words and concepts that have been co-opted into radicalizing Islam rather than acting to liberalize it as more adherents of the faith seek to live among Westerners—who have a heritage of liberal freedoms which stand in contrast to elements of the Islamic faith and doctrine, especially in its radical or Islamist aspects.

The field of philosophy has dealt for many years with a concept it calls "toleration." Professor Andrew Fiala, writing on the concept in the *Internet Encyclopedia of Philosophy*, states that for a person to practice toleration he or she must accept three conditions:

· (1)He must hold a negative judgment about this thing;

· (2)He must have the power to negate this thing; and

· (3)He must deliberately refrain from negation of this thing.

Sir Karl Popper, the great Austrian/British philosopher lived through the cataclysmic events of Stalinism and Nazism and argued that these totalitarian movements created a paradox for philosophical toleration. He put it this way:

> If we extend unlimited tolerance even to those who are intolerant, if we are not prepared to defend a tolerant society against the onslaught of the intolerant, then the tolerant will be destroyed, and tolerance with them. … We should therefore claim, in the name of tolerance, the right not to tolerate the intolerant.

Philosopher John Rawls devoted a section of his influential book *A Theory of Justice* to this problem: whether a just society should or should not tolerate the intolerant. He also addressed the related issue of whether or not the intolerant have any right to complain when they are not tolerated, within their society.

Rawls concluded that a just society must be tolerant; therefore, the intolerant must be tolerated, for otherwise, the society would then itself be intolerant, and thus unjust. However, Rawls qualified this conclusion by insisting, like Popper, that society and its social institutions have a reasonable right of self-preservation that supersedes the principle of tolerance. Hence, the intolerant must be tolerated but *only insofar as they do not endanger the tolerant society and its institutions*. Indeed, Popper himself wrote in 1981's *Toleration and Intellectual Responsibility* that we should tolerate intolerant minorities who wish to simply publish their theories as rational proposals, and that we should simply bring to their attention that tolerance is based on mutuality and reciprocity, and that our duty to tolerate a minority ends when they resort to violence.

More difficult, says Popper, is when an intolerant minority passes from rational thought to violence – for example, what of incitement to violence or conspiracy to overthrow liberal democratic institutions? Popper says that the difficulty in finding the dividing line between criminal and non-criminal acts or words should not pose more of a problem here than in other areas of the law, where illegality is a matter of degree and jurisprudence.

Popper warns of the difference between a political party pledged to uphold all the institutions and laws of liberal democracy even if it obtains a majority which would allow it to do otherwise, and a party that conspires, either openly or in secret, to abolish liberal democracy. Such a party will necessarily resort to violence, and to Popper it is clear that we must not submit to such illiberal acts, even if that party has obtained a majority.

To Popper, then, it is clear that should such a party claim a right to be tolerated, the theory of liberal democracy should say no. Popper states: **"We must not tolerate even the threat of intolerance; and we must not tolerate it if the threat is getting serious."**

This does not mean that we should give up on rational refutations of their intolerant ideas, and their advocacy of violence. Popper argues that almost all such parties seek to justify their violence in a similar way: they allege that our tolerance and our democracy is just a sham, and that we, the allegedly tolerant, were first to use violence and in fact we use violence all the time. Popper draws on the events of his lifetime: he notes how in 1917 it was argued in support of the Communist violence that it was Capitalism that was really the violent system. This was of course followed by an orgy of killing and imprisonment by the Communists. Then came the horror of the Nazi years and the pursuit of the utopia of the Third Reich, based on the slaughter of millions.

Says Popper: **"After these events in Germany, I gave up my absolute commitment to non-violence. I realized there was a limit to toleration."**

But, the reader shall surely wonder whether Popper's theories are useful in practice.

Would that every individual could approach every issue with the logical approach of the great philosophers; the reality is that individuals instead are either indifferent or skeptical or otherwise impatient of the philosophical approach. Popper himself warned of the undue deference given by Mills and others to the concept of individual autonomy, when he wrote that, "No rational argument will have a rational effect on a man who does not want to adopt a rational attitude."

Popper was wise enough to warn of the power of intellectuals: "we the intellectuals, have done the most terrible harm for thousands of years. Mass murder in the name of an idea, a doctrine, a theory, a religion—that is all 'our' doing, 'our' invention: the invention of the intellectuals."

And yet he warned of the fear of freedom when the common man must confront the limits of toleration: Popper picks up, in his work, on the Freudian refrain that there exists a conflict between the demands of civilized society and the instincts implanted in every person, as he writes: "… most people do not really want freedom, because freedom involves responsibility, and most people are frightened of responsibility."

And so, in my view, for the intellectual pursuing a grand Idea, or the common person afraid to take the responsibility of freedom, both filter their words and actions through a world view, and that world view is Ideology.

And the ideology of excessive faith in philosophical toleration is what I call tolerism.

The problem is that tolerists, having adopted tolerance as their overriding value and principle to the exclusion of all other ideas, cannot undertake the exercise that Rawls took when dealing with a solution of Popper's paradox. Of course, the debate should be, as Rawls formulated it, that the intolerant must be tolerated *only insofar as they do not endanger the tolerant society and its institutions.* Sadly, the ideology of tolerism uses the idea of tolerance not as a starting point for debate, but as a way to *close off* further debate. Their ideology has contaminated philosophical toleration. For the tolerists, the sole measure of the good life is how lenient they can be to the intolerant others, and in fact how much they can run from the responsibilities of freedom to negate their own liberal democracies and embrace relativism and moral skepticism.

Running from the responsibility that the exercise of freedom, and its maintenance under the threats of the intolerant, results in the supposed tolerists being the least committed of all to the responsibilities of dealing with the threats to our values. It is far too easy to censor, to embrace human rights commissions, non-governmental organizations and the United Nations and abrogate all decisions to them. To the extent that tolerism chooses that route, we should not be surprised when our enemies outvote us and our lower middle classes embrace parties of the far right.

One of the great tragedies of our education system in the modern era, is that after seeing the mischief of fascist and communist ideologies, especially in the Second World War, we have failed to make scrutiny of ideologies our primary focus. This has in turn led to the silliness professed by today's liberals that they are somehow "post ideological." They argue, with a straight face, that if one is truly tolerant, fair and pacifist, then one is free of the ideologies that plague the so-called right wing or the so-called Marxist left.

This of course is preposterous. The position that one is free of ideology is actually an ideology itself – the ideology of thinking that one is capable of divorcing oneself from all the cultural values and ways of seeing the world that are inherent in today's fashionable commentators, educational institutions and politicians.

Of course, ideology is easier to see when one looks backwards. It is also easier to see when one looks at those with whom one disagrees. But I can think of nothing as important in a democracy for educators to help students understand the origins and transmission of cultural values and ideologies.

And so, I have coined the term *tolerism* to try to understand the ideology so dominating the West today. I do not expect my views to be exactly welcomed by those whom this book critiques. For one of the very essences of tolerism is the intolerant response to criticism, and in fact the shunning of those like Phyllis Chesler who dare to examine the politically incorrect topics.

Nevertheless, as a lifelong student of the Nazi ideology that made possible the murder of my grandparents and aunt in the gas chambers of Auschwitz, I struggle constantly with the fear that contemporary ideologies are again making the murder of Jewish children or grandparents respectable. How else can one make sense of the lack of critical response to the Palestinian suicide bombers sent by their parents to kill as many civilians as possible, on their way to an Islamist heaven of virgins awaiting? Having spent time in Israel and knowing the Israeli longing for peace and even accepting for many years the idea of a two-state solution with genocidal Palestinians given land within firing distance, and knowing that Arab Israelis are the freest Arabs in the mid-East, I know that, while Israel is far from perfect, it is far from morally equivalent to the totalitarian Islamist indoctrination of murder and hate inculcated in controlled media, education systems and mosques.

Regarding those who purport to be beacons of tolerance yet are in fact complicit in the various ideologies of hate and totalitarian violence, it is apparent that their excessive tolerance and leniency for those who are in fact *enemies* of our political freedoms, has gone beyond tolerance and into the realm of the ideology of *tolerism*. Then, we ask in this new book, does tolerism conduce to an eventual ideology of submission?

How else can one understand that the Europeans' harshest criticism was not for the suicide bombers, but for the Israelis who were forced to put up fences and walls to stop the suicide bombers from their near daily atrocities in 2001 to 2003, before the fences had their effect? And how can one fail to understand that the moral failings of Europe in the twentieth century should probably disentitle it from passing judgment on anyone? From colonial and imperial abuses to the fascist acts or complicity with the Nazis, Europe has lost the moral authority it thinks it has. The nerve of countries like Belgium and Spain to set themselves up as having the authority to judge Israelis is preposterous. Belgium, which pulled its soldiers out of Rwanda which made the genocide there more probable, has no right to lecture anybody. Spain, which has the highest incidence of anti-Semitism in all of Europe, should take care of its own intolerance before making tolerist speeches against others.

As the Jews, and hence the Jewish state, are essentially the "canaries" in the mine, the failure of Western morality to understand the manipulation of truth and journalism in favor of totalitarian regimes and against liberal democracies, amounts to a modern tragedy.

Accordingly, having a family history and a religious orientation and an occupation (I am a retired lawyer) that all stress justice as a more important value than tolerance, I am predisposed to an investigation of the *limits* of tolerance. And accordingly, we have taken a look at the philosophic position of Karl Popper and others and the quest to understand just where there might be limits to the concept of tolerance or, as the philosophers call it, toleration. We can summarize my book on tolerism as follows:

In the chapter on the ideology of tolerism, we considered tolerism as an excessive tolerance, in fact a leniency, for the intolerant and unsupportable views that threaten our very freedoms. We concluded that tolerism is the skill in consuming massive quantities of political correctness, and moral and cultural relativism, without displaying the obvious signs of the drunken leniency toward, and even taking pleasure in, the slow ascendancy of Islamist values of terrorism, breach of human rights, and attempted reversals of the wonderful liberties and advances made in western societies, where church and state have been successfully separated, and an enormous degree of freedom reigns.

We considered ten aspects of how tolerist ideology works in practice to distort the morality of our political positions. We examined the work of one brave anti-tolerist. We examined how tolerism shuns the truly courageous in their advocacy of human rights and rewards those who simply join the politically correct to heap inappropriate abuse on America and/or Israel.

The Tale of Two University Bombings shows the double standards being applied to Israel. It is the application of double standards which takes such double standards out of the realm of "anti-Zionism" and into the realm of "anti-Semitism." Tolerists routinely try to argue that they are anti-Israel, not anti-Semitic, but the use of flagrant double standards used only against the Jewish state exposes the anti-Semitic strain in tolerism.

Unfortunately, what the world should have learned with the Nazis is that what starts with the Jews seldom stays only with the Jews, and who is next is anybody's guess. We should counsel our gay friends, for example, to stop supporting countries that would imprison them in a minute, and start supporting Israel where a gay soldier can be openly gay, which is more progressive than the situation in America.

To show how the vile ideology of tolerism has even infected the liberal Jews who have organized the various Holocaust museums, commemorations and educational programs, we have a chapter tracing how tolerist views have distorted the very message of such. Too many programs state that they are trying to keep alive the memory of what the Holocaust teaches us, but are too politically correct and tolerist to even state what the supposed message is. And from no message at all, these have now morphed into a vague tolerist invocation of "tolerance" as the message of the Holocaust, when it is the exact opposite. Nothing, in my view, shows how prevalent is tolerism than this contamination of Jewish organizations.

When an ideology is powerful enough to cause such a distortion in the thinking of otherwise good people, it is in fact appropriate to examine the ideology for abnormal thinking, from a psychological viewpoint. And so, I have not hesitated to examine the masochist stream in tolerism and the aspects of delusional thinking and aspects of how terrorism creates abnormal thinking, in the case of our cultural Stockholm syndrome.

Moreover, tolerism has almost become a religion where the use of shunning disposes of the heretics.

Nothing portrays the stark difference between tolerism and justice than an examination of the reaction of the French and Hollywood elites to the arrest of convicted child rapist Roman Polanski and his flight from America to France.

To really understand how an ideology grows in a culture, one has to examine literature and film-making and other cultural realms. These cultural sectors, both reflect tolerist thinking and help spread such thinking to an ever wider group of people. My examination of certain movies for anti-Semitism and tolerism of immoral positions is one of the most important chapters of the book. It is indeed unfortunate that more people will get their history from Spielberg et al. than from the great historians. This is a catastrophe of our era.

This catastrophic cultural abnegation operates in tandem with the ridiculous resolutions by the totalitarian and other corrupted nations that control the United Nations and the moral corruption of Barack Obama awarding a Medal of Freedom to that proprietress of the Durban hatefest, Mary Robinson. All of these matters create cultural symbols which teach our young what is admired and what is rejected, and who are the young people going to believe – the Founding Fathers from hundreds of years ago, or the hip Mr. Obama?

Tolerism as a value seems to be most attractive to those without the traditional values espoused by patriotic Americans. Our exploration of the "multiphrenic" President Obama is meant to examine how confused identities in the post-modern era are conducing to tolerism. The *Singer in the Market* shows that the post-modern confusion, along with masochistic tendencies, are not confined to America but have even contaminated the Israeli public discourse. We shall see, however, later in this new book, how Israel avoids the pitfalls of that type of confusion, by having a strong social resilience that makes terrorism less of a threat than to other western countries.

My essay about tolerism at Berkeley is meant to show just how silly and juvenile that tolerism can make a university. The University of California system, especially the campuses at Irvine and Santa Barbara are infected with such a degree of anti-Israelism and false double standards, that Jewish parents are being warned by Jewish institutions not to send their children to these campuses. Then the

University of California Press thought it was appropriate to publish a recent book by provocateur and now dismissed professor, Norman Finkelstein. While tolerists worry about whether a mentally ill nudist has the right to be nude on campus, they ignore that their campuses are so anti-Semitic that they are becoming Judenrein. California, granted, is not fully representative of the rest of the country. But from Columbia University with its bizarre Middle Eastern Studies Department, and its welcoming of Ahemadinejad, to University of South Florida whose computer engineering professor Sami Al-Arian, was finally arrested as the North American leader of Palestinian Islamic Jihad responsible for killing hundreds of Israeli civilians, and from Harvard welcoming the bizarre anti-intellectual tirade of Iran's Khatami, and over to Berkeley, there is a cancer attacking the intellectual foundations of American universities. Academic freedom should not mean the abnegation of all standards that is inherent in tolerism.

We explored tolerist censorship and how it has affected our political leadership in the West. We looked at Phyllis Chesler and how mainstream feminism has been infected with tolerism. And we looked at Karen Armstrong's attempts to make compassion into another tolerist term of moral equivalency.

We studied how tolerism involves a form of cultural "masochism" and how tolerism has conduced to an ideology of "denialism." These psychological factors are so important, we shall return later to the topic of the ideology of denialism, as this is a major stepping stone on the pathway from tolerism to submission.

The selection of words like "tolerance" and "compassion" as values which supposedly supersede traditional western notions of justice is meant to obfuscate the actual power politics that is inherent in every situation. Proponents of tolerance and compassion are meant to become docile and naive tolerists whose compassion for the enemy continues right up to the time of torture or death. "Turning the other cheek" may appeal to some Christian theologians, but fighting for justice and freedom seems to me a better idea.

One of the most dangerous tolerists in the world today is a former nun named Karen Armstrong who sees herself as an expert on world religions including Islam. She is criticized constantly by students of Islam like Robert Spencer, who see her as an apologist for the excesses of radical Islam, and a symptom of self-hatred in the West. Her ideology of "compassion" to me is a stepping stone to submission.

One of the big problems facing the West today is the issue of self-appointed NGOs (Non-Governmental Organizations) whose agendas are often not clear, who are not responsible in any democratic sense, and who, once they establish a reputation and a financial base, are too often accepted by naive western journalists as having some moral authority.

Karen Armstrong is the moving force behind a new organization called the Charter for Compassion. The organization picked a number of international theologians to draft and vet the document she calls the Charter for Compassion. But the two biggest problems with the whole enterprise are the political and religious values of the organizer, Ms. Armstrong, and the people she has selected to be the international group defining Compassion.

Critics of Armstrong such as Raymond Ibrahim, writing in May 2007 in *National Review Online*, and Robert Spencer, writing in July 2005 in *FrontpageMagazine.com* have discussed in detail how her books have frequently ignored problematic areas of Islamic law, and how she has been, according to Spencer, "propagating ... a highly tendentious version of Islam, as benign as Quakerism and as expansive as the most liberal form of Anglicanism." In *Islam: A Short History*, she blames Christians for the misapprehension that Islam is not a peaceful religion.

We cannot defeat an enemy like Islamism, when there are too many like Armstrong – who believe that tolerant liberal Americans and intolerant illiberal terrorists all need just an equal dose of compassion.

Look at Armstrong's conclusion in *Islam: A Short History*:

> The West has not been wholly responsible for the extreme forms of Islam, which have cultivated a violence that violates the most sacred canons of religion. But the West has certainly contributed to this development and, to assuage the fear and despair that lies at the root of all fundamentalist vision, should cultivate a more accurate appreciation of Islam.

And so, ignoring those parts of Islamic texts that are embarrassing for Armstrong's idealized vision of Islam, and emphasizing that it is not forces within Islam that has caused violence, but the West's 'contribut(ion)', are typically tolerist in nature.

In a September, 2009 interview with the *Vancouver Sun's* Douglas Todd, Armstrong is said by Todd to argue that there is not much true compassion being practiced in the West these days. He then quotes her: "This is not a compassionate society, no matter what we tell ourselves. We are a superficial and frequently unkind society."

But as to Islam, Armstrong waxes enthusiastically that it is a religion devoted to the "ethics of compassion." She quotes from the Hadith: "Not one of you can (truly) believe if you do not want for your (believing) brother what you want for yourself."

The problem with Armstrong is that she is starting from a position that there is moral equivalency between "the frequently unkind" West and the Muslim countries who have no developed human rights law like the West but are somehow compassionate. Ask an Egyptian Coptic Christian how "compassionate" is the Islamic regime in Egypt or an Yzedi or Christian how compassionate are the Arab Muslims of Syria and Iraq.

Do we think that Armstrong is doing anything real to temper religious extremism? Or is she really about legitimizing Islamic fundamentalism as part of her pattern of moral equivalency?

Rabbi Brad Hirschfield, president of CLAL – The National Jewish Center for Learning and Leadership, is an Orthodox Rabbi, and he too is concerned with compassion and the problems caused by fanaticism. In fact, he authored a book entitled, *You Don't Have to Be Wrong For Me to Be Right: Finding Faith Without Fanaticism.*

But Rabbi Hirschfield is not a fan of Armstrong's approach; he is a moderate, modern Orthodox Jewish leader, who writes against extremism, and sums up the argument against Armstrong's approach:

> I have never met anyone who is opposed to compassion in theory, including people ... who are engaged in violence against those who do not share their faith ... And so, what we really need is not a charter about how we ought to feel about others, to which all will attach their names and then begin making exceptions. What we need is an agreement about how we understand our own belief, how to practice the kind of modesty which assures that we not seek the destruction of those with whom we have genuine difference.

> Before we start engaging people in grand declarations about how they ought to feel, I would settle for a year of teaching the faithful in every community about the sacredness of modesty, humility, questioning, and even doubt as expressions of real faith. When people experience that posture as rooted in the depths of the tradition they love, be it a faith, philosophy or politics, fewer people around the world will die in the names of those traditions. That would be more than enough for most of us, I think, at least for now.

I don't think that Rabbi Hirschfield is a captive of moral equivalency. His argument, to me, in fact, is useful to negate the moral equivalency which I feel is endemic in Karen Armstrong's work; that is, without equating our traditions of liberal freedoms and tolerance with those who in fact have little in the way of freedoms and tolerance (which to me is the flaw in the Charter of Compassion), it is better for well meaning people of all traditions to come together to renounce violent conquest, terrorist attempts at forcing submission to their values, and the power politics implicit in immigrating to other countries and then demanding that they change their liberal traditions because they are "offensive" to those who disagree with the freedoms in the countries to which they have immigrated.

To me, the moral equivalency of Karen Armstrong and her undue deference to Islam as practiced in some of the world's most oppressive regimes is simply an act of tolerism. To me, the values that are important are freedom and justice. My fear is that Armstrong's work submits to values that are inimical to freedom and justice, all in the name of a value – Compassion – which, I agree with Rabbi Hirschfield, cannot withstand the culture and value wars being fought with illiberal forces in the world today. Writers like Armstrong who blame, to any degree, the liberal West for the illiberal forces in Islam, cannot be trusted as moral leaders in today's crazy world.

And so, we arrived through our study of tolerism at our reluctant, but considered conclusion:

The generations born into the freest, richest, most attractive societies in the history of mankind have too often failed to use their opportunities to pass on to their children a legacy of justice and adherence to the best, most righteous moral values. Instead, we leave a huge legacy of government debt and we have demonstrated a failure to take individual responsibility and a desire to blame others, including the long suffering target of the periodic evil inclinations of Western civilization, those canaries in the mine, the Jews.

Europeans relish the chance to reverse their historical evils by finding moral equivalency everywhere. Most shamefully, they seek to assuage their historical guilt by allegations that the Jews are the new Nazis and the Palestinians are the new Jews. The only problem is that they are speaking nonsense, and such positions are only understandable to analysts of abnormal psychology. The fear of freedom continues; the European love affair with violence and totalitarianism continues—for the Left, through their Islamist proxies, and for the Right (too often) through the revived nationalist/fascist parties, which are the common man's resistance to the dead end provided by their leftist elites.

I devoted much attention in the book to the sad case of the Palestinians. That is because I believe that without the tolerism shown to them, the tolerance of their inculcation of hatred in their children, the tolerance of hijackings, then suicide bombings, and now the tolerance of Iranian terrorist proxies like Hamas and Hezbollah, there would be no Palestinian problem. They would have long since accepted Israeli proposals for an independent state in most of the West Bank and Gaza and they would have long since been working with Israel for the economic benefit of their people. Instead, the tolerists, especially in Europe, but also in the United States (Clinton repeatedly welcomed the arch-terrorist Arafat to the White House), rewarded bad behavior and refrained from asking the Palestinians to take some responsibility for peace. So, to those who disagree with me on the Israel-Palestinian problem, I am sorry, but it is the clearest case, and therefore the example most cited in this book, of the mischief caused by tolerism.

Being threatened the most by Islamists, Israeli security experts like Lior Akerman, formerly of the Shin Bet security service, have studied the situation the most. He believes that the two organizations pledged to Israel's destruction, Hamas and Hezbollah, grow every year and every year increase their military strength. Akerman, writing in the *Jerusalem Post* on February 9, 2017, "We can't let radical Islam take over the world," says that Sunni Hamas has some 15,000 to 20,000 fighters as well as tens of thousands of supporters. Shiite Hezbollah has about 35,000 regular and reserve fighters and tens of thousands of volunteers.

Adding in the 25,000 ISIS fighters (who may now be declining in number as they begin to lose their war) and various groups in Afghanistan and Pakistan and Boko Haram in Africa, we know that there are now hundreds of thousands of radical Muslim terrorists, together with many supporters and tolerists, all in support of a world-wide caliphate. So, Akerman, argues that, although less than 0.01% of the 1.5 billion Muslims in the world are actively involved in terrorism, and a little less than 0.1% support terrorist organizations, and a maximum of 10% of Muslims support the Islamist religious struggle to obliterate other religions and install a world-wide caliphate, those figures are sufficient to have a state of fear spreading around the world.

And what is the reason for the fear and increased power of the terrorists and their supporters? Akerman writes, "(W)hen Western leaders display weakness, are fearful of using military might, and obey strict international laws regarding military actions and punishing terrorists, this only serves to encourage terrorist organizations."

His view is clear:

> ISIS has operated unhindered for years now. Boko Haram has murdered tens of thousands of people in Africa without anyone batting an eye. And this is how Hamas has remained in power all these years despite its reign of terror. And thus the Western World sits powerless in the face of these terrorist organizations.

Akerman, the security expert, says that we can change this, but a change in mindset is needed, especially among the EU countries. In other words, the EU is the worst case scenario for what I claim are the results of ideological problems. Says Akerman, "There needs to be cooperation by world leaders if we are to take back control from this relatively small number of terrorists who are wreaking havoc on civilians the world over."

I suggest that the world should look after itself and its civilians' safety by leaving Israel alone in its defense against Islamist genocidal terrorism, and stop picking on minor issues like Trump's latest tweet, and come together to fight this problem, which Obama would not do. We are in a war with the Islamists. This is wartime, and certain steps must be taken in wartime.

Let's listen to Akerman:

> Making a successful change would involve imposing emergency regulations in Western countries and carrying out legislative changes that would enable security and intelligence forces to do their jobs properly. Western militaries must engage in action without fearing legal restrictions. Intelligence gathering agencies must share intel and carry out preventative actions that would neutralize terrorist cells. All of this activity must be backed by international law enforcement agencies.

The issue to me involves whether our tolerist governments have passed the point of no return on the path to submission. We hope not.

A significant number of our opinion leaders have begun to hate our goodness and worship the evil aspects of our enemies. They pretend to be tolerant, but are so intolerant of opposing viewpoints that they censor and shun. These people have begun to be masochistic, delusional and, having critiqued all traditional values, have failed to find anything to replace them with. They seem to now pretend to be too sophisticated to worship God but instead worship those who practice infanticide as a means of terror and spousal abuse as a means of social control, and whose every illiberal action are the opposite of what the tolerists purport to rank as important values.

Our opinion leaders are blind to the important debauched symbols of the West and the symbols of Islamofascist rage, destruction, and totalitarianism.

This member of the Second Generation, the children of Holocaust survivors, sees right through the purveyors of mindless tolerance with no limits, the ideologues of tolerism; they are not tolerant at all, except in their embrace of yet another revolt against Good and yet another dance with Evil. They scoff at the concepts of Good and Evil, but their actions are all the proof we need. Believing in nothing, they purport to tolerate everything, but it is not an intellectual position; it is a delusional ideology. Samuel Johnson said that patriotism is the last refuge of scoundrels, but perhaps it is time to say that tolerism is the last refuge of scoundrels. Patriotism, when it applies to a country with a liberal Constitution rather than to one with a dictatorial demagogue, is a positive value; tolerism, when it applies to a liberal society that has lost the will to confront evil, is a negative value. It has the potential to make anything tolerable, including the murder of little children, the abuse of women, the worship of hate and violence in the name of religion, and the abandonment of the lessons of History itself. Therefore, tolerism has a shaky foundation, and is bound to fail as a reasoned and reasonable world view. One hopes that it will be seen for what it is, before too many have died and too many have suffered, from the transformation of the normally positive trait of tolerance into the destructive force of ideological tolerism.

Chapter 1: Starting Down the Path to Submission

Is there reason for any optimism at all? Is it possible that tolerism will be unmasked for the self-destructive ideology that it is?

In the short term, I am pessimistic, mainly because of the lasting influence of President Obama and his tolerist team of advisers. It is incomprehensible that liberal Americans almost elected the corrupt Hillary Clinton (whose close associate Huma Abedin has ties to the Islamist Muslim Brotherhood). I believe that domestic issues of the deficit, the economy, international trade and health care will continue to so absorb the public's attention, that the naivety of the new American appeasement of Radical Islam will be off the radar screen of public concern for awhile. But, since radical Islam intends to march on in its quest for domination and acceptance of its ideological and religious agenda, and since Trump is willing to tackle the difficult issue of vetting Islamic immigrants to America for anti-American Islamist beliefs, Americans will eventually return their attention to the problem that will not go away, and understand that this is wartime.

I am also pessimistic when I hear Tucker Carlson, a conservative commentator on *Fox News*, ask a question of Ayaan Hirsi Ali on his show of March 22, 2017: "There is this feeling that we don't have the moral standing in the West to criticize Islamism." I know that Carlson himself likely does not agree with that statement, but the fact that he inserted this question at the beginning of the interview, shows how prevalent this cultural suicide is becoming. Ali responded that this in part comes from the Islamists who "remind us that we don't have that moral standing, because the Islamists see non-Muslim, even non-Islamist ideas as illegitimate as against the idea of God."

She continued: "I think we empower them, because every time we appease and appease and appease, they see that as in God's hand as making it easier for them to advance their agenda. They don't see us as a decent civilized society that is trying to understand them and give them time..."

The election of Donald Trump is encouraging in that he is willing to stand up to the tolerists, even as they go to ridiculous lengths to delegitimize him. Ayaan Hirsi Ali said to Tucker Carlson, when she was defending the travel ban (although she said it was "clumsily" done):

> I listened to his speech in Youngstown Ohio, and he first of all named the problem – we are at war with *radical Islamic Ideology* – and he put this ideology in the same sequence as fascism, national socialism and communism. Islamists' objective is to get a Sharia-compliant world and he said that is the ideology of the day.

The tolerist media continues to be blind to the nature of its own ideology and continues to name-call instead of understanding the big ideological issues, and focus on the War that we are not winning. To the extent that the media fixates on the often ill-advised "tweets" and off the cuff comments of President Trump, the ideological pathway from tolerism to submission, my basic fear in this new book, could come to pass—in an America where supposedly liberal women march to the orders of Islamists who discriminate against women's basic rights. The fact that the Muslim Brotherhood-tainted Linda Sarsour was an organizer of the large women's march shortly after Trump's election is troubling, to say the least.

Why does the left turn to Islamist radicals for leadership in our own organizations? Robert Laurie writing in *Canada Free Press* in March, 2017, notes:

In addition to Linda Sarsour, Palestinian Rasmea Odeh was a leftist heroine for her prominence with the Women's March and another protest called "A Day Without a Woman." This "leader" was involved in a couple of 1969 supermarket bombings in Israel which ended in the deaths of two students. She spent ten years in prison, before entering the United States on false pretenses.

Finally, Rasmea Odeh will be stripped of her U.S citizenship and forced to leave the country and return to Jordan after failing to disclose to immigration authorities that she had been imprisoned in Israel for committing two terror attacks.

To the women who march under the direction of Sarsour and Odeh, you have one foot in the grave of submission. When the Islamists issue your marching orders, you are certainly not soldiers of freedom.

The quest for petro-dollars will of course skew the policy of Europeans, as European morality continues to flounder. For example, Britain released the terrorist behind the Lockerbie bombing to Libya, where he received a hero's welcome. The release was justified on humanitarian grounds as the terrorist has cancer. But reports suggest that the real reason for this grand humanitarian gesture of tolerance and compassion was further oil deals with Libya.

I believe that Brexit, Britain's exit from the European Union, will have a positive effect on a Britain now more able to formulate an independent policy towards Islamist immigration and domination.

But, granting that Europe may be slipping into Eurabia, the real question is the future of the United States as a bulwark for liberal democracy and the main defense against Islamist terror and totalitarianism. In this connection, we must, I suppose, hope that the better American minds will eventually discover that appeasement of the Islamists is not seen by them as an appreciated compromise, but justification for the methods of terrorism and intimidation as techniques for maximalist aims.

The United States will find out eventually what Israel found out during the Oslo process – the Arabs are not interested in compromise. Israel's Left basically self-destructed after arguing that gifting a state in stages to the Palestinians (without any quid pro quos) on most of the West Bank and Gaza would lead to peace. In fact, it led to the suicide bombing of the Second Intifada, and more and more demands and ever more bizarre demands. As we noted in the case of the Hamas spiritual leader who said that it was a "war crime" to put Holocaust study on the curriculum of Gaza schools, the definition of "war crime" will grow ever wider as long as there is a willing audience for this nonsense.

A couple more examples will suffice. Firstly, the late, great Canadian/American poet, songwriter and performer Leonard Cohen, a non-political type, decided to give a concert in Tel Aviv to be called *A Concert for Reconciliation, Tolerance and Peace*, with proceeds to go to a fund established by Cohen whose mandate was "to provide financial support for organizations and individuals to achieve reconciliation, tolerance and peace between Israelis and Palestinians and thereby advance the recognition and full expression of human rights in this region."

The Palestinians however seem to have well learned from the tolerists that tolerance is meant to be a one-way street: Omar Barghouti of the Palestinian Campaign for the Academic and Cultural Boycott of Israel (PACBI) said:

> This ill-considered project ... is clearly intended to whitewash Israel's violations of international law and human rights." And the Palestinian NGO Network believed the concert "legitimiz(es) the abnormal situation in Palestine, and especially in Gaza, where war crimes were committed by Israel a few months ago, and remain unpunished.

This supposedly "ill-considered project" intended to fund such beneficiaries as The Parents Circle – Families Forum, which seeks to unite bereaved Palestinian and Israeli parents, and promote peace by arranging positive encounters between people who might otherwise have considered each other enemies. It will eventually be recognized by those whose tolerist blinkers are not too tight that the Palestinian leaders who resist these types of projects do so precisely because they oppose peace, they oppose positive encounters and it is in their perceived interest to continue training families and children for hate and for suicide bombing.

Cohen actually wanted to do two concerts, one in Tel Aviv and one in Ramallah. The boycott crowd opposed Cohen going to Judea and Samaria (also known as the West Bank), while some said it would be all right as long as he canceled the Tel Aviv concert.

The idiocy of the tolerist crowd opposing tolerance when it is extended equally to Palestinians and Israelis will hopefully be the eventual undoing of tolerism as a credible ideology. *Tolerism* included a lot of information on the Israel-Palestinian problem, due to my view that it is not an isolated problem, but rather a template for the future. Those who do not learn from it, to paraphrase the famous quote, will be compelled to relive it in their own neighborhoods.

The other example that shows the banality of the evil that is being applied to Israel comes from the 2009 Toronto International Film Festival. The Festival decided to do a "City to City Spotlight" on Tel Aviv, which was celebrating its 100th anniversary as a city. The Festival's website promised that the 10-movie series would "explore the evolving urban experience while presenting the best documentary and fiction films from and about a selected city." John Greyson, a professor at York University's film department, and a leading director of gay-themed movies, decided to pull his movie from the Festival's regular program. His reason was Israel's "occupation" of the West Bank and also that the movies were too uncritical of Israel. (Anyone who monitors the Israeli movie and art scene, the literary scene and the media, know that self-criticism of Israel is a major art form in Israel.)

How long will it take before the mainstream will start to understand that people like Greyson are either outright anti-Semites or just plain stupid, or both? The Israeli movies shown included *The Bubble* by Eytan Fox, about a gay relationship between an Israeli Jew and a Palestinian Arab, and *Jaffa*, a contemporary Romeo and Juliet story about a doomed romance between a Jewish woman and an Arab mechanic who works in her father's garage. They also included *Bena* by Niv Klainer about a father who tries to keep his schizophrenic son out of a psychiatric institution by bringing home an illegal Thai alien to care for his son, and *Kirot* by Danny Lerner about a Russian illegal immigrant who is forced into violence.

In other words the brilliant Professor Greyson is boycotting the Israeli film series that takes on the difficult themes of gay relationships between Israelis and Palestinians, heterosexual relationships between them, illegal immigrants, mental illness, and violence. In other words, in Israel's film industry, very little is taboo, most themes are "tolerated." There is nothing comparable in the entire Muslim world.

Israel has a culturally rich and thriving gay scene, with Pride parades in Tel Aviv and even in Jerusalem. As Jerusalem is in large part Orthodox Jewish, it shows that freedom for gays is more important to Israelis than offending the religious sensibilities of a significant religious group. That is a lesson for Western tolerists who constantly worry about giving offense to Islamists and other Muslims and tolerate an erosion of our liberties to prevent that. Greyson cannot see that, of course, because an ideology of hate has put blinkers on him. Israel is one of the few countries in the world where gays can serve in the Army as acknowledged gays without limiting their careers.

For North American gays to make common cause with Palestinians (where gays are persecuted) against Israel (where gays have equal rights) is indicative that their hatred for the Jewish state is greater than their commitment to gay rights. Surely some gays will start to recognize the ludicrousness of that position. Tolerism that tolerates the persecutors of gays while denying the legitimacy of the one country in the Middle East that gives rights to gays, is a dead end position and one has to have confidence that it will be seen as such.

Greyson's decision was later supported by some 50 signatories to a letter accusing the Film Festival of becoming "complicit in the Israeli propaganda machine." Such signatories, including actors Jane Fonda and Danny Glover, anti-Israel Jew Naomi Klein and author Alice Walker, appear not to understand the difference between a free arts scene in Israel and the totalitarian states where propaganda is in fact possible. The headline of their open letter was "No celebration of occupation." This seemed to imply that Tel Aviv was somehow occupied territory, rather than being the heart of Israel, where the first neighborhoods were built out of sand dunes in 1887. Robert Lantos, the award-winning film producer, was so disgusted that, in a column in Canada's *Globe and Mail* on September 10, 2009, wrote: "If (Tel Aviv) is disputed territory, then Ms. Klein and her armchair storm troopers are clamouring for nothing short of the annihilation of the Jewish state. They are effectively Mahmoud Ahmadinejad's local fifth column."

(The confused Ms. Klein had written a letter to the film festival which included the following telling remark: "The city of Jaffa (was) Palestine's main cultural hub until 1948." Lantos commented that "This seemingly factual statement fails to mention the detail that there was no such thing as Palestine prior to 1948.")

Greyson, a few years later, found himself, most ironically, a tortured and beaten detainee, without charges filed, in an Egyptian jail, when he and a physician friend, stopped in Egypt, on their way to help Hamas in Gaza. Seeing a protest, the physician started treating some injured protesters and Greyson began filming, a sequence of events that ended up with their incarceration in the Egyptian jail for a month.

Almost all mainstream Canadian media omitted completely any mention of Greyson's political activities against Israel, including the fact that he has been a leader of Queers Against Israeli Apartheid, and also that his physician friend, Dr. Lobani was an activist with the militantly anti-Israel International Solidarity Movement and was once arrested for his activities in the so-called West Bank area.

Many weeks went by before a *Globe and Mail* columnist, the courageous Margaret Wente, did a column exposing the pair as "grandstanders" with a radical agenda, who should have known better than to get involved in any way in an Egyptian protest. Wente was immediately faced with a barrage of criticism from the Left that she should not have mentioned in her column that Greyson is a gay activist and maker of gay-themed films, despite the fact that Greyson's entire persona revolves around his homosexuality and nearly every internet posting about him confirms that. One would also think it relevant to report that gays in Egypt are persecuted, but mainstream media are reluctant to report that.

All of Greyson's earlier actions regarding the Toronto film festival, and his leftist support, resembles, chillingly, McCarthyism in the 1950s in the United States, where filmmakers publicly betrayed their colleagues as Communist to have them silenced for their political beliefs. Now, Jane Fonda betrays Israeli filmmakers. Who will she betray next – will it be an American pro-Israel filmmaker? Will it be me? Where it stops, nobody knows.

One can view all this as the ultimate dumbing down of Canada/America brought on by the tolerist ideology, and the beginning of a long, dark era. However, one who has confidence in the morality of Americans, in the age of Trump, might hope that in fact these excesses might signal the beginning of the end of this dangerous but silly thinking, as more people start to take offense at the tolerist agenda. But it shall only be the beginning of the end if the advocates of freedom and liberalism actually step forward to shed the light of ideological clear-thinking on this nonsense. If not, my two books on tolerism shall be unhappily prescient if we continue along the path from tolerism to submission, the steps for which are the subject of this book.

Hopefully, Trump will reverse the ideology of "globalism," which conduces to submission in two ways: First, it concentrates both economic power and jobs outside of one's own nation, concentrating power to the "global supra-national elites," who can use that economic power and the power of non-governmental organizations against liberal nation-states; second, it gives political power to international organizations, dominated by Islamists or Leftists, and supports "open borders." As such, globalism has more in common with communism than it does with the American Constitution.

We must understand that the Americans and Europeans who want to delegitimize Israel by boycotting every product or service from that liberal country are in fact precisely anti-Semitic and self-hating of freedom. We must critique them in that light. The challenge is to do this in such a way that we can maintain our sanity and our enjoyment of the goodness that life has to offer, lest our children run away from our values due to a perception that they create too sad and difficult a life for the proponents of such values, while the adoption of tolerist ideology offers an easy way out. Ultimately, we must prevent this by teaching our children that freedom and justice take work and constant vigilance, but the satisfactions of life in a liberal democracy, where justice rules, are well worth the effort.

In this connection, Professor Gil Troy of Montreal's McGill University, counseled those who are fighting the anti-Semitic demonization of Israel: "The best response to all this ugliness is to foster as much beauty as possible in the modern Jewish state. Better to spend more time building an enlightened, just, democratic, fair, prosperous and fun country than fighting calumnies." But Professor Troy might be underestimating the extent to which many Arabs and western leftists have come to hate the beauty and joy of the Israelis, just as they hate its freedoms.

And so, we must show the world that while tolerance is important, it has limits. We must show the world that justice is compatible with Joy, but the excessive leniency of tolerism and the steps based on the sad ideologies (stemming from tolerism) and exposed in this book, will eradicate both justice and joy, within a generation.

Our leaders of human rights organizations, even Jewish organizations, must rise to a greater moral and political standing by demanding action to negate the words and actions of these self-hating tolerists, in the name of preserving freedom, justice and happiness in the world. We must understand that Israel is just one battleground in a world-wide war, which has already distorted British liberal democracy, and could soon do the same in North America. We must not be shy about articulately negating the very bizarre assumptions behind the tolerist arguments, and where necessary, refusing to grant them the dignity of being taken seriously. That is not censorship; instead it is the very necessary step of upholding intellectual and moral standards in the face of totalitarian attempts to use our tolerance against us.

Now, we are in danger of the tolerists, even leftist tolerist Jews, leading the way to a submission to Islamist values. For example, the hysterically anti-Israel and anti-Trump columnist for the *New York Times*, Thomas Friedman, on February 15, 2017, had the nerve to charge Israel that by "legalizing this land grab by settlers deep in Palestinian (sic) areas, (it) is not an act of security — it will actually create security problems. It is an act of moral turpitude that will make it even harder to ever find that Palestinian partner and will undermine the moral foundations of the state. This is about right versus wrong." Mr. Friedman's inability to understand that the Arabs have since 1948 been the ones to wage war to "grab" land, and the Israelis have only been defending themselves against genocide, including armed attacks rockets fired intentionally on Israeli civilians including school buses and kindergartens, is the act of "moral turpitude."

Israel does not need to listen to Friedman's ilk as it is has offered repeatedly to buy peace through land transfers to the Palestinians when its offers, as in the case of the Oslo Process, have been answered with murder. Friedman goes so far as to take it upon himself to argue that the debate over Israel handing over more land to the militants and terrorists now launching missiles from Gaza, is going to divide the Jewish people, when it is my belief that it is the absurd anti-Israelism of Friedman and his colleague Roger Cohen and folks like Peter Beinart, which are dividing the Jewish people. Friedman would lead, if he could, the Jewish people into complete submission.

It is my hope that understanding the nature of the tolerist ideology, like understanding the nature of any enemy, is the first step in defeating that enemy. The book that follows shows why defeating tolerism is so important. It seeks to expose the ideological confusion that could further a submission, whether it is an extremely utopian acceptance of radical Islam, or more possible, a slow appeasement and tolerance of mainstream Muslim values by a culturally tired West, which does not understand that there is a culture war between their "group rights" against our "liberal individualistic" human rights. The extent to which a culturally tired West questions its own "moral standing" to criticize and otherwise resist the Islamists, is the extent to which we have started along the pathway to submission.

To start, we must explore carefully the difference between Islam and Islamism; and only later will it become clear what is the real problem and what is it that we must be fighting against, lest we fall into submission.

CHAPTER 2: ISLAM AND ISLAMISM

Discerning the Various Islams

I use the term "Islamism" to describe the ideology of members of radical Islam—and those who are complicit with them—who believe that the West must "submit" to Islam and who use violence and other illegal acts, and who define "jihad" as an outer-directed struggle to create a restored caliphate, rather than an inner-directed struggle for goodness., and who believe in Daar Al-Islam, meaning that once a territory is ruled by Islam it must never be ruled by anyone else, (and hence Israel and Spain, as two examples, must return to Islamic control), and who believe that wherever Muslims settle they should be governed by Sharia law rather than the secular law of the land.

Islam is a religion with various problems in its Holy books that must be reformed or interpreted so that illiberal and hateful aspects be removed. It would help discussions of "Islamophobia" to understand that there are many types of Islam, not just Sunni versus Shiite, but types that have more or less fidelity to certain practices found objectionable by the liberal West. Islamism is the powerful movement that seeks to use those very illiberal aspects to control their own people and wage an asymmetrical war against the West and implement Sharia law in a world wide caliphate, enforcing submission to its dictates. Like so much of what passes for politics, it is a game all about power. It is time to stop the denial that the situation is otherwise.

We must overcome our denial and our psychological fantasies that cause us to think we can control Islamism. The only way to do it, is to overcome our reluctance to tell people of religion that certain matters will not be tolerated in the West; from honor killings to female genital mutilation, to strict Sharia law enforcement for crimes, to the abuse of women, gays and ethnic or religious minorities, it is time to declare, courageously and unapologetically that we welcome as immigrants only those willing to be part of a reformed Islam— without the barbaric cultural practices that should have been left in the Middle Ages. It is not our fault that Islam has developed in such a way that it is threatening our freedoms, but it is our duty to plainly distinguish Islamism from Islam and act to defeat Islamism. In this way we shall help people to have the power to make Islam more compatible with a culture of liberty and human rights. After the Obama administration's abject failure in this regard, we have no time to waste.

But to be clear, it is up to Muslims to reform themselves if they wish to participate in Western political culture; people like me cannot do it for them. We can reasonably expect Muslim immigrants to the West to pledge allegiance to our Constitutions and confirm that taking up residence in the West means that where Sharia law and our Constitutions conflict, they will be loyal to our Constitutions. I understand the many bloggers and commentators who argue that Islam itself contains the seeds of Islamism; but we cannot wage war against more than a billion people practicing Islam who are not a direct threat to us. In my opinion, we must acknowledge the way that the Islamist enemy feeds off of Islam, but while in theory we could starve the Islamists by attacking their food source, and attack all Muslims, in practice that is very wrong. On the other hand, we must stand for freedom and justice and western values based on such, not appeasing concepts like diversity or multiculturalism, which ultimately lead to submission.

Yes, I know that Turkey, once a secular Muslim state under Ataturk, has become Islamist under Erdogan, and in the modern era, Islamic states tend to become more Islamist than less Islamist over time. And yes, I know that Erdogan has said, "The Term 'Moderate Islam' Is Ugly And Offensive; There Is No Moderate Islam; Islam Is Islam."

Erdogan is an Islamist and therefore his comments are suspect and let us look at why they are suspect.

Daniel Pipes quotes from comments Erdogan made in the United States back in 2004. Reacting to the term, "Islamic terrorism," Erdogan stated:

> Such a definition saddens not only the Muslims, but also those who believe in other religions. No religion permits terrorism. Therefore, it is very ugly to put the word *Islam* before *terrorism*. You may say *religious terrorist* but you can't say *Islamic terrorist*.

Reacting to the term, "moderate Islam," Erdogan, who has moved Turkey closer to Islamism, stated:

> Turkey is not a country where moderate Islam prevails. This expression is wrong. The word Islam is uninflected, it is only Islam. If you say *moderate Islam*, then an alternative is created, and that is *immoderate Islam*. As a Muslim, I can't accept such a concept. Islam rejects extreme concepts. I am not an extreme Muslim. We are Muslims who have found a middle road.

Erdogan, despite Turkey's membership in NATO which predates him, is quite wrong. Saying that there is only one Islam, and that is the Islam promoted by an Islamist like Erdogan, validates the equally incorrect view of the hard-core anti-Muslim crowd, who say that we must oppose all Islam. Such thinking places us in a corner where hard core Islamists and hard-core anti-Muslims both agree about the one extreme Islam, that it cannot be reformed. Then those of us in the middle have nobody to listen to us, when we say that it is up to Muslims to make Islam acceptable to the western liberal world; that their problems are not the fault of the West; that it is up to them, not us, to solve the problem of Islamism; and if they do not fix the problem on their own, we shall start applying not only the "extreme vetting" that Trump promises for prospective Muslim immigrants, but "extreme intolerance" for Islamism in any mask it assumes. We must bear in mind that Islamism, feeding off of Islam, has declared war against the West, and we are ready to fight that war. In wartime, we should remember, certain liberties must be limited to win the war, and such a thing (advocated by Obama) as giving Islamist terrorists the same rights in criminal law as a criminal citizen would have, is just preposterous.

We must understand that the above comments by Erdogan, represent, says Daniel Pipes, writing in *Middle East Forum* in June 2003 "the standard verbal deception that Islamists routinely engage in, hiding their radical utopianism behind the integrity of the Islamic religion. (For a Western analogy, think of Communists who hid behind the label of socialist.)" Later in this book, we shall return to some of Erdogan's more recent mischief as he seeks to control the Turkish Muslim Diaspora, especially in Germany, which is a clear challenge to Western Europe's sovereignty over its citizens.

What then do we make of experts on national security like Jon Guandolo, a former FBI agent, who has a website entitled *Understanding the Threat*, and who provides "strategic and operational training and consulting on the threat of the global Islamic movement?" Let's take a look at his position, based on his understanding of national security.

In an essay on February 26, 2017 entitled "Unfit for Duty", Guandolo criticizes President Trump's choice of new national security adviser – Lieutenant General Herbert Raymond McMaster – and the counter-terrorism adviser to the president of the United States – Sebastian Gorka, on the basis that both unequivocally state the "terrorist" threat America faces has nothing to do with "true" Islam. Guandolo goes so far as to say that "Both men are catastrophically wrong and, therefore, are leading America down a disastrous road towards defeat." Guandolo states:

> 100% of all Islamic doctrine, from elementary, junior high, and high school Islamic text books as well as the highest authorities in Islamic jurisprudence, to include Al Azhar University in Egypt, all clearly and doctrinally state Islam is a "complete way of life (social, cultural, political, military, religious) governed by sharia (Islamic Law)". 100% of all sharia mandates jihad until the world is under Islamic rule, and 100% of sharia only defines "jihad" as warfare against non-Muslims.

He points out that the most widely used junior high text book in U.S. Islamic schools, *What Islam is All About* emphasizes that "The duty of the Muslim citizen is to be loyal to the Islamic state."

I suggest that a good starting point in our struggle for peace and justice in our lands, would be to outlaw teaching materials for young people that direct them as a matter of "duty" to be loyal to the Islamic State. The Islamic State ISIS is an evil entity and I do not accept any ideological or religious argument otherwise. There are plenty of arguments that this book makes to try to persuade the tolerists and the deniers about Islamism. Now that the Democratic Party tolerists of Islamism have lost power, we see a unique opportunity in America to attack Islamism in the name of our values and constitutions and for us to induce those Muslims who want to live here with us, to also attack Islamism and to reform the elements of Sharia law, violent jihadism, anti-non-Muslim, anti-female, anti-gay elements. If they do not want to do this, then I agree that they should not reside here, but should stay in Muslim-majority states. After the tragedies in Iraq and Syria and the near constant warfare in the Muslim world, it is an opportune time to take a strong position in this regard.

It has been about 20 years now that the American scholar Daniel Pipes has been writing about the Middle East and insisting on the differences between Islam and Islamism. In his important 1998 essay, "Islam and Islamism", he brings an important historical perspective to the issue:

> The religion of Islam is essentially a religion of success; it is a winners' religion. The prophet Muhammad fled the city of Mecca in A.D. 622. By 630, only eight years later, he was back in Mecca, now as ruler. The Muslims began as an obscure group in Arabia and within a century ruled a territory from Spain to India. In the year 1000, say, Islam was on top no matter what index of worldly success one looks at—health, wealth, literacy, culture, power. This association became customary and assumed: to be a Muslim, was to be a favorite of God, a winner.
>
> The trauma of modern history that began 200 years ago involved failure. Failure began when Napoleon landed in Alexandria and has continued since then in almost every walk of life—in health, wealth, literacy, culture, and power. Muslims are no longer on top. As the mufti of Jerusalem put it some months ago, "Before, we were masters of the world, and now we're not even master of our own mosques." Herein lies the great trauma, as Wilfred Cantwell Smith pointed out forty years ago in his ground-breaking book *Islam in Modern History*.

It is the response to this failure, and the ever-increasing humiliations for Muslims in the modern world, that fuels Islamism. The Jews, perceived as interlopers, despite historical validation that they are in fact the indigenous people of their area, have built a highly cultured, modern, technologically sophisticated (including high tech and the latest military equipment), nation, which sits there, constantly humiliating the Muslims who in both national entities and terrorist organizations fail to defeat this aspect of liberal modernity in their backyard.

I argue that while we have no right to invade Muslim countries to defeat their Islamist governments (unless, like Iran, they explicitly threaten to exterminate non-Muslim countries like Israel or pose a threat to us), we do have the right to demand of any Muslims who wish to immigrate to the West that they adopt our ways—a secularism, reducing Islam to the private sphere and a reformism, which means modification of illiberal intolerant religious doctrines that make Islam irreconcilable with host countries steeped in the liberal democratic traditions. We in the West must repudiate the ideology of Islamism wherever we see it on our shores, and make its abandonment a prerequisite for Islamic immigration to our countries or participation in government. Otherwise wrapping themselves in the Western doctrine of freedom of religion, the Islamists turn our freedoms against ourselves as they apply supremacist, jihadist, and illiberal Sharia law in lands that cannot accept such cultural and legal warfare.

To those who think that it is an impossible task to separate out Islamist beliefs and practices from basic Islam, I answer this way: If an American Christian man wanted to marry a 13 year old girl or practice polygamy, we don't have to think too hard to say that we would not tolerate such a breach of our basic values. Then, although the task is difficult, we should be able to agree on what other practices promoted by the Islamists are against our values. Instead what we claim to be most important to us—our values based on the Constitution in America—are seldom discussed in the realm of immigration and education and criminal law. We must have a national discussion, not promoting diversity in the abstract, but what diverse values and behavior are acceptable in the name of religion. In the case of Islam, we shall term as "Islamist" the actions that are not acceptable and term as "Muslim" the private religious practices of an Islam, reformed in such a way as to be acceptable to liberal democracies. It will be difficult and time-consuming, and delayed by many lawsuits, but respectfully done, with the aid of the best Muslim reformist minds, it can be done.

Failure to insist on a repudiation of Islamism, makes us appear to Muslims everywhere, weak and unsuccessful and promotes further reliance on Islamism to overcome Islam's failures and humiliations in the last two hundred years. Barack Hussein Obama was a tragedy from which the United States must recover.

Pipes argues that:

> Islamists, not all Muslims, are the problem; they, not all Muslims, must urgently be excluded from the United States and other Western countries. Not just that, but anti-Islamist Muslims are the key to ending the Islamist surge, as they alone can offer a humane and modern alternative to Islamist obscurantism.

Whether this is feasible, it is surely very difficult, especially given the Islamist doctrine of sacred lying, the doctrines emanating from stories about Mohammed, and termed taqiyya (sacred deception and dissimulation), kitman (half-truths) and khodeh (trickery and deceit). The Sunnis advocate Adarorah (the end justifies the means).

Pipes has been, in the way of readership and influence, eclipsed by the anti-Muslim bloggers' world, including Robert Spencer, Pamela Geller, and the like, whose reaction to Islamic illiberal and violent doctrines has been to stipulate that Islam itself is the problem and is unlikely to be reformed enough to remove the threat. On the other hand, Pipes differs from the bloggers by his understanding and even respect for major aspects of the Muslim religion, and his realism that we cannot be at war with a billion Muslims. I believe that exercising our power over our own societies and the laws that govern them with an eye to severing the Islamist response to the role of Muslims in the modern world is necessary and in fact is a kindness to most Muslims; either the Islamists shall submit to us or we shall submit to them. Right now, after eight years of Obama and pro-Islamist administration figures like John Brennan, Valerie Jarrett, and Huma Abedin, the Islamists are on the ascendancy. That is a major failure of the Obama administration. Correcting this is the difficult, yet necessary, role of the Trump administration. With the recent removal by Trump of his anti-Islamist adviser Steve Bannon, it is not clear if Trump will be listening to other anti-Islamist advisers. In any event, anti-Islamists will find themselves hindered every step of the way by the tolerist mainstream media.

After many years of study and reviewing the anti-Muslim blogging world, I believe that Pipes still offers the most realistic and informed way to reduce the power of the Islamists. I suppose his realism as to what is possible is one thing that appeals to me. This book is being written a couple of months after the start of the Trump administration, where President Donald Trump issued an executive order on Jan. 27 establishing radically new procedures to deal with foreigners who apply to enter the United States. Building on his earlier notion of "extreme vetting," the order explains that:

> To protect Americans, the United States must ensure that those admitted to this country do not bear hostile attitudes toward it and its founding principles. The United States cannot, and should not, admit those who do not support the Constitution, or those who would place violent ideologies over American law. In addition, the United States should not admit those who engage in acts of bigotry or hatred (including "honor" killings, other forms of violence against women, or the persecution of those who practice religions different from their own) or those who would oppress Americans of any race, gender, or sexual orientation.

The Democratic Party, the mainstream media, and left liberals in general reacted hysterically to what they term a "ban" on Muslim immigration, which in fact is confined to seven majority Muslim governments where radical Islamists exercise control. (It was later reduced to six.) They have found allies in courts willing to strike down executive action. It is more appropriate to use the word "pause" on such immigration rather than "ban." But as we see, the silly American media, joined by those around the world who have demonstrated time and again their ineptitude dealing with the Islamist problem, are the most vocal in putting down Trump's very necessary attempts to control America's borders. Daniel Pipes again brings a degree of erudition to the issue, lacking in most other commentators:

> This passage raises several questions of translating extreme vetting in practice: How does one distinguish

foreigners who "do not bear hostile attitudes toward it and its founding principles" from those who do? How do government officials figure out "those who would place violent ideologies over American law"? More specifically, given that the new procedures almost exclusively concern the fear of allowing more Islamists into the country, how does one identify them?

Pipes, in his important essay, "Smoking Out Islamists via Extreme Vetting" in *Middle East Quarterly*, Spring 2017, says that "these are doable tasks and the executive order provides the basis to achieve them. At the same time, they are expensive and time-consuming, demanding great skill. Keeping out Islamists can be done, but not easily."

Pipes points out how difficult it can be for immigration officials to know whether an individual is Islamist. But in the above-mentioned article he lists 93 questions that could be used to vet prospective immigrants, in the areas of Islamic doctrine, Islamic pluralism, the State and Islam, female rights, marriage and divorce, sexual activity, schools, criticism of Muslims, fighting Islamism, views on non-Muslims in general, specific views as they relate to Muslims in Dar al-Islam and Dar al-Harb, violence, Western countries, and truth and lying.

Pipes agrees that to truly to protect the country from Islamists requires a major commitment of talent, resources, and time. But, he says that these questions offer a mechanism to separate enemy from friend among Muslims. They also have the benefit of slowing down immigration, as he argues that the West has been taking in too many immigrants too fast, without proper vetting. He quotes a Pew Research Center study that in America, immigrants totaled 5 percent of the population in 1965, 14 percent today, and are projected to make up 18 percent in 2065.

When one looks at the magnitude of the task of vetting immigrants from countries or ideologies that are at war with us, it seems the whole process should be slowed down to ascertain that we get this right, as the effects of failure are a life and death matter.

It seems where the tolerist ideology is strongest, such as Germany and Sweden, the vetting is the weakest, and thus Germany and

Sweden admitted many single males some of whom have participated in sexual assaults and other criminal activity. In the United States under Trump, we can be fairly certain that Pipes' suggestions will be followed. In Canada, there are some concerns, mainly caused by the Government under Justin Trudeau making the admission of a certain number of immigrants by a certain date an election promise, which puts pressure on those doing the vetting and suggests that the vetting will be done in a rushed fashion.

So far, in Canada, we have had certain government documents released to *National Post* newspaper under the Access to Information Act, and reported on February 28, 2017. They seem to show admission to mostly families, often small businessmen or tradesmen, who were working in Lebanon and who were able to freely move between Lebanon and Syria. They contained among them many Armenians and other Christians. These documents, although far from complete, show the numbers and reasons for refusals of Syrian refugees.

The refusal rate for Syrian refugees was 4 per cent according to the documents, which, though released only recently, date to the early stages of the Syrian refugee program, when the Liberal government was trying to fulfill a campaign promise to resettle 25,000 by the end of 2015.

To those who argue that the Koran and the Hadiths all contain anti-Jewish and anti-Christian elements, you are surely right, but Christianity can be interpreted, and has been interpreted, in a very anti-Semitic way, and to be frank there are hundreds of Christian clergy holding vile anti-Israel positions (but there are also hundreds who have goodwill to Israel and the Jewish people.) We must stop being fearful of pushing our agenda based on the great traditions of Judeo-Christian ethics, and extend our hand to the third branch of the Abrahamic religions to join us in giving our people liberal freedoms and separation of religion and politics. If the Islamists want to label us Islamophobic, our future depends on stripping away the power of the Islamists and using every tool at our disposal to convince Muslim immigrants that we accept immigrants who follow a liberal Islam but not Islamism. We must also be clear that not one Muslim majority country welcomes Jews and therefore the anti-

Semitism and anti-Israelism that pervades the Muslim world requires us to insist that not one anti-Semitic Muslim should be allowed to immigrate to the West. On this, we must be firm. A country that gives admission to anti-Semites is declaring war on its Jews. It is bizarre that most Jews do not see it in these terms.

Magnus Norell is an astute commentator in this area and he writes often for Huffington Post. He is an Adjunct Scholar at the Washington Institute for Near East Policy in Washington DC as well as Senior Policy Advisor at the European Foundation for Democracy in Brussels. His research focus is mainly on International Terrorism (particularly of the religiously motivated kind), Political Violence and tensions between religion and politics.

Norell believes as I do, that:

> Islam is a disparate and decentralized religious tradition with a great many different interpretations. By Islamists effectively acquiring the position as representative for Muslim communities, other Muslim groups were marginalized in the sense of who could represent Muslims in relation to political and economic power.

Norell and I both believe that we have been misled to accept the concept that only one definition of Islam exists. The Islamists have been able to set the definition of which is the only "correct" and "true" version. Norell argues that the Muslim Brotherhood and all its successors have been very successful in winning the battle over whose definition of Islam is the "true" one.

He holds that there are two important reasons for this success:

> Firstly, the fact that Western organizational and administrative systems benefited the most well-organized Muslims, since they were the ones who most rapidly and efficiently understood the benefits of organizing themselves and thus present the authorities with a party with which to conduct negotiations. These groups were originally made up of Islamists in general and the Muslim Brotherhood in particular.
>
> Secondly, the internal Muslim debate about Islam plays a major role. Naturally, those who refuse to believe that Islam really needs to play a part in how society is structured and governed have no reason to organize themselves into various Islamic movements. Those representing a more liberal (i.e. a privatized vision of

Islam) and/or a reformist view are thus removed from the agenda already at the outset. The whole point of the Western approach—that various religious movements are endowed with certain representatives—is rendered null and void when individuals show no interest in being defined based on their religious stance and therefore do not consider themselves in need of any religious representatives.

This is where I differ slightly from Norell. I believe that we in the liberal West in order to win the cultural and religious war declared against us, must require Muslim immigrants and organizations that receive public funds to support reformist Muslim organizations, by banning the Islamists. We must realize that abandoning the playing field to the Islamists is deadly and therefore liberal Muslims must advocate, and we must cooperate in such, for a privatized or reformist Western Islam. Yes, I know that many will argue that we have no business messing with anyone's religious beliefs, but my whole point is that tolerism towards Islamism, which is more than a religion, leads to submission; therefore we must be intolerant when it comes to upholding the preservation of liberty, human rights for women, children and gays, etc. Before the Islamists start to acquire the huge political power of attaining the balance of power in our elections, we must reward and support reformist Muslims. Perhaps Norell thinks it is already too late for this, and I am hoping that under Trump, America might assert some control over its Muslim community dominated by Islamists.

And indeed there are groups worthy of support; to prevent submission to the evil part of Islam we must support them. In the United States, there is M. Zuhdi Jasser, M.D., the founder and president of the American Islamic Forum for Democracy (AIFD) and author of *A Battle for the Soul of Islam: An American Muslim Patriot's Fight to Save His Faith* (Simon & Schuster, June 2012). The AIFD has the slogan, "Engaging in the War of Ideas against the ideology of Political Islam." The American Government under Trump should disempower the Muslim Brotherhood associated organizations like CAIR and the Islamic Society of North America, and empower the AIFD. Americans have that choice and must overcome the tolerist ideology that there is only one Islam and that one Islam is radical

Islam or Islamism. It is the most important choice to be made and Trump is correct to pause Muslim immigration from certain countries until a way forward to this end can be organized and inform the immigration system.

In Canada, I am familiar with the leadership of the group Council of Muslims Facing Tomorrow (MFT) (muslimsfacingtomorrow.com). Their president is the great Canadian Muslim woman, Raheel Raza, author of the book *Their Jihad – Not My Jihad*. Their vice-president is the brilliant Canadian Professor of Political Theory at Western University, Salim Mansur, who is the author of the award-winning book, *Delectable Lie: a liberal repudiation of multiculturalism*. Here is the MFT mission statement:

Whereas in the contemporary world the values of individual freedom, human rights and gender equality, science and democracy are cherished universal ideals, yet Muslims and non-Muslim minorities espousing these ideals in countries that are member states of the Organization of Islamic Cooperation face abuse, persecution, and violence; and

Whereas Muslims and people of all other faith traditions need to come together in opposing bigotry in the name of Islam as preached and practiced in the mainstream mosques in Canada and across the Muslim world;

Therefore

Our mission is to reclaim Islam for, as the word itself means, securing Peace for all people, and to oppose extremism, fanaticism and violence in the name of religion; and

Our vision is to advance among Muslims the principle of individual rights and freedoms, and for Muslims to embrace the idea of openness, of relating to others as equal and deserving of equal respect, and of defending freedom of speech as the basis of all other freedoms enunciated in the constitutions of liberal democracies, such as ours in Canada; and, accordingly,

We consider our effort is consistent with the forward-looking reading of the principle enunciated in the Qur'an, "There is no compulsion in religion;" and

We believe our mission and vision are intimately bound with the struggle for Enlightenment among Muslims and Reform of Islam in the modern world; and

In order to succeed we are dedicated to nurturing harmonious coexistence among people of all faith traditions, to supporting open and free intellectual discourse about our history beset with problems that need to be publicly discussed, and to celebrating as Canadians our cultural diversity in all of its aspects.

Norell is correct in stating:

There is no actual non-political Islam to contrast with Islamism. The Christian division "unto Caesar what belongs to Caesar and to God what belongs to God" cannot be applied to Islam. In Islam, religion and politics are intimately intertwined, which makes it very difficult for Muslims who are trying to reform and/or liberalize Islam...over time the Islamists consolidated the power to define Islam both for their "own" group of Muslims and towards European authorities and politicians ... Since it was critical for the Brotherhood to be able to dominate the Muslim group, the result was an unholy alliance between Islamists and the authorities and politicians, who in the midst of their awkwardness and estrangement walked down a treacherous path, ignoring the fact that democratic and secular countries refrain from defining individuals based on religion and ethnicity.

Islamists of all stripes have taken the opportunity to exploit the system. This is logical given how important it is for Islamists to be the ones who decide what Islam is. It is also logical because this implies a sharp division between Muslims and non-Muslims in society. Segregation is promoted for the reason of maintaining control. The many (and more frequent) alarming reports coming out of our more or less ghettoized suburbs detailing how women in particular are oppressed by men attempting to rule over Muslim inhabitants by means of religious dogma are proof of how far this process has gone.

The interesting and remarkable thing is that our politicians and authorities have allowed this to happen. For decades, Islamist organizations have received large sums of money from public funds. This has contributed to increased segregation, problems of integration and an increasing proportion of individuals who decide to act violently.

Our tolerism must stop. We must divorce Western politicians from Islamist, including Muslim Brotherhood, organizations, individuals and funders such as the Wahabist Saudi Arabia.

French Prime Minister Manuel Valls said in January 2015 following the *Charlie Hebdo* shooting,

> It is very important to make clear to people that Islam has nothing to do with ISIS. There is a prejudice in society about this, but on the other hand, I refuse to use this term "Islamophobia," because those who use this word are trying to invalidate any criticism at all of Islamist ideology. The charge of "Islamophobia" is used to silence people.

(theatlantic.com/international/archive/2015/01/french-prime-minister-manuel-valls-on-islamophobia/384592/)

If Prime Minister Valls is right, charges of Islamophobia against critics of Islamism are meant not as a shield against racism, but as a sword to promote submission. The more Islamophobia an Islamist extremist can whip up, the more that Islamist can justify his ideology. The more he can make his case that all westerners are by nature Islamophobic, the more power that Islamist acquires as the charge of Islamophobia becomes self-fulfilling. These Islamists revel in extremist statements and actions, such as promoting the caliphate, Sharia law, threatening Jews and the State of Israel, strict control over women, beheading enemies, etc.

A good example of this reversal of sword and shield is the British Islamist, Anjem Choudary, now in jail. Choudary, born in Britain of Palestinian parents, is not an Islamic scholar. He started out in university studying medicine, but failed his examinations. He then studied law and graduated but was more drawn to Islamism than legal practice. He found that the more extreme he could be, the more publicity he received, and notwithstanding that mainstream Islam in Britain did not support him, he was successful in drawing in a band of disaffected young Muslims, and could count on media coverage. When his hateful message was badly received, that was not because it was hateful, he contends, but because the listeners are Islamophobic.

In Canada, Iqra Khalid, a Liberal Party member of parliament, presented a motion in the House of Commons on December 5, 2016. Motion 103 calls on the government to "condemn Islamophobia and all forms of systemic racism and religious discrimination," asks the government to "recognize the need to quell the increasing public climate of hate and fear," and request for the:

> Commons heritage committee to study how the government could develop a government-wide approach to reducing or

eliminating systemic racism and religious discrimination, including Islamophobia, and collect data to provide context for hate crime reports and to conduct needs assessments for impacted communities. Findings are to be presented within eight months.

Khalid has been "unwilling to entertain any compromise on the specific wording" of Motion 103.

Laws giving special attention to the ill-defined "Islamophobia," (the so-called "Islamic Blasphemy Laws") do in fact restrict free expression in a way that empowers the Islamists who want protection for their extremist views against the light that should be shone on them in a liberal society. Accordingly, Canadian government motion M103, which expresses government intent for future policy, is problematical. Interim Conservative leader Rona Ambrose said she was concerned that charges of "Islamophobia" would be used "to intimidate rather than to inform." Ambrose added: "I do worry that some of my work trying to empower women and girls in Muslim communities could be branded as 'Islamophobic' if I criticize practices that I believe are oppressive."

Conrad Black, *National Post*, February 24, 2017, in his article entitled "Parliament can't simply demand people feel good about Islam", writes about the private members motion in the Canadian Parliament:

> The principal role in strengthening the prestige of the Muslim world will have to be played by the secular and clerical leaders of Islam to enable the other four-fifths of the world to distinguish more easily between the violent fanatics and their fellow travelers and the reasonable majority of Muslims, and to discourage and punish acts of criminal violence against non-Muslim minorities in their midst. The Coptic minority in Egypt, much larger than the Muslim minority in any Western country, and the Christians in Syria and Iraq, have been treated with disgusting brutality and it has scarcely elicited an audible reproof from the civil and ecclesiastical leaders of Islam (or of Western governments, except the Vatican). ...
>
> ... The Islamic leaders are not remotely doing all they can to reassure the world, including the people of this country, of the tolerant spirit of the Muslim majority. Not one per cent of Canadians has any problem with Muslims

and anyone else having and practicing their religion and cultural traditions, as long as they are not an affront to the laws of this country. Islamophobia, in the sense of a visceral dislike of everyone who is a Muslim, is "infinitesimally small" in this country. But those who seek greater respect for Islam have to earn it, not just require it from Parliament, which has no jurisdiction to confect or confer it.

Norell in mid 2015, was optimistic enough to show "a way forward" with respect to international Islamism in an essay at *Huffington Post* which is so good that it deserves a lengthy quote: "A Way Forward—Countering Militant Islamism in the MENA-Region":

> ... it may be fair to ask what possible steps to take in order to counter the trend of increasing terrorist violence across the MENA (Middle East North Africa)-region, as well as in Europe. It's a dark picture to be sure, made even worse by the rise of the Islamic State (IS). But what the rise of IS has also brought forth is a new and more assertive debate in the region about the reasons for this sorry state of affairs. This is a discussion that to a new extent has placed the roots of this religiously motivated Islamist violence in the region itself, pointing out—like for instance Egyptian President Al Sisi did at Davos already in January of this year—that it's an indigenous interpretation of Islam that give IS (and every other like-minded group or organization) a religious sanction in its quest.
>
> This is a very hopeful development, because it means that the people most affected by this violence, are really the only ones that can effectively counter this and reverse the trend. So even if the situation is dire in much of the region there actually are a number of examples of how to combat and even defeat militant Islamism. There are three countries in particular that, in various ways and to different degrees, has successfully bucked the trend and been able— so far at least—to stay stable and fighting off the Islamist threat at the same time;
>
> Morocco, on the North-Western tip of Africa is the Arab country that most successfully has implemented a strategic program in tackling militant Islamism at its core, namely in its religious teachings. This was seen most recently in the newly inaugurated Institute; "Mohammed VI Foundation for African Ulemas." It's an Institute set up to train hundreds of African religious scholars and Imams in ways to counter

religious extremism and violence. In addition, Morocco has made it very costly to join and/or assist the Islamists of the IS (and others). It hasn't stopped volunteers from Morocco to travel to Iraq and Syria, but it has tackled the problem at its root at the same time as it has been able to preserve stability and security back home. And, most importantly perhaps, it has done this at the same time as having implemented a long-term strategic program of democratizing and reforming the country, showing in the process that it is actually possible to effectively combat Islamism on several levels simultaneously.

The second example is Israel, the only truly liberal democracy in the region. What the Israeli example shows more than anything else is that it is possible to successfully develop efficient means of countering militant Islamism without severely curtailing the fundamentals of a solid democracy. Israel faces the same threats concerning terrorism as her Arab neighbors, but does not have the same problems as Moslem countries when it comes to countering volunteers to Islamist groups or organizations. Furthermore, one of the things Islamists are in agreement about is a vicious enmity towards Israel and Jews. Violent anti-Semitism is a constant here. So it's no surprise that Israel and several of her neighbors have found common ground in facing a common threat.

The third example is in some ways the most astounding, by its mere existence. It's the Kurdish Regional Government (KRG). Like Morocco the KRG is juggling a democratizing process with a fight against Islamism. But the Kurds are facing a much more acute situation of course, being on the front-lines of the struggle with IS and also having to deal with the fact that neither Iraq, Iran, Syria nor Turkey are particularly interested in seeing an independent Kurdish state. Nevertheless, the KRG has been able to deal both with external threats, at the same time as handling domestic challenges in pursuing democratic reform-work and trying not to alienate her neighbors.

By 2016, Norell seemed to be getting more pessimistic about reform in Islam. One can hardly blame him as he watches his own country of Sweden ally itself ever more closely with the Islamists. The Swedish tolerism prevents their politicians from seeing that the Islam/Islamist divorce should be their main gift to their Swedish Muslim citizens.

Is his pessimism just realism or is it surrender to the Islamists? Certainly the following is an astutely realistic account of the problem viewed internationally (huffingtonpost.com/magnus-norell/militant-jihadism-a-strat_b_5546469.html):

> ... for the countries in question, militant Islamist violence is fueling everything from civil war to an increase in criminal activity. Several of these countries already suffer from weak (or in some areas non-existent) central governments and are rife with internal ethnic and religious conflicts, adding to the complexity of the situation. Thus, underlying weaknesses with major social and economic problems that have been allowed to fester for decades play right into the hands of organizations that recognize no borders and abhor secular or non-divine authority.
>
> It is important to name the 'white elephant in the room' here. As Gaza lecturer Subhi Al-Yazji was stressing on the Hamas-owned Al-Aqsa TV channel on June 6, (2014), it is a firm belief in the Islamic faith that makes some people embark on Jihad and martyrdom missions (i.e. suicide-attacks). Most of the jihadists are 'rational and mature,' according to Al-Yazji. It is paramount not to discard Al-Yazji as just another extreme preacher. He is just the latest example of a religious scholar, lecturer and/or preacher with an Islamist bent, that are repeating what has been known for decades; that the most important driving force behind much of Islamist-driven violence are a deep and strong religious conviction.
>
> The idea that the activists who are driving all these organizations are either brainwashed or poor and unemployed, are not only proved wrong empirically. It is too often a westernized mode of trying to down-play the religious motivations behind Islamist violence. That is a mistake that the secular, individual-oriented liberal West keeps repeating. The result is a constant inability to look at some of the underlying driving forces behind militant Islamist violence, making the problem much harder to deal with and making it virtually impossible to even make a dent in the trend that keeps seeing individuals leaving the West to pursue jihad in the MENA-region and western and central Asia.

We must acknowledge the enormity of the task before us. For example one can start with the very first chapter (called the "Opening" or Al-Fatihah) of the Koran, especially verses six and seven.

There are differing interpretations for verses 6 and 7. The phrase "the Path journeyed by those upon whom You showered blessings" is usually seen as referring to Muslims. The phrase "those who made themselves liable to criminal cognizance/arrest" (more clearly translated as "those who have incurred Your wrath") is usually seen as referring to the Jews and the phrase "those who are the neglectful wanderers" (more clearly translated as "those who have gone astray") is seen as referring to the Christians. *The Quran: An Encyclopedia*, authored by 43 Muslim and non-Muslim academics says, "The Prophet interpreted those who incurred God's wrath as the Jews and the misguided as the Christians."

Australian scholar in linguistics and theology Mark Durie wrote in his internet blog on December 3, 2009:

> To be genuine and effective, reconciliation between Muslims and those they refer to as 'People of the Book' (Jews and Christians), requires that Al-Fatihah and its meaning be discussed openly. That devout Muslims are daily declaring before Allah that Christians have gone astray and Jews are objects of divine wrath, must be considered a matter of central importance for interfaith relations. This is all the more so because the interpretation of verse 7 which relates it to Christians and Jews is soundly based upon the words of Muhammad himself. As Al-Fatihah is the daily worship of Muslims, and represents the very essence of Islam itself, the meaning of these words cannot be ignored or glossed over.

There must be some kind of consensus published widely by Muslim scholars that these verses do not refer to any particular religious community. For example, Mahmoud M. Ayoub, on page 49 of his *The Qur'an and Its Interpreters: v.1: Vol 1*. State University of New York Press, refers to some alternate interpretations.

This is of great importance. Andrew Bostom points out in *PJ Media* on January 24, 2017, that at the interfaith prayer service for the inauguration of President Donald Trump, Sajid Tarar, from the Medina Masjid, Baltimore, Maryland, recited the Surah Fatiha. Bostom said because of the contentious aspects of this Surah its use on state occasions such as this should be *reconsidered* as a "basic principle of true ecumenism, and basic civility."

If Islam is to be a part of the religious mainstream in the West, the wider Muslim community must insist that their scholars re-interpret such problematic sections of the Koran.

As Daniel Pipes has put it, anti-Islamist Muslims are the key to ending the Islamist surge, as they alone can offer a humane and modern alternative to Islamist obscurantism.

However, anti-Islamist Muslims, religious or secular, have a very difficult task when they speak out against the radicals. One example is the Pakistani born Canadian commentator Tarek Fatah. Most critics of Islamism do not know quite what to make of him, as he does reflect certain attitudes that make them uncomfortable. For example, Robert Spencer, of *JihadWatch*, noted on February 27, 2017, that:

> Fatah is a paradoxical figure; indeed, he personifies the paradoxes of most moderate Muslims. He speaks out strongly against Muslim Brotherhood organizations and Sharia encroachment in the West, but is extraordinarily concerned at the same to absolve Islam of all responsibility for the crimes done in its name and in accord with its teachings.

Fatah has lately been doing television in India where his views, that might not arouse so much passion in Canada, are incendiary to the ears of the Islamists. So much so, that an Indian Muslim group has offered a $15,000 reward to anyone who beheads him. Spencer, who could be seen as squarely in the camp that Islam is by its nature violent and illiberal, therefore cannot accept Fatah's sincerity as an anti-Islamist, and goes so far as to characterize him as a practitioner of Taqiyah or as a pseudo-reformer. He writes:

> And now there is a bounty on his head from the All-India Faisan-e-Madina Council, which only shows that the All-India Faisan-e-Madina Council, in its hatred, bloodlust, and savagery, doesn't realize who its true friends are. In any case, however, this just illustrates yet again the uphill battle that Islamic reformers, and even pseudo-reformers such as Tarek Fatah, face: when they speak out against Islamic practices that have a foundation in the Qur'an and Sunnah, they're threatened with death as heretics or apostates. That's why we don't see more Islamic reformers, even insincere and opportunistic ones.

Fatah may not have found a stable "center" between Islamistphobes and Islamists. Spencer's article continues:

"Tarek Fatah is conspiring to disrupt harmony between Hindus and Muslims. He is as an agent of our enemies. He must be stopped at any cost and our organisation will pay Rs 10,00,786 (Rs 10 lakh) to any person who will decapitate him," said Moeen Siddique, head of the council.

"He and his programme are being funded by foreign enemies of our country and the government must initiate an inquiry against him," Siddique said.

[He] is known for his secular views against Islamic fundamentalism.

"In his programme, he claims that it is not required to wear a burqa and terms triple talaq [an instant divorce proclaimed by the husband] as haram. Muslims must not listen to his advice and come forward against him," said Siddique.

Other Muslim social organisations too voiced their resentment against Fatah.

Jamat Raza-e-Mustafa, another social organisation that works under the aegis of Dargah-e Ala Hazrat, has written a letter to the President Pranab Mukherjee, demanding a ban on the television programme and expulsion of Fatah from the country... .

Fatah, speaking to the Toronto Sun on February 26, 2017, stated that not only had the Islamic cleric put a bounty on his head (but) as well on the head of Dr. Subhas Chandra, the head of India's leading TV news network, Zee News (which airs Fatah's program).

The Sun, for which Fatah has periodically written a column, asked:

What has Fatah done that's so wrong on his talk show, Fatah Ka Fatwa (Fatah's Fatwa)?

In his own words, 'we grapple with issues that for centuries have never been fully discussed openly in public, outside the confines of Muslim homes.

'These include polygamy, child marriage, the institution of Muta'a (a temporary marriage that provides a theological cover for prostitution) and contempt for 'kafirs', meaning non-Muslims.'

The Sun, considered a "right-wing" paper, is almost alone in speaking out for Fatah's attempts to promote liberal values, which is what *The Sun*, unlike Prime Minister Trudeau, believes to be Canada's main value.

The road away from Islamism requires courage and it requires support from liberal Canadians and Americans. Tolerism is the wrong approach. On the other extreme, Fatah must be given a bit of latitude, even if we do not agree with all his positions. The debate over reforming or moderating Islam when it resides in the West, is necessary and Fatah shows why the truly courageous will defend him.

The road away from Islamism also requires Muslim action against the problem that conversion to Islam is so easily done and requires no religious figure to mentor the convert's views and actions after the conversion.

Some very terrible violent jihadist attacks have been done by people who were converts to Islam, a very worrying trend especially since the rise of the Islamic state which welcomes unstable converts as weapons in their Islamist war against the West. The Islamic State, writes Adnan Khan October 27, 2014 in Canada's *Maclean's* magazine "appears to be attracting some of the most troubled individuals across the Western world, including the U.K., France, Germany, Canada and the U.S.—young men defined by fractured lives and violence, embracing a corrupted and debased version of faith to justify their rage."

Khan notes that some Muslims are asking:

> Why has Islam become a magnet for the deranged, the lost and the psychologically unstable ... and what can be done to either keep these people out or support them once they have converted? We might add that there needs to be some attention paid to the many jailed criminals who are converting in prison – how much are they following Islam when they are released, and how much are they just attracted to militant Islamism?

"We're helpless," says Yusuf Badat, 34, imam at the Islamic Foundation in Toronto and vice-chair of the Canadian Council of Imams. "We can't see into the inner motivations of a person who wants to convert to Islam. Many of these people are coming from broken backgrounds. They're looking for an escape."

The problem, recognized by this imam, is that conversion to Islam is relatively straightforward: A person announces his or her intention, then recites the Shahada, a declaration of faith, three times. There does not even have to be witnesses. There is no formal procedure. Once a person has converted however, the onus remains on the individual to learn about his new faith. This is unlike Christianity, where conversion usually plays out in a church setting with the minister being involved and the congregation providing support, or Orthodox Judaism, where a convert must study with a rabbi for months, and demonstrate adherence to Jewish law, before he or she is allowed to convert before a rabbinical court; a convert to Islam may be on his or her own and attach himself to any guide, no matter how radical, or he may rely on the Internet, full of radical views, for guidance.

Badat says this is dangerous. "Given the current context, there needs to be some kind of protocol put in place, be it background checks or criminal-record checks."

Badat is correct. Islam in the West cannot be tainted with troubled converts who are specifically attracted to the violence and supremacism of Islamism. This is another case where it is up to Muslims who want to be accepted in the West, to clean up a problem of Islamism. This is another case where an element of Islamic law, the conversion, needs to be reformed or added to, to provide some control over who speaks for Islam or acts as an Islamist. Again, I have no standing to tell Muslims what to do religiously; but we in the West have every right to try to set some guidelines of who will be accepted as immigrants or what will be accepted in the name of religious freedom. Unfortunately, there is not one central authority for all Muslims, so Imam Badat's wish to have "some kind of protocol put in place," may be admirable, but may have little chance of being realized. Those of us who are really interested in the welfare of fellow citizens who are Muslims should encourage those who want to be seen as "moderate" to work with the reformers on this problem.

It is a monumental task for America to disentangle itself from support for Islamist organizations like the Muslim Brotherhood and the various groups and committees that have spun off from the Muslim Brotherhood. While America slept in the Bush and Obama years, the Muslim Brotherhood ascended to a position of influence and power that is shocking. We need to understand exactly how influential the Islamist Muslim Brotherhood has become, so that we can plan the major effort required to disempower this traitorous organization.

John Guandolo at UnderstandingTheThreat.com not only enlightens us about the Muslim Brotherhood, but he also provides some key information about who is behind attempts to thwart President Trump's attempts to improve national security by pausing immigration from certain Muslim majority countries that have little in the way of functioning governments.

When President Trump issued his second Executive Order designed to keep individuals from hostile nations from entering the United States, the Attorney General of Hawaii announced he will file suit against the Trump administration. The plaintiff listed in Hawaii's lawsuit is Dr. Ismail Elshikh, the imam of the Muslim Association of Hawaii, notes Guandolo.

Guandolo says that the address of the Muslim Association of Hawaii is 1935 Aleo Place, Honolulu, Hawaii. The property records for Honolulu reveal this property is owned by the North American Islamic Trust (NAIT) – the bank for the Muslim Brotherhood in North America.

Guandolo submits: "The Muslim Association of Hawaii is a Muslim Brotherhood organization, which means the Muslim Brotherhood is directly confronting the President of the United States and challenging his authority."

NAIT was created in 1973 by the Muslim Brotherhood's Muslim Students Association as stated on its own website.

Guandolo has posted on his website a declassified document from the FBI's Indianapolis office dated December 15, 1987 which states:

> The North American Islamic Trust (NAIT) was organized by the leaders of the Muslim Students Association of the United States and Canada (MSA) in 1973 as the parent organization of various Muslim groups in the U.S. and Canada. The leadership of NAIT, MSA and other Muslim groups are inter-related with many leaders and members of NAIT having been identified as supporters of the Islamic Revolution as advocated by the Government of Iran (GOI). Their support of JIHAD (a holy war) in the U.S. has been evidenced by the financial and organizational support provided through NAIT from Middle East countries to Muslims residing in the U.S. and Canada.

Evidence entered in the largest terrorism financing and Hamas trial ever successfully prosecuted in American history (US v Holy Land Foundation for Relief and Development, Dallas, 2008) – 15 year FBI investigation – identified the North American Islamic Trust (NAIT) as a member of the U.S. Muslim Brotherhood which directly funded Hamas (TERRORISTS) leaders and organizations.

On the last page of the U.S. Muslim Brotherhood's strategic document (*An Explanatory Memorandum*), the MB identifies NAIT as one of their organizations.

The stated objective of the Muslim Brotherhood in the United States is to wage civilization jihad "by OUR hands" to overthrow our government and replace it with an Islamic government ruled by sharia – Islamic law. See *An Explanatory Memorandum*, page 7 of 18.

Guandolo argues:

If this offensive assault by the Muslim Brotherhood [through Dr. Ismail Elshikh, the Imam of the Muslim Association of Hawaii] against the President of the United States and his effort to secure our nation and keep our enemies out is not met with significant force by the U.S. government, the Muslim Brotherhood will view this as more weakness and push harder and more violently in the coming months.

And we should think carefully about Guandolo's prescription to cleanse America of the Islamist Muslim Brotherhood:

The Department of Justice should indict NAIT and the affiliated Muslim Brotherhood Islamic Centers, mosques and other organizations, arrest all Muslim Brotherhood leaders in the United States, legally seize all NAIT and Muslim Brotherhood property, and utterly dismantle their jihadi network.

Better late than never.

When we get to the final chapter of this book, we shall face the "catch-22" that I fear is inherent in our journey. If we are successful in the West in a fight against the Islamists and in support for a reformed version of Islam, might that make it *more* likely for a culturally-weakened West, tired of fights between Left and Right, to convert or otherwise submit to Islam? And if that is so, we note that once moderate countries like Turkey and Indonesia are moving rightwards to a more Islamist stance; in that case, a submission to

Islam may start out as submission to a moderate Islam, which ends up becoming more Islamist over time. This is a problem that should be occupying our very best minds.

Islamophobia, Islamistocriticism and Islamophilia

I do not think that the term "Islamophobia" is very helpful in any discussion of Islam or Islamism. Those who use it are very often loath to actually define it.

Paul Jackson writing back in 2001,(*The EDL: Britain's 'New Far Right' Social Movement* (PDF). RMN Publications, University of Northampton. pp. 10–11), argued that both jihadi Islamists and far-right activists use the term "to deflect attention away from more nuanced discussions on the make-up of Muslim communities," feeding "a language of polarised polemics"… it can be used "to close down discussion on genuine areas of criticism" regarding jihadi ideologies, which in turn has resulted in all accusations of Islamophobia to be dismissed as "spurious" by far right activists. Consequently, the term is "losing much [of its] analytical value." Certainly, its widespread usage since 2001 leaves us with no alternative but to study the term and hope that a better understanding of the relationship of Islam to Islamism will lead to more sophisticated discourse, both on Left and Right, Muslims and non-Muslims.

The term Islamophobia entered discussions of public policy with the report by the Runnymede Trust's Commission on British Muslims and Islamophobia (CBMI) entitled *Islamophobia: A Challenge for Us All* (1997). The introduction of the term was justified by the report's assessment that "anti-Muslim prejudice has grown so considerably and so rapidly in recent years that a new item in the vocabulary is needed."

But using the suffix, "phobia" contained the inherent problem that a "phobia" is often seen as an *irrational* fear. Thus it was not a neutral term between those who felt Islam, or at least Islamism, included certain ideas and behaviors that were in fact fearful, with good reason, to proponents of women's rights, gays rights, non-Muslims living alongside Muslims, especially as minorities, and liberal political theory. Islamists themselves could browbeat any critics of their ideology with a term that implied an irrational fear.

And so, a better term would be *Islamistocritic*.

That would conduce to a better understanding of what criticism is in liberal traditions valid and fair, and what criticism is irrational. And so we note, the term Islamophobia, has become used as much as a sword by Islamists as a shield by Muslims in general to unfair or racist hatred or prejudice. An Islamistocritic, could be anyone, Muslim or not, who feels that homophobic, misogynist, jihadist, honor-killing, or any illiberal parts of Islam need to be discussed and that Islam needs to be purged of its illiberal and Islamist notions to make it reconcilable with Western liberal traditions.

Once we accomplish this linguistic reform, we could go on to discuss Islamophilia or Arabophilia, because it is clear to me that there are many in the West who have embraced the ideologies of "love thy enemy" or tolerism with respect to groups of Muslims who themselves are intolerant and often hateful. But a divorce between Islamism and Islam, would give better credibility to those who find some aspects of Islam tolerable or even praiseworthy, but need the distinction in their love between Islam and Islamism, as the latter should hardly be tolerated let alone loved.

Professor Mohammad H. Tamdgidi of the University of Massachusetts, Boston in his critique of the methodology used by the above-mentioned Runnymeade Trust study warns against the linguistic

> ... trap of regarding Islam monolithically, in turn as being characterized by one or another trait, and ... not adequately express(ing) the complex heterogeneity of a historical phenomenon whose contradictory interpretations, traditions, and sociopolitical trends have been shaped and has in turn been shaped, as in the case of any world tradition, by other world-historical forces.

((2012, Spring): Beyond Islamophobia and Islamophilia as Western Epistemic Racisms: Revisiting Runnymede Trust's Definition in a World-History Context. *Islamophobia Studies Journal*, 1(1), p.76.)

There is no doubt in my mind that Islamophilia or Arabophilia exists in a substantial way. It is found most often among the groups that, promptly after any jihadist terrorist attack, seek to show that such terror is not a part of the mainstream religion that should be loved on the basis of the ideological "inclusive diversity" that we discuss in more detail later, or tolerism; or that such terrorism is found is a small percentage of all Muslims or even all Arabs. Those who express such love, compassion, empathy, tolerance and respect for ALL Muslims must be engaged in discussion by critics who profess that the critics' criticisms are actually more helpful to the welfare of the average Muslim, compared to the appeasement of Islamism shown by the Islamophiles.

On the other hand, we might have to be careful with prescriptions for moderation from the classically Liberal crowd, including myself. What results in the religion and culture of a reformed Islam might be attractive to our intellectuals who are tired and searching in a secularist era for slightly more authoritarian religious guidance? Later in this book, we shall discuss some recent writings about submission by French intellectuals.

Islamists induce and love words or behavior that they can term, with the support of Leftists in the West, "Islamophobia." And so, President Trump is routinely called an Islamophobe for his temporary restriction on certain Muslim immigration, while other American presidents did something similar. Jimmy Carter (the most Arabophile of any American president) in reaction to the Iranian abduction of American diplomats following the 1979 Iranian hostage crisis during which the U.S. embassy in Tehran was stormed and 52 Americans were held hostage for 444 days, cut diplomatic relations with and imposed sanctions on Iran. He also banned Iranians from entering the country.

As Ann M. Simmons and Alan Zarembo reported in the *Los Angeles Times* on January 31, 2017, Trump relied on a 65-year-old provision of the federal Immigration and Nationality Act.

> The provision gives presidents broad authority to ban individual immigrants or groups of immigrants. Presidents haven't hesitated to use it.

Barack Obama invoked it 19 times, Bill Clinton 12 times, George W. Bush six times and Ronald Reagan five times. George H.W. Bush invoked it once.

Obama, they point out, turned to the provision more than any other recent president, using it to bar people who conducted certain transactions with North Korea, engaged in cyberattacks aimed at undermining democracy, or contributed to the destabilization of Libya, Burundi, Central African Republic or Ukraine.

According to these reporters from the *LA Times*, Obama's broadest application of the law came in 2011, when he suspended entry of foreigners "who participate in serious human rights and humanitarian law violations and other abuses," including "widespread or systemic violence against any civilian population" based on, among other factors, race, color, disability, language, religion, ethnicity, political opinion, national origin, sexual orientation or gender identity.

Obama also used the law to block anybody involved in "grave human rights abuses by the governments of Iran and Syria" through the use of communications technology to disrupt computer networks or provide monitoring or tracking.

So, it is telling that only Donald Trump was called an Islamophobe for using the provision.

Simmons and Zarembo report that the bipartisan Congressional Research Service pointed out in a report this year, the law does not place "any firm legal limits" on how it can be used. It doesn't say what factors should be considered in deciding who would be "detrimental" to U.S. interests or what constitutes "appropriate" restrictions. However, since Trump's order has been appealed to court, and will probably end up in the Supreme Court, we can expect a battle over how far the Supreme Court can place its opinion ahead of the president's opinion on these matters. Democrats who are all for tying Trump's hands, may think very differently if in the future, there is a conservative Supreme Court filled with Trump appointees that asserts the ultimate control over a Democratic party president.

Thank you to *the Los Angeles Times* for reporting these facts, because in our current media manipulation of facts against President Trump, there is a dearth of reporting of these kinds of facts. That is why President Trump, surely against the wishes of many of his media advisers, keeps poking the mainstream media for reporting "false facts" and being biased. To understand the extent of the media hostility to this president, we need only consider:

As of October 25, 2016, *Politico* reported:

> Clinton received more than 200 endorsements from daily and weekly newspapers in the United States. A dozen or so papers have endorsed not-Trump, and one endorsed not-Clinton, but a striking 38 papers have chosen to endorse no one in this presidential election. So far the number of papers that have endorsed Donald Trump ... stands at six.

(politico.com/magazine/story/2016/10/donald-trump-newspaper-endorsements-214390)

By November 7, 2016, Rebecca Harrington of *Business Insider* reported that while Democratic nominee Hillary Clinton garnered the support of more than 240 editorial boards, her Republican rival Donald Trump only received 19. Most were newspapers from mid-size cities concentrated in the mid-West and South.

Since we know that the media in general did not explain that Trump's policy about an immigration ban (or, more properly, a pause) was not radically different from previous presidents, one would have to conclude that there is an ideology that unites almost all American mainstream media in order for it to be so uniform in their support of a flawed candidate like Clinton. That support, we think, is *ideological* in nature. We wish it could be discussed as such, rather than using terms like "fake news" to critique ideological opposition based on ideologies that need full discussion for the benefit of the American people.

And so, I allege that the mainstream media in the West is *Trumpophobic*. Its failure to report in depth on Hillary Clinton's close friend and adviser from Saudi Arabia, Huma Abedin, could be seen as evidence of Islamophilia or even Islamistphilia. Can we imagine what would have happened to President Kennedy should it have been discovered that his closest friend and adviser was a Communist? Saudi Arabia, although Americans are happy to do business with it, is the originator and funder of Wahabist Islamism. The Saudis are not a good love match for Americans.

In *Tolerism: The Ideology Revealed*, I explained my view that much Islamophilia (and Arabophilia) is based on ideological phenomena, such as a *cultural Stockholm syndrome*, a *masochism*, or a self-hatred inculcated by leftist educational institutions in the West and sadly, a resurgence of anti-Semitism where a hatred of the individual Jew or the Jewish community as minorities in host nations has been replaced by a hatred of the Jewish State, Israel. Like the great Natan Sharansky, I hold that criticism of Israel passes from fair comment to anti-Semitism, if it is based on *delegitimization, demonization* or the use of *double standards*, the so-called 3D test. And so love of those who promise genocide for the Jews is in fact anti-Semitism, not true love. Perhaps we need the term Islam*ist*philia in addition to the term Islamophilia.

It is clear that our media and our politicians are more loving of Islam than phobic of it. In Ontario, the most populous province in Canada, at any rate, October is now officially recognized as Islamic Heritage Month, starting in 2016. It began as a New Democratic Party (the most left-wing party) private members' bill, and party leader Andrea Horwath said it was an opportunity to celebrate and learn about the history of Islamic culture. The resolution on this was supported *unanimously* and no one questioned why only Islamic heritage had to be celebrated and not Hindu, Buddhist or Jewish heritage, or for that matter, atheism.

Horwath says she also hopes it's also a step toward eliminating Islamophobia, noting that in her city of Hamilton, a fire was set at a mosque recently.

Canadian Islamic History Month has been officially recognized federally since 2007.

If you want to see Islamophilia in action, see: huffingtonpost.ca/ 2017/03/08/daughters-of-the-vote-islamophobia_n_15247066.html. A young Muslim student stood in a Conservative MP's seat in the House of Commons in March, 2017, to deliver a harsh statement about "Islamophobia."

Srosh Hassana represented her home riding of Sherwood Park— Fort Saskatchewan, a federal seat held by Garnet Genuis, for a "Daughters of the Vote" takeover of the House to mark International Women's Day.

The University of Alberta student spoke about being a Muslim woman of color caught facing "overwhelming stigma" and a "growing culture of ignorance" from those who justify xenophobia and prejudice "under the veil of free speech." She was met with rousing applause and tears. But here is where the problem lies:

Her hyperbolic speech during this love-in actually stated, "I fear being *othered, profiled and killed* in a country I call my own. My identity is challenged and my actions are heavily scrutinized," she said. "I am simultaneously silenced into shame while being expected to apologize for the actions of a small group of people that do not represent me or anything I am."

In Hamilton, Ontario, a medium sized city which has taken in some 1400 government sponsored, or privately sponsored refugees this year (mostly Syrian) compared to 250 the year before, the Police Services Board in its March 2017 report on hate crimes for the year 2016, says that about 30 hate crimes were against blacks, 20 against Jews, and only 10 against Muslims. (hamiltonnews.com/news-story/ 7183236-hate-crime-up-slightly-in-hamilton-says-chief-eric-girt/) One would never know that Jews are twice as likely, and blacks three times as likely, as Muslims to be subject to hate crimes, if one just reads the constant cries by Islamists about a supposed Islamophobia, including the University of Alberta student's remarks.

This is bizarre, as she is not in danger of being profiled or killed. As a Jew, who has been attacked by Islamists at a lecture, I am in far greater danger than she is. As a Jew standing up for fundamental freedoms, no one has invited me to speak to parliament. This young woman gives a speech during a love-in at Parliament and then tells us she is stigmatized. She is using the so-called Islamophobia as a sword to beat down naive Canadian politicians who have decided to meet Islamism with love and then will wonder what happened later on to fundamental freedoms. Notice this university student has been given the special privilege of being her riding's spokesperson for the day – hardly Islamophobic (it is in fact, Islamophilia) and she disingenuously takes this opportunity to deny that the Islamist leadership in Canada "represent" her; because that is the meaning when Muslims refer to the "small group of people" who are radicals. In fact that small group of people controls most Muslim organizations, and has she ever made a speech in support of a more moderate leadership for Muslim groups in Canada?

Query whether she has ever gone to a meeting of the Muslim Students Association which is affiliated with the Islamist Muslim Brotherhood? Or has she attended a speech by any one of the dozens of Islamist radicals making speeches in Canada? Our Members of Parliament were too busy loving her with constant nods of approval and applause to actually think about what is going on. The Islamophiles should check out her background thoroughly so as to understand whether they are Islamophiles or in fact Islamistphiles, where the latter is very dangerous.

Her words come weeks after the Official Opposition challenged a Liberal MP's non-binding motion — referred to as M-103 — to condemn "all forms" of Islamophobia. The challenge was based on the special mention of Islamophobia made in the motion when no other ethnic group, religion or race was similarly mentioned. Members, especially in the official Opposition Conservatives, have been condemned as Islamophobes for suggesting that specific use of the term Islamophobia as a concern for racist statements, should have in addition, an opposition to other specified religions being hated. Most Conservatives argue the use of the term without a definition of what it means is problematic because it could suppress debates on issues such as the niqab.

The Islamist allegations of Islamophobia are of course exaggerated, precisely to encourage more tolerism and empathy towards the Islamists. The Canadian writer and blogger Diane Bederman on *dianebederman.com* provides the facts on whether "Islamophobia" is more widespread, or anti-Semitism:

> In 2016, the Jewish community, which makes up 3.8% of the religious population in the Toronto area, was victimized in approximately 30% of the total hate/bias crimes while the Muslim community, which makes up 8.2% of the population, was victimized in approximately 15% of the hate/bias crimes. Hate/bias crimes include assault, assault with a weapon, criminal harassment, mischief, interfere with property, threatening bodily harm, threatening death and willful promotion of hatred. Out of 66 hate/bias occurrences involving religion, Jews were targeted 43 times and Muslims were targeted 22 times.

Bederman notes the Islamist anti-Semitism heard in Canada:

> On December 23, 2016 Sheikh Muhammad bin Musa Al Nasr, a Jordanian cleric led the Friday prayer at Dar Al-Arqam mosque in Montreal and called the Jews the "most evil of mankind" and "human demons" emphasizing that their fate was predetermined by Allah to be killed by the hands of the Muslims.

Bederman writes also of Sheikh Abdulqani Mursal, imam at Masjid Al Hikma mosque in Toronto who also is of the opinion that the fate of the Jews is destined to be killed by the Muslims. At a lecture, he read the chapter *Turmoil And Portents Of The Last Hour* from Sahih Muslim (hadith collection, meaning narrations attributed to Mohammad), including the following narration: "You will fight against the Jews and you will kill them until even a stone would say: Come here, Muslim, there is a Jew (hiding himself behind me); kill him."

Islamist anti-Semitism is against Canadian law and should be against all western legal systems. The very first action to be taken against the Islamists is to prosecute them for hate crimes where appropriate and deport foreign Islamists who would incite western Muslims to anti-Semitism.

In a Canada based on tolerance and inclusive diversity, we tend to look at what we need to do to help new immigrants smooth their transition into being Canadians. However, it is fair, when a significant number of Muslims, while not Islamists themselves, tolerate and support to some degree, Islamists in their own countries and in Canada, that we ask our immigrants to repudiate the Islamists, in return for all the help.

For example, in Hamilton Ontario, *The Hamilton Spectator* on April 19, 2017 reports (thespec.com/news-story/7251482-hamilton-organization-aims-to-build-a-warmer-welcome-for-newcomers/) that pursuant to a federal program, a local body has devised a plan to make Hamilton more "welcoming" to immigrants and refugees. It reports that the Hamilton Immigration Partnership Council hopes to implement by 2020:

- A campaign to counter negative immigrant stereotypes;
- A yearly Newcomer Day;

· A mobile settlement information hub;

· An annual conference;

· An updated immigration profile of the city;

· University research on Syrian integration into the labour market.

We are told that Hamilton received 1400 government or privately sponsored refugees last year, when it normally gets about 250. A recent chair of the group says, "Many (Syrian refugees) came with large families and had low language skills or were illiterate in their own language." I am all for helping newcomers integrate. There is just one glaring omission in the plan: where is the training to make the refugees good Canadian citizens, to learn that Canada, while being very tolerant, does not tolerate the kind of racism and genocide against minorities that exists in the countries they have left, and to realize that they must repudiate Islamism and the Islamist leaders, both abroad and within Canada. We need to impress upon them that Islam in Canada is respected, but only to the extent it repudiates the jihad, the supremacist notion of the caliphate, and the separate Sharia law.

Is that too much to ask in return for all the help we are prepared to give? Or does our Islamophilia know no bounds?

And so we must always remember that true love is evidenced by reciprocity; too much of Islamophilia without understanding that it may be *Islamist*philia is not requited love, but submission. That is why an ideological approach to this topic is necessary.

CHAPTER 4:   DENIALISM AS THE MAJOR STEPPING STONE ON THE PATH TO SUBMISSION

Any strong ideological belief carries with it a risk of denying those facts that do not support the ideology.

In *Tolerism* we noted that the denial of certain facts approaches an ideology of *denialism* when the facts denied seem incontrovertible. So if there is doubt, for example by Islamist radicals concerning the fact of the Holocaust, that denial of fact must arise from a strong ideology, in this case a hatred of the Jewish people and the wish to excise the Jewish presence in the Middle East.

Since the writing of my book *The Second Catastrophe*, in 2002, I have felt we ought to take seriously the threat of a second Holocaust, this time at the hands of Islamists, encouraged by their leftist supporters and the state sponsors of anti-Israel and anti-Jewish propaganda. Are we in *denial* or are we prepared to *tolerate* another Holocaust against the Jews?

I have also been concerned about the increasing genocide against Christians in Arab countries and the persecution of other minority religions in Asia and Africa. What is the relationship between denial and tolerance and how is denialism an essential stepping stone in the ideological path to submission? This is important enough to reproduce and then expand upon certain arguments made in *Tolerism*.

We discussed that the ideology of denialism is based on the psychological concept of *denial*.

American psychologist Kendra Cherry has summarized psychological denial as follows:

> **Denial** is probably one of the best known defense mechanisms, used often to describe situations in which people seem unable to face reality or admit an obvious truth (i.e. "He's in denial."). Denial is an outright refusal to admit or recognize that something has occurred or is currently occurring. Drug addicts or alcoholics often deny

that they have a problem, while victims of traumatic events may deny that the event ever occurred.

Denial functions to protect the ego from things that the individual cannot cope with. While this may save us from anxiety or pain, denial also requires a substantial investment of energy. Because of this, other defenses are also used to keep these unacceptable feelings from consciousness.

Note the importance to denial of the need to use this defense mechanism as a way to deal with anxieties and fears that an individual cannot cope with.

In late 2012 and early 2013 there were election campaigns in two liberal democracies much at risk from Islamist terrorism and jihad – America and Israel. Yet a study of both election campaigns show how little attention was actually paid in the threat of Iranian nuclear weapons and support for terrorist groups like Hezbollah, which in the past has taken hundreds of American and Israeli lives.

"Bread and butter" issues like jobs, health care, and the economy completely dwarfed international relations in this most dangerous era of world history. In the 2012 candidate's debate for the U.S. presidency, Mitt Romney probably lost the election by not pressing Obama hard on his numerous foreign policy mistakes. With the terrorist-supporting Iranian regime on the verge of obtaining nuclear weapons in the next decade, Americans and Israelis seem to be in a state of denial.

One would think that no educated politician in this era would ever mimic Neville Chamberlain's infamous phrase justifying his sell-out of Czechoslovakia for "peace for our time," spoken the day before the Germans occupied Sudetenland and less than a year before the Germans occupied Poland. Chamberlain's silly words are quite often quoted as "peace *in* our time," but he actually used "peace for our time." Barack Obama, in his speech on his inauguration for his second term in office, actually stated:

We will support democracy from Asia to Africa, from the Americas to the Middle East, because our interests and our conscience compel us to act on behalf of those who long for freedom. And we must be a source of hope to the poor, the sick, the marginalized, the victims of prejudice. Not out of mere charity, but because **peace in our time** requires the constant advance of those principles that our common creed describes.

Note how Obama believes that the world of Islamist dictatorships and theocracies shares a "common creed" with an America immersed in liberal democracy and constitutional government. Tolerance? Denial?

Tolerism and denialism have a strong link: to tolerate evil or to tolerate facts that might cause a great evil is to show a *denial* of the danger of the evil or the facts that might create the evil.

An example of denialism was the reaction of President Obama and Secretary of State Hillary Clinton to the September 11, 2012 terrorist attack on the American embassy in Benghazi Libya and the murder of ambassador Chris Stephens and three other Americans—and the acceptance by American media (with certain exceptions such as Fox News) of what was surely a misleading, if not untruthful, explanation by the Obama administration.

Despite its knowledge to the contrary, Obama and Clinton *denied* that this was in fact an organized terrorist attack and attempted to frame it as a spontaneous uprising against a silly anti-Islam video by an American Coptic Christian.

Moreover, when finally Clinton had to appear in front of a Congressional investigation, she had the nerve to state, "What difference does it make?" to the important question of whether this was an organized terrorist attack. Only members of an Administration in absolute denial over the extent of the Islamist terrorist threat and the danger of the Muslim Brotherhood and its associated organizations, could suggest that the facts about the Benghazi attack do not make a "difference."

In fact, hours before U.S. Ambassador Christopher Stevens died in a terrorist attack in Libya, he sent Secretary of State Hillary Clinton a cable warning that local militias were threatening to take away security officers guarding the U.S. diplomats.

The cable, which Stevens submitted on the morning of Sept. 11, 2012, relayed the warning that Libyan militia *"would not continue to guarantee security in Benghazi, a critical function they asserted they were currently providing."* Militia leaders had previously expressed anger at U.S. support of a certain candidate for Libyan prime minister and consequentially planned to extract their security.

Stevens' cable reached Clinton hours before terrorists attacked the U.S. consulate in Benghazi and killed the ambassador and three other

Americans. The cable was publicly released by the chairman of the U.S. House Oversight and Government Reform Committee, Rep. Darrell Issa, and includes 160 pages of documents outlining the violence surrounding Benghazi.

The cable also refers to a Sept. 2 meeting in which the commander of Benghazi's Security Council expressed deep concern about police and security forces being too weak to protect the country from terrorists.

One paragraph refers to the "expanding Islamist influence in Derna" and a "troubling increase in violence and Islamist influence".

Another example of denialism emanates from the Roman Catholic Church. Pope Francis has given a pass to the Islamists as being just a small minority of violent fundamentalists, and equates that to what happens in other religions. In fact, he has said (as quoted by Raymond Ibrahim in *Frontpage Magazine* on August 2, 2016):

> ... he doesn't like speaking about Islamic violence because there is plenty of Christian violence as well... [He] said that every day when he browses the newspapers, he sees violence in Italy perpetrated by Christians: "this one who has murdered his girlfriend, another who has murdered the mother-in-law... and these are baptized Catholics! There are violent Catholics! If I speak of Islamic violence, I must speak of Catholic violence. And no, not all Muslims are violent, not all Catholics are violent. It is like a fruit salad; there's everything."

Ibrahim quotes the pope as saying,

> "I had a long conversation with the imam, the Grand Imam of the Al-Azhar University, and I know how they think. They [Muslims] seek peace, encounter."

Ibrahim says that

> Dr. Ahmed al-Tayeb, the Grand Imam of Al-Azhar, arguably the most authoritative Islamic institution in the world, did indeed recently visit Francis and inform him of how Muslims desire peace and harmony with the world.
>
> But back home in Egypt, the grand imam and Al Azhar promote an Islam that is virtually indistinguishable from that of ISIS. Indeed, days before he went to take pictures hugging the pope, Tayeb said that it is a criminal offense to apostatize from Islam, and the punishment is death.

The pope reflects a denial that there is a significant branch of Islam, that has more power than any other Muslims and has this power precisely because the pope and other western leaders treat the Islamist leaders with too much tolerance, when they are supremacist Muslims. Just think how much easier winning the war declared upon us by the Islamists would be if the pope took sides and shunned the Islamists and what they stand for and only accepted visits from reformist Muslims.

But how can the pope act differently when he apparently believes that terrorism has nothing to do with Islam, notwithstanding it is the main tool of the Islamists. The pope actually thinks terrorism springs from poverty. Ibrahim quotes the pope as follows:

> "Terrorism grows when there are no other options, and when the center of the global economy is the god of money and not the person – men and women – this is already the first terrorism! You have cast out the wonder of creation – man and woman – and you have put money in its place. This is a basic terrorism against all of humanity! Think about it!"

Pope Francis seems to ignore the problems inherent in Islam itself, which in this book I have argued should be reformed out of the religion by those who want to live in the West peacefully. He also seems to ignore the true nature of the Islamists and does not seem to understand when he is meeting with an Islamist or a non-Islamist.

Denial of facts that make us uncomfortable or anxious is a common psychological behavior. When a denial of a whole set of facts, for example, in the political domain, becomes an ideology or belief system, it passes into the ideology of denialism. Some psychologists and philosophers have even studied the rhetorical devices used to support such denialism.

Anthropologist Didier Fassin distinguishes between *denial*, defined as "the empirical observation that reality and truth are being denied," and *denialism*, which he defines as "an ideological position whereby one systematically reacts by refusing reality and truth."

Given Iran's nuclear weapons program and it missile program, and given Iran's extensive arming of Hezbollah in Lebanon and Syria for the purpose of war against Israel, it is denialism to fail to understand the extent of Iranian threats to Israel and to America and its interests abroad.

Mark Hoofnagle, writing in the *Guardian* in March 2009 has described denialism as:

> The employment of rhetorical tactics to give the appearance of argument or legitimate debate, when in actuality there is none." It is a process that operates by employing one or more of the following five tactics in order to maintain the appearance of legitimate controversy.
>
> · 1.Conspiracy theories — Dismissing the data or observation by suggesting opponents are involved in 'a conspiracy to suppress the truth'.
>
> · 2.Cherry picking — Selecting an anomalous critical paper supporting their idea, or using outdated, flawed, and discredited papers in order to make their opponents look as though they base their ideas on weak research.
>
> · 3.False experts — Paying an expert in the field, or another field, to lend supporting evidence or credibility.
>
> · 4.Moving the goalpost — Dismissing evidence presented in response to a specific claim by continually demanding some other (often unfulfillable) piece of evidence.
>
> · 5.Other logical fallacies — Usually one or more of false analogy, appeal to consequences, straw man, or red herring.

Denialism, as it is based on the psychological tactic of denial, contains within it the seeds of other ideologies, and this is perhaps the scariest part. Dr. Carl Alasko, writing in *Psychology Today* in April, 2012, claims:

> There is an immutable fact about denial: it does not work—long term. Reality always wins. And when it does, the next step in the process is blame, which shifts responsibility onto someone or something else. "I only did it because of you! If you hadn't done that, I wouldn't have done this." So where there's denial, blame is always *available to ease the pain when reality bites*.

So when denial runs up against the reality of certain facts, says Alasko, blame is sure to follow. And that is where denialism and tolerism morph into the oldest blame of all – the blame for everything wrong in the world on the Jews, and now on the Jewish State.

It may be that denialism results in either blame or tolerism. The scoundrels resort to blame and the uncaring majority feel more comfortable in their tolerism, as it allows them to turn their negative immorality or uncaring about a just world into a pseudo-tolerance. This in fact makes it easier for those, doing the blaming and resorting to violence, not to be challenged by the silent majority.

Finally, some excellent work has been done in this area by American writer and head of the *Middle East Forum*, Daniel Pipes, and by American writer Bill Siegel in his 2012 book, *The Control Factor: Our Struggle to See the True Threat*. They do disagree, however, on the contentious issue of separating Islam and Islamism.

Pipes, in his essay, "Denying Islam's Role in Terror" in the spring 2013 *Middle East Quarterly*, argued:

> The establishment – law enforcement, officials, the media, and academics – has shied away from seeing this (terrorist) violence as jihadi. Why? First, officialdom wants to assure Muslims that it is not biased against them. They worry that being perceived as anti-Islam will inspire even more alienation and violence. Second, officials want to avoid the many implications of focusing specifically on violence by Muslims, which upsets the modern liberal ethos. These motives are worthy but wrongheaded. Common safety and the survival of Western civilization both require those in positions of authority candidly to inform the public about the nature of Muslim-on-non-Muslim violence, and then the press to report on it.

Siegel's book actually emphasizes not so much denial but *self-deception* in failing to recognize and deal with the threat of Islamism. Hence he sees a psychological process that endangers us all since Islamism dominates Islam. This psychological process he labels the "Control Factor". Siegel argues:

> It is that creative part of our minds that actively and continuously seeks to assure us that the threat we feel, see, hear, and think about is largely under our control, when in reality it is not." He contends that we have no control over a three-pronged Islamic threat: blatant

terrorism, infiltration into and manipulation of Western society from within, and the pressure exerted upon us by international organizations.

In truth, we are in a war – a Holy War, as defined by the enemy itself. We are unsure how to defend ourselves in such a war much less how to fight it aggressively. This uncertainty, complicated by our asymmetrical adherence to rules and moral codes which our Constitution and national identity impress upon us but which our enemy does not share, has led many to a deep anxiety – a sense of too little control over our present circumstances and exponentially less over future ones. To ease this anxiety, the Control Factor's organizing principle is to recast our perceptions, thoughts and beliefs to restore the sense of control; that is what it is created to do. The self-deception that results is at least as dangerous to us as any enemy weapon.

Pipes pointed out that three years after Maj. Nidal Malik Hasan's massacre at Ft. Hood, Texas, in November 2009, the classification of his crime remains in dispute. He notes that "the Department of Defense, supported by law enforcement, politicians, journalists, and academics, deems the killing of thirteen and wounding of forty-three to be 'workplace violence.'" For example, the 86-page study by the Department of Defense dated January 2010 on preventing a repeat episode, *Protecting the Force: Lessons from Fort Hood*, mentions "workplace violence" sixteen times. *Protecting the Force* mentions 'Muslim' and 'jihad' not a single time, and 'Islam' only once, in a footnote. Pipes alleges: "The military leadership willfully ignores what stares them in the face, namely Hasan's clear and evident Islamist inspiration." And so Pipes concludes that the massacre "officially still remains unconnected to terrorism or Islam."

The establishment, in its desire not to lose support among Muslims or to be charged with stoking the fires of Islamist violence, avoids a clear discussing of the need to sever off Islamism from Islam. We know that Islamism can point to Islamic sources in support of its form of Islam that seeks to make Muslims dominant through an extreme, totalistic, and rigid application of Islamic law, the Sharia. We know that Islamism represents the leading global cause of terrorism and that it acts medievally in its aspiration to create a caliphate that rules humanity. Certainly Islamism expands on Islam's public law that appears to elevate Muslims over non-Muslims, and males over females; and Islamic sources endorse the use of force to spread Muslim rule. In recent decades, Islamists (the adherents of this vision of Islam) have established an unparalleled record of terrorism, and Pipes in his spring 2013 essay refers to website TheReligionOfPeace.com counting 20,000 assaults in the name of Islam since 9/11, or about five a day.

Accordingly, fear of *offending* Muslims has been so pervasive and thorough that it must surely give succor to the Islamists who feel that they will not be challenged as they use "Islamophobia" as a sword, or seek special privileges, or push for western opposition to the Jewish state, Israel.

Even the death of 3000 civilians on 9/11 was inadequate for the American establishment to name the Islamists as the enemy: *Dateline*, NBC, on September 21, 2001, reported that just one day after 9/11, U.S. Secretary of State Colin Powell set the tone by asserting that the just-committed atrocities "should not be seen as something done by Arabs or Islamics; it is something that was done by terrorists."

Pipes says that the avoidance of discussing Islam in connection with terrorism has reasons deeper than political correctness, ignorance, or appeasement. According to him those reasons are firstly, not wanting to alienate Muslims and secondly not wanting to "re-order" society.

The first was often seen in the Obama Administration, as Obama felt he had some unique skill at winning the "hearts and minds" of Muslims both in America and throughout the world. Query whether leaning over backwards wins Islamic friends or demonstrates the kind of weakness and appeasement that encourages Islamists and the rest of Islam to think that the Islamic world caliphate is on its way to success, thereby creating more support for hardline Islamists among more moderate and less political Muslims.

Pipes' second reason to inhibit one's talk about Islam concerns the "apprehension that this implies a large and undesirable shift away from how secular Western societies are ordered." Avoiding the true Islamist causes of terror allows Westerners not to confront troubling issues concerning Islam and Islamism. Says Pipes:

When one notes that Islamist terrorism is almost exclusively the work of Muslims acting out of Islamic convictions, the implication follows that Muslims must be singled out for special scrutiny whether they are government employees in law enforcement, the military or the diplomatic corps and need to be watched for connections to terrorism, as do Muslim chaplains in prisons and the armed forces.

Then we would have to support Trump-like checks of visitors and immigrants and perhaps have periodic suspensions of immigration from certain countries. Just look at how such a policy, although it is well supported by the majority of Americans, arouses vehement allegations of racism from the Left, the media and the university communities. Furthermore, mosques would require a special scrutiny for hate speech and extremist literature beyond that applied to churches, synagogues, and temples.

Applying police surveillance and security checks on one community that is defined by its religion, Pipes notes,

flies in the face of liberal, multicultural, and politically correct values; it also will be portrayed as illegal and perhaps unconstitutional. It means distinguishing on the basis of a person's group characteristics. It involves profiling. These changes have unsettling implications which will be condemned as "racist" and "Islamophobic," accusations that can ruin careers in today's public environment.

And so, Siegel's "Control Factor" of psychological maneuvers to avoid seeing the Islamist threat before us, meets Pipes' understanding of the need for restraint in language and counterterrorism, due to America's ideological liberal multiculturalism. But even Pipes argues that we must recognize the elephant in the room by discussing honestly the nature of Islamism. Even Pipes notes that the majority of Muslims who would be seriously offended by this discussion are actually Islamists posing as moderate Muslims.

I believe that there exists a large number of Muslims who would welcome the negative attention to be given to the Islamists as part of a war against them, with a Western resolve to be honest on the nature of the fight, and the need to reform Islam itself if Muslims want to embrace the totality of citizenship in Western countries. Our politicians and other elites have appeased the Islamist beast, and forbade us from advocating against it and in favor of the necessary reform of Islam.

This too is a serious form of denial, and our ideologies can only avoid submission to the Islamists by supporting the small but growing number of reformists, even if they are hardly "moderates."

We conclude this chapter with a personal story. About thirty years ago, I was living in Waterloo Ontario and through my community activism and my law practice, I became acquainted and friendly with two Muslim women. One was an advocate for intercultural relations and edited a magazine meant to provide better understanding between religious and ethnic groups. She identified as a secular Muslim, and she and her secular Muslim husband hailed from Egypt, where a sufficiently sized group of secularists jockey for power with the Muslim Brotherhood folks and their religious supporters. The other was a devout Muslim and she and her husband were also from Egypt. She dressed in black headcovering and black burka, and her husband wore a long beard. They were a hardworking family, with many children, and operated a nice Egyptian restaurant. I acted as their business lawyer, and I would often visit their restaurant for vegetarian cuisine and enjoyed the company of both the husband and the wife.

Once I gave a lecture about my pro-Israel novel, *The Second Catastrophe: A Novel about a Book and its Author*, in a large Waterloo bookstore. I was shouted down during the lecture by a couple of Islamist recent immigrants, while the bookstore employee left in charge, who was wearing a hijab, smiled and took no action as they shouted that I should not be allowed to give a pro-Israel lecture and that I was a "f---ing Jew." I have written previously about the incident and the non-support of the literary community and even the Jewish community. After it happened I decided to meet with my two Muslim friends to see what they suggested.

The reaction was very interesting and informative. They both regretted the incident, but more importantly they bemoaned that the power structure among Muslims in Waterloo favored the radicals, the Islamists. Then they mentioned how local Muslim engineering professor Mohammed Elmasry was in charge of a Muslim organization. This is the same man who on a television interview show took the position that all Israelis were fair game for terrorists because each Israeli could potentially serve in the military.

Both of them respected me I suppose for my position as a lawyer, a Jewish community leader, and an activist for race relations. I was amazed however when they both turned to me and asked *me* if I could do something about Elmasry's role and how to get rid of him from his position of power.

To me, this drove home, the reluctance of good Muslim folks to challenge or antagonize the radicals, the Islamists. This is probably a carry-over from the lands of their origin where Islamists maintain control by various violent and abusive means. Yet here were two good ladies, one active in race relations as a magazine editor and the other a businesswoman whose husband was active in the local mosque, both reluctant to cause waves in reaction to the hate shown to their Jewish lawyer and friend.

Bill Siegel posits the dirty little secret that underlies much of the examples of tolerance—those in which we accept that somehow *we* are the cause of the enemy's behavior and thus move our focus away from the enemy and onto endless consideration about what else we can do. This is part of his idea of a self-deceptive "Control Factor" maneuver; we can easily believe that if we change our behavior theirs will change as well.

Hence the peace process, which Siegel calls "the extortion process" where there is an endless recycling of Palestinian "demands" and Israeli "concessions" implying that Israel causes Palestinian terrorism not the Palestinian leadership that incites their people. What is too frightening is the realization that there is nothing Israel or its Western counterparts can do to please the Islamists except national suicide, when it comes to stopping terrorism. We do not control or cause the Islamist beast, and we have to stop pretending that it is possible.

It is pure denialism to neglect to have our governments in the West both vet and re-educate Muslim immigrants so that they understand the primacy of liberal values here and also the separation of church and state. To those who want to call me an Islamophobe for suggesting this, I think you in fact are the Islamophobes by refusing to help the vast numbers of Muslims who, like all human beings, have an inclination towards freedom and human rights. To those who refuse to help sever Islamism from Islam, you are not only denialists but you are anti-Muslim. I am brave enough to incur the wrath of the Islamists and do so out of feelings of goodwill to ordinary Muslims who want to worship the Divine without a culture of hate and violence.

Chapter 5: Tolerism in the World View of President Obama

Barack Obama showed very early in his administration that he had an ideology that was very different than past American presidents. First, he awarded America's highest civilian award—the Medal of Freedom—to Mary Robinson who presided over the infamous Durban Conference of 2001, where Islamic countries were allowed to hijack a conference about racism into a hatefest against the one country in the Middle East (Israel) that has a functioning justice system protecting minority rights.

Then he went to Cairo and showed his intentions to appease radical Islam by accepting that tension between the West and Islam has had nothing to do with Muslim actions against the West but was "fed by colonialism that denied rights and opportunities to many Muslims, and a Cold War in which Muslim-majority countries were too often treated as proxies without regard to their own aspirations."

And then he uttered the infamous words, equating the glorious tradition of justice, freedom and tolerance in America with that of totalitarian countries like Egypt, Syria, Iran, and Saudi Arabia: Obama contended that America and Muslim countries "share common principles—principles of justice and progress; tolerance and the dignity of all human beings."

As a lawyer myself, I can tell you that the American justice system is not perfect, but I would much rather be tried for a crime in America, Israel or Canada than any of the Muslim countries. And, as a Jew, the idea that Muslim countries, most of which have ethnically cleansed themselves of Jews (and now have been doing the same with Christians) share the same degree of "tolerance" as do we in the West, is, quite simply, an obscenity.

In 2010, Obama visited his boyhood home of Indonesia. Granted, Indonesia does have some form of democracy, perhaps the most democracy in the Islamic world. But, once again, Obama sought to further western submission to radical Islam by morally equating America with far lesser lights when it comes to liberal democracy. Specifically, he stated in Indonesia that the United States and Indonesia have "shared values" and that "our nations show that hundreds of millions who hold different beliefs can be united in freedom under one flag." He claimed that in Indonesia, under its Muslim majority (87% of the population is Muslim) "people choose to worship God as they please. Islam flourishes, but so do other faiths."

The biggest problem with these words was that they were blatantly false. The other problem is why would an American president, sworn to uphold the Constitution of the United States, travel the Islamic world, with the message that America is responsible for the Islamic sense of victimization, and that Islamists are correct in the sense that the Islamic notion of democracy under Sharia law and the dictates of the Koran is equivalent to the Judeo-Christian notion of liberal democracy, based on separation of church and state, and an emphasis on justice? All the talk of "tolerance" in the Islamic world obviously refers to something very different to what I see as tolerance.

For let us look at Indonesia. Although the Western media does not seem too interested, there is a disturbing recent history of violence and oppression of minority religions, especially towards Christians around the time of the East Timor independence movement, and more recently towards a minority Islamic sect called Ahmadiyah.

With respect to Christian persecution, read about the atrocities in the central Indonesian area called Sulawesi and about the extremist Islamists (tolerated by authorities) called the Laskar Jihad.

The January, 1999, anti-Christian violence resulted in the death of tens of thousands. Chris Wilson documented the ethnic cleansing in North Maluku in his book *Ethno-Religious Violence in Indonesia: From Soil to God.* (Oxon: Routledge, 2008).

The Asian Human Rights Commission in a study released last February concluded that there is no religious freedom in Indonesia. It stated that:

> There is continuing concern at the distinctions made in legal documents between the six recognized religions of Islam, Protestantism, Catholicism, Hinduism, Buddhism and Confucianism, and the adverse impact on the freedom of thought, conscience and religion of people belonging to minorities, ethnic groups and indigenous peoples in Indonesia.

There are lesser rights for non-recognized religions like Judaism, or for those who accept no religion and are atheists. A blasphemy law criminalizes speech and other expression by those outside the officially recognized religions.

Read on the internet about the terrible persecution of the Ahmadiyah minority Muslim sect, which is under violent intimidation in both Indonesia and Pakistan. But of course wars *between* Muslim sects (such as Sunni versus Shi'a) are a continuous problem in the supposed tolerant world of Islam.

Indonesia does not recognize Israel; that is, it does not believe that Jews can live in peace in the small historic Jewish homeland, surrounded by hostile Muslim states. Israelis are not allowed to travel to Indonesia. I do not believe it has ever objected to any of the numerous statements from radical Islamist groups and states that Israel should be "wiped out."

Moreover, during the very time that Western tolerists praise Indonesia as a "moderate" Islamic state, there is in fact a concerted effort by Islamists there to implement Sharia law and fight its secularism. Jon Emont, writing in the *New York Times* in early 2017 ("Shariah Law Erodes Indonesia's Secularism") points out that Aceh province, once a bastion of late night bars and secularism, especially in the seaside town of Banda Aceh, now has established Sharia law, and women are required to dress modestly, alcohol is prohibited, and numerous offenses are punishable by public whipping. Sharia police raid hotel rooms and beaches looking for "immoral" activity.

Aceh Province back in 2001 received special authority from the central government in a bid to stop separatist activity. Now Aceh has become the model for other areas that wish to implement Sharia and reduce secularism. Those who oppose it, according to the vice-speaker of the Aceh provincial legislature aren't "brave enough to say anything," and there was little public debate even though he says that a "silent majority" thinks the government has gone too far.

I hazard the guess that Indonesia's favorite American, Barack Obama, will not speak out against the Islamist trends in formerly more open Islamic societies. In fact, he promoted the Muslim Brotherhood in its takeover of Egypt, now reversed by the military. It is my opinion that western support of Islamists amounts to complicity in the loss of freedoms imposed by the Islamists.

And so, to the American president who reserved his criticisms for Israel's homebuilding around its historic capital of Jerusalem, there is no criticizing Indonesian Muslims, Egyptian Muslims, or Palestinian Muslims. There is only continued praise for them and insistence that Americans and Muslims share similar values. There was never a request that Muslims take responsibility for their problems, only an appeasement-like agreement that their problems would disappear if Americans and Israelis would only submit a little more to this tolerant religion of peace.

And so it is important to realize that the Obama era laid the foundation for a tolerance leading to a submission. Americans were given by their ancestors a precious legacy of freedom. While the mainstream media did not often question Obama's ideological emphasis on what I have called tolerism, a significant portion of the American people came to an understanding by the last year of Obama's term that their legacy was being squandered on the altar of moral relativism and false notions of tolerance. The failure of the mainstream media to deal with the issue forthrightly led directly to the election of Donald Trump, as he was the only candidate willing to address the issue of tolerism and its effects on American freedoms. The reaction to his order about pausing certain immigration showed us something very interesting. As John Hayward put it in *Breitbart.com* on January 29, 2017:

> The hysterical reaction to Trump's order illustrated the very thing that worries advocates of strong immigration security: American's security is the lowest priority, far below progressive ideology, crass political opportunism and emotional theater. We're being effectively told by the theatrical class to tolerate a certain amount of Islamic terrorism because their feelings would be hurt by tough measures.

Obama's big problem was that he could only see that Muslim dictatorships, supported by the West, were the big problem. From Libya to Egypt to Iraq and Syria, he and his advisers could recognize that Muslim dictators were bad for political culture, kill extra-judicially and their repression foments violence.

Recognizing that the primary opponents of these dictators were the populist Islamists, meant that Obama could only think as far as aiding the Islamists, which this book decries as the worst reaction possible. Obama could see that they wanted to vote which gave an appearance of democracy; if he had a better appreciation of the dangers of Iran, he would have understood that after voting they want to appoint an extra-constitutional body of clerics to strike down legislation they do not approve of.

Faced with these two possibilities, Obama and his administration failed to understand the wisdom of the third option, advocated here: The demand that Muslims who want domicile in the West or Western military assistance must follow a reformed Islam completely divorced from Islamism and a theological view of civil society.

Obama's tolerism with respect to radical Islam, the Islamists, robbed Americans of the power to actually help the Islamic world by empowering those working for a healthier political culture and escape from the barbaric practices that we were told were intrinsic to Islam. In Obama's case, raised as a Muslim, but attending church for 20 years with a black liberation theology, and schooled in community organizing and power politics, Chicago-style, meant that a little knowledge (of Islam) was a bad thing. He missed the chance to empower the reformers and prevent a submission to Islamism, which if not unchecked, has the potential to destroy freedom and liberal values. For that, he will one day be considered one of the worst presidents in American history.

CHAPTER 6:   WHEN DENIAL BECOMES COMPLICITY

Obama and Clinton Deny the Islamist War Against the West

In my opinion 9/11 was a clear declaration of the Islamist war against America. Since that time we have witnessed Islamist attacks, most recently in Orlando and San Bernardino, but also at Fort Hood (against the American military!), the Boston Marathon, and the Seattle Jewish Federation. Those commentators who seek to minimize the continuing danger of more Islamist attacks by citing other non-Muslim mass murders are being, I believe, disingenuous, as one cannot win one war by saying we are losing another war. That is surrender.

Around the world Islamists have murdered in Paris, Brussels, Madrid, London, Berlin, and throughout Scandinavia and Germany where the attacks take the form of sexual assault against non-Muslim women. In fact all over the world, where Muslims live with non-Muslims, there are constant attacks in places as diverse as the Philippines, Nigeria, Russia, and of course, Israel.

Astoundingly, what we call the Mainstream Media, with its main values of tolerance, moral and cultural relativism and moral equivalency, after each attack, work hard to deny the obvious: that there is a war against the West by Islamism, and while not all Muslims are Islamist radicals, there tends to be, among the majority, a certain tolerance and reluctance to take active steps to prevent terrorism; expressions of sympathy, after each horrible attack, are not enough. That is to say, Muslims who are serious about stopping Islamist terrorism must not just denounce it with words, but prevent mosques being used as indoctrination centers, stop the Muslim Brotherhood-supported Muslim Students Association from ideological indoctrination of their university age children, and support western values like separation of church and state, respect for gays, Jews and other ethnic and religious minorities including dissident Muslims (remember the acquiescence in what happened to Salman Rushdie and other subjects of fatwas).

Again, in Orlando, we see the media rush to distort the event, by trying to make the case that the moral of the massacre is the need for more gun control, and that the FBI can do nothing about so-called "lone wolves," even though the perpetrator had given off danger signals. And then, the event is distorted into proof of continued hostility for gays, lesbians and transgendered, even though that battle in the West has been won, and the only holdouts balk at marriage rights. Further still, the ideologues of moral equivalency try to argue that Christianity and Judaism also outlaw homosexuality, when there is no moral equivalency and you have likely never heard of Christians and Jews attacking gay bars or throwing gay people off of buildings as happens in several countries of the Muslim world.

The abuse of language by those in whose interest it is to minimize or obscure this War is well-known. Obama characterized the Fort Hood massacre by an Islamist shouting Allah Akbar and dressed in Islamic robes as "workplace violence." After Orlando, the FBI, most politicians and left-liberal media, quickly decided that he was a "lone wolf" just as the Canadians did when a gunman killed a Canadian soldier outside Parliament and then stormed the Parliament building. This is of course a blatant attempt to mislead the public who should be worried about the preponderance of Islamist ideology in media, in universities, and on the internet where any disaffected Muslim can access all elements of Islamist violent and anti-Western ideology. One can only characterize such people as "lone" if you ignore all the influences on them of Islamism including family influences. For example, the Orlando murderer of 49 in a gay nightclub is often said to be "American born" as if that makes any difference, when his father is a Taliban-supporting Afghan immigrant, who had a pro-Taliban radio show and an extensive series of pro-Taliban YouTube videos. With a father like that, and, as it turns out, a friend at his mosque who became a suicide bomber in Syria, how can he be said to be a "lone wolf"? Anyone who wants to ignore all context to his life, which is that he became an enemy combatant, simply doesn't understand the nature of the war against us.

You see, the Arabs in and around Israel, learned the lesson in 1948, 1956, 1967, and 1973, that they could not use conventional forces to commit genocide against a people so motivated to never again let a genocide happen, who would fight to the last man or woman, if necessary. What the so-called Palestinian Arabs learned however, was that terrorism, "suicide" bombers and alliances with leftist anti-Semites in the West could give them the power they lacked in conventional armies. Iran, by using terrorist proxies like Hamas and Hezbollah, could be at war against Israel at the same time as Obama (who insisted he supported Israel) was signing agreements and removing sanctions from Iran, the major funder and organizer of the War against the West, now proven to have been behind the bombing of the Jewish Community Center in Buenos Aires, killing 80 and injuring 300.

Let us examine the two most important leaders in America of tolerance, even empathy, for the enemy in this new form of war – a form of war that the media wants to obscure by turning our attention to "lone wolves," mental illness, homophobia, and the need for more gun control. It is obvious to me that any enemies of Islamism, such as gays, Jews, Yazidis, dissident Muslims, and young women "immodestly dressed" must all carry handguns and be trained in how to use them. If one gay or any other person at the nightclub had a handgun, over 40 lives could be saved. Many young Israelis carry rifles and they are almost never used in mass murders or individual murders. The effect of further gun control is to circumvent the Second Amendment by preventing good people from defending themselves against the enemy who will find ways to get assault rifles to use in their war against us. So who are the leaders who have surrendered America's interests?

In 2008, Americans were fooled into believing that electing Barack Hussein Obama was something of a redress for historical mistreatment of black Americans, especially slavery. The only problem was that Obama was not a black American: the skin-tone he inherited from the Kenyan who impregnated his mother and then ran away did not make him a black American. A black American is in fact someone who is descended in whole or even in a small part from African slaves imported to pre-Civil War

America. As such, the inadequate assimilation into mainstream culture for the freed slaves, especially male slaves who were short on the skills of adherence to family responsibilities, resulted in a culture of absent fathers, over-representation by far in prisons, public welfare assistance and drug dealing and the like.

In fact, Obama's white maternal ancestors were "occupiers" of Native indigenous land in Oklahoma and Kansas, cleared by violence, and given to American "settlers." Obama and his left-liberals have a lot of nerve to categorize the indigenous Jews of historical Israel as occupiers when such Jews lived on the land for centuries before Islam was even invented, considering America's historical record with respect to its indigenous Natives. Such is the submission to Arab Islamist narratives – terrorism works, unless the terrorized have strong values and clear ideologies to resist the terrorist Stockholm syndrome.

With the assistance of affirmative action programs and both the inherent and learned feelings of fairness and goodwill by many Americans, and with the riches emanating from successful careers in sports, business and entertainment, many black Americans have risen to success in business and the professions and just about every aspect of American life, including politics. No doubt, much remains to be done, but a good start has been made. But Barack Obama, raised partly in Indonesia by his mother's second husband Soetoro, a general in the 1965 genocide of more than a million ethnic Chinese and Communists (the reward for which was a plum position in a government oil company), and partly by his mothers' mother, (who got him into a Hawaii private school as a "foreign student"), has little in common with most black Americans.

And so, upon his inauguration, Obama's priorities seemed to revolve around assuring terrorist supporting Muslim states that he considered that they have had the same history of justice and tolerance as do the Americans, whose founding fathers wanted to create a new Israel, a "light unto the nations." Obama has wanted to create an "anti-Israel," with cultural and moral relativism replacing the Judeo-Christian ethic, heretofore the foundation for American values.

Obama's America was not the same nation that reacted to Pearl Harbor with an entry into World War 2. Obama's America doesn't pay too much regard to 9/11, and doesn't understand that it was the opening major attack in World War 3, the Islamist war against the West. America all but ignored Osama bin Laden's revealing comment that 9/11 was meant to remind the world that Islamism was still angry about the 12th century defeat in Andalusia, where the Muslim invaders into Europe were turned back. Ask a sampling of Americans what bin Laden meant when he said "Remember the Andalusia" and I doubt one out of ten will know what it means. Instead of seriously fighting Islamism, America responds with empathy and tolerance and suggests that the war can be won by more understanding and less Islamophobia (sic).

One of the ways in which a pacifist tolerist ideology is working against an American victory over the Islamists can be seen in the media and Democratic Party opposition to the use of enhanced interrogation techniques (EIT). While there have been isolated cases of prisoner abuse such as that by military police at Abu Ghraib, a U.S.-run Iraqi detention facility for terrorist detainees, the reality is that EIT thwarted terrorist plans and potentially saved thousands of American lives.

Writing in *American Thinker*, on March 5, 2017, Janet Levy reviews the new book, *Enhanced Interrogation: Inside the Minds and Motives of Islamic Terrorists Trying to Destroy America* (Crown Forum, 2016) by psychologist and retired Air Force lieutenant colonel, Dr. James E. Mitchell. In it he describes the author's involvement in the development and implementation of the CIA's enhanced interrogation program from its inception in 2002 until it was shut down by Obama in 2009. Levy concludes that "the book is an eye-opening account of how thoughtfully and judiciously enhanced interrogation techniques were developed, how they were applied, how much valuable intelligence was gleaned from their use and how effectively they thwarted potentially deadly attacks."

Political gamesmanship combined with ideological pacifism so that the "same Democratic members of the House and Senate intelligence committees that condemned the program were fully briefed ahead of time and supported it before it became politically useful to denounce it."

CIA head, George Tenet, the DOJ, White House lawyers, then national security adviser Condoleezza Rice, VP Cheney and President Bush, all approved the use of these techniques including waterboarding.

Continued waterboarding as time went on against major Al Qaeda operatives, resulted in, not a useless torture operation, as later claimed, but the uncovering of a treasure trove of information about terrorists and their plans to launch horrific attacks that could now be thwarted. The book discusses countless terrorist attacks on civilian sites in America that were thwarted.

Enhanced Interrogation makes clear that the CIA's interrogation program was a success and provided much information about terrorist organizational structure, leadership financing and planning. Without EIT, according to Mitchell, the United States would never have killed Al Qaeda leader Osama bin Laden.

"When it comes to the limited use of approved non-life threatening enhanced interrogation techniques EIT," Levy concludes,

> Americans must ask what they value most: the so-called rights of terrorists intent on destroying America or the safety and security of the American people. Should U.S. authorities stop people who see themselves as being at war with us and our way of life by employing a pre-emptive, war-focused intelligence gathering approach or do we use an ex post facto law enforcement or criminal approach of convicting terrorists in a court of law? Surely, the former pro-active perspective offers the best chance for keeping Americans safe.

Obama's ideology, to treat your enemies in wartime the same as you would treat your citizens, constituted a movement towards submission.

Someone who worshiped with Reverend Wright who invoked God to "damn America" could maintain an anti-American world view with a media that had abnegated its role of defender of liberty and justice in favor of the prosaic political correctness of the era. Who even noticed when Obama backed every popular Islamist uprising against long-time Islamic dictators except for the pro-freedom attempted 2009 Green Revolution in Iran? With Iran, there was to be cooperation and agreements giving them what they wanted in legitimizing their nuclear program and obtaining the end of embargoes and sanctions and release of large sums of money.

Iran, it must always be remembered, is a major state sponsor of terrorism, including the dastardly Hezbollah in Lebanon and Hamas in Gaza. The latter showed the world what nightmares Israel could expect should it listen to so-called "progressives" in Europe and America to give more land and sovereignty to those whose main goal is the destruction of Israel and the murder of its people. The former showed America could never learn the lesson of Iran's leadership of Hezbollah's murder of hundreds of U.S. troops stationed in Lebanon during the Reagan era, and Iran's role in the mass murder of Argentinean Jews at the Buenos Aires Jewish Community bombings. Both Iranian leadership and masses call for death to America and Israel.

Saudi Arabia, the American ally, not only has a medieval human rights policy but is the main exporter and funder of the radical notion of Islam called Wahabism. By funding Islamist takeovers of mosques around the world, some of which previously had moderate imams, and by funding more radical imams in mosques and university programs, Saudi Arabia is a strange ally indeed.

In 2011, a consortium of American defense contractors were allowed to sell $29 billion dollars worth of advanced fighter jets to Saudi Arabia.

The *International Business Times* investigated the arms sales and reported:

> In the years before Hillary Clinton became secretary of state, the Kingdom of Saudi Arabia contributed at least $10 million to the Clinton Foundation, the philanthropic enterprise she has overseen with her husband, former president Bill Clinton. Just two months before the deal was finalized, Boeing—the defense contractor that manufactures one of the fighter jets the Saudis were especially keen to acquire, the F-15—contributed $900,000 to the Clinton Foundation, according to a company press release.
>
> The Saudi deal was one of dozens of arms sales approved by Hillary Clinton's State Department that placed weapons in the hands of governments that had also donated money to the Clinton family philanthropic empire, an *International Business Times* investigation has found.

Hillary Clinton not only has funding contacts with the Saudis, but her best friend is a Saudi raised operative of the Muslim Brotherhood, who took a salary from the White House at the same time she was working for a Muslim Brotherhood journal (the Muslim Brotherhood being an Islamist organization).

Huma Abedin, progressed quickly from an aide to Hillary, to her chief aide, and even to the co-Chair of her election campaign. Whether or not the two have just a friendship and work relationship, or are as some claim, romantically involved, only they know. The role of Abedin however raises substantial issues, even worse, in my opinion, than Hillary's notorious use of non-governmental insecure email servers for the most confidential of security-related matters. But in an era of problematic infiltration of Muslim Brotherhood supporters into various American security organizations and non-governmental organizations, Abedin's success in getting so close to a presidential candidate is bizarre and worrisome.

Obama has become infamous for his mischaracterizations of anything terrorist and Islamist. Major Dr. Hussein, the Fort Hood terrorist, was, despite all words and actions to the contrary, only reflecting "workplace violence" according to the president. He joined with Hillary Clinton in withholding from the American people the facts that the Benghazi attack on the American ambassador and others was a terrorist attack by the Islamist terrorist group Ansar al-Sharia, and making up a lie that it was some spontaneous reaction to an anti-Muslim movie made by a Coptic Christian in the United States. The purpose of this lie was to prevent the matter of Islamist terrorism against American targets from becoming an issue in the 2012 presidential election. To me, hiding key security information from the American people in order to increase his chances in the election, smacks of treason by Obama. Hillary's relationship with Abedin and the Muslim Brotherhood and the Saudis also reflects treason.

The failure to protect the border and to properly vet Muslim immigrants to remove ones that are Islamists or support Islamists is also a failure of military leadership that reflects the treason of putting American interests behind his attempts to minimize American exceptionalism and increase the chances of great diplomatic power for him personally after the end of his presidency.

Yes, healthcare, tax equity, environmental matters and the economy all are important issues.

But the treason of Obama and Hillary Clinton was a turning point along the path to submission.

CHAPTER 7: FUN AND FOOLISHNESS AS A RESPONSE TO JIHADIST WAR

Recently social networking site *Badoo.com* conducted a survey among its readers (mostly in their twenties and thirties) on which country was the most "fun." The actual question was: "How often would you say that you really have fun and a good time?"

The top two countries were Argentina and Mexico, with reports of days per month spent having fun being 14.8 and 13.7, respectively. The percentage of those having fun "most days" was 41.6 and 36.8, respectively. The United States finished sixth, so young people in the United States report they are having a lot of fun.

Most of us who follow international affairs know that Argentina and Mexico are highly corrupted countries. Argentina's corruption led to a "deal" made with Iran not to prosecute Iranian government officials and politicians found to be behind the Hezbollah terrorist bombing of the Jewish Community Center in Buenos Aires, in order to preserve trade relations. Mexico, of course, continues to struggle with drug and crime cartels and a corrupted justice system.

Given the views of most conservative writers that the West is facing a crisis brought on domestically by over-spending and internationally by the terrorist war by Islamism for Western submission to Islamist values and influence, this cultural emphasis on fun gives us pause.

If "fun" is the new cultural core value of the West, are we happy with that? With an ideology of "fun-seeking," are we prepared to fight the ideological aspects of the Islamist war against the West? Do we even know what the word "fun" means? Shouldn't we discuss it more?

It might be useful to understand its derivation first. According to *Dictionary.com*, the word derives from between 1300 and 1350 and from the Middle English word "fond," which in turn stemmed from "fonned" (the past participle of "fonnen" to be foolish, originally, to lose flavor, sour).

It is also suggested that by the 1680s, the word was used as a verb to mean "to cheat or hoax," which was probably a variant of "fon" or "befool." Later, it was used often in the sense of "it is all in fun," that is playfully or not seriously.

Only later, it seems, did "fun" take on the predominant meaning of "amusement," "mirth," and even "pleasure."

So, we note that "fun" has seemed to pass from a concept of foolishness and playfulness to the serious business of a cultural value.

A Western culture that promotes the fun-ness of video games over the pleasure of reading a good book and the fun of gambling over the hard work of honest toil, may be worshiping at a rather bizarre altar.

When one looks at the tremendous problems of modern society, and in particular the threat to our fundamental freedoms from Islamist terrorism and jihad against liberal values, how do we defend ourselves when we are busy, engaged in "foolishness" in the name of fun?

American presidents have often enjoyed golf (a game I also enjoy and would play more of, if only I had the time), but President Obama seemed to have always been playing golf when national emergencies struck – during the run up to the capture of Osama bin Laden, during the first bout of violence in Egypt in July 2013, and again in the middle of August as the military fight with Muslim Brotherhood protesters took a more deadly turn, and for three days a couple of weeks before the looming March 1st, 2013 deadline with Congress to avert automatic massive spending cuts.

George Bush for the first part of his presidency did the same thing. Margaret Talev writes for *Bloomberg* that, after Palestinian terrorists staged attacks in Israel, including the suicide bombing of a bus in August 2002, Bush gave the U.S. reaction from a golf course near his family's vacation compound in Kennebunkport, Maine.

"I call upon all nations to do everything they can to stop these terrorist killers," Bush said, adding, "Thank you. Now watch this drive."

Bush, however, realized that his "fun" was looking increasingly "foolish": In a 2008 interview with Politico, cited by Talev, Bush said he gave up golfing because it sent the "wrong signal" as the United States was engaged in a war. "I don't want some mom whose son may have recently died to see the commander in chief playing golf," he said in the interview.

Obama also went golfing during the Gulf oil spill crisis. Of course, good mental health requires some downtime in such an important and stressful job. Obama however is reported to have gone golfing six or seven times during the 58 days of the Gulf oil spill crisis.

Obama is supposed to have received daily briefings during his August 2013 vacation, when he golfed nearly every day, and which culminated in a round with Seinfeld show co-creator Larry David. David, whose wildly popular show about "nothing" and the fun-filled lives of four underemployed narcissistic New York liberals, earned his way into the realm of presidential golf partners.

The big problem is that the Egyptian crisis (along with the Iranian nuclear bomb) has in some ways defined his presidency. Obama shocked scholars of radical Islam by favoring the Muslim Brotherhood (along with former Secretary of State Hillary Clinton, whose adviser and close personal friend Huma Abedin has never hidden her continuing relationship with Muslim Brotherhood officials, including her family members).

Obama seemed unable to interrupt his fun vacation to ask the Brotherhood to stop killing Christians or comment on the burning and looting of 40 churches and the heavy damage of 23 others during the week of his golf vacation. His only public comment for the week was to ask the Egyptian government and military to stop *their* violence. He appeared not to reflect upon the serious problem that encouraging "democracy" without constitutional or judicial powers to protect human rights and fundamental liberties is a recipe for more abominations like the Iranian ayatollahs or Hamas in Gaza. Was he having too much fun to even care about these crucial world issues, which surely impacted world peace? Is it more *fun* to golf with Larry David?

Did Winston Churchill golf his way through World War II six hours at a time?

It is *fun* to spend money and not so much fun to *save*. That is why our politicians like to make their marks by spending on new programs and monuments to themselves. It is not fun to tell people the truth that spending trillions more than we take in as taxes will result in bankruptcy within two generations.

When my parents grew up in the 1920s, the word "fun" was probably used about 5% of the time it is used today. Today's children in the West spend half their waking hours engaged in the *fun* of video games, texting, and watching television and movies, a significant portion of which are action and horror films where the educational benefit to the young viewer is marginal. How much Internet surfing is spent in acquiring knowledge and how much in mere foolishness, including pornography and gossip and celebrity sites?

What education our children do receive is meant to be *fun* and is meant to teach them that there can be education without values, respect without being respected and tolerance without being tolerated. It is more fun for the teachers to avoid the whole issue of values and pretend that it is possible to separate values and ideology from informed discussions.

My day job is as a (lawyer turned) real estate developer of socially just, and culturally enhancing, real estate projects, including affordable rental housing for low-income working people and conversion and restoration of heritage institutional and industrial buildings for new affordable uses. In the evening and on weekends, I should be having "fun" but instead I read and write articles and books, and publish books through my publishing house, Mantua Books, for international conservative authors who are being shunned by mainstream left liberal publishing houses. It is not often *fun*, but it is *necessary* if my grandchildren are to grow up with the freedoms we too often take for granted.

Many of us spend our lives in the pursuit of money, fame and pleasure. The real pleasures are more than momentary fun, more than drug or alcohol or sexually induced highs, and consist of a deep enjoyment of living a good and meaningful life in loving relationships;

in doing good for others and promoting liberal freedoms as a constitutional right for every man, woman and child.

Within that context of a meaningful life, and meaningful love, there is lots of room for fun, but fun is not the ultimate goal, although it is nice when it, to some degree, accompanies our other deeper goals.

However, I fear that we are making *fun* the ultimate measure of our lives. Moreover, if we appear in the West to be focused only on *fun*, those Islamists who enjoy *jihad* more than fun can easily surmise that they have a good chance of winning, and making a world-wide caliphate when their opposition is too busy having fun to take up arms in defense of their own liberty.

The historical sense of "fun" as "foolishness" should be a warning to us all.

CHAPTER 8: DIVERSITY AND TOO MUCH DIVERSITY

From Jerry Seinfeld to Haneen Zoabi

I believe that "political correctness" has now taken us to the point where every area of human endeavor must reflect gender, race and religious diversity.

In 2014, I noted that two very different sources were blowing back at the enforced diversity that the left-liberal do-gooders are seeking to impose.

One was the great Jewish comedian Jerry Seinfeld. Melissa Clyne, writing in *Newsmax*, notes that in an interview with *CBS This Morning*, Seinfeld responded to a question about whether his new web series, *Comedians in Cars Getting Coffee*, is stacked with white men like himself. Seinfeld thought the question was silly. He asked whether "people think it's the census or something?" "We represent the actual pie chart of America? Who cares? I have no interest in gender or race or anything like that."

According to Jerry: "Everyone else is calculating, is this the exact right mix? To me, it's anti-comedy. It's more about PC nonsense than, are you making us laugh?"

But it wasn't long until the PC Police started to pounce. Lily Rothman of *Time* magazine in a column told Seinfeld that he was on the losing side of this issue:

> A continued lack of diversity on his show would prove his detractors' point — and make him look racist and sexist, even if he's merely failing to actively think about matters of race and sex — while increased diversity would seem to acknowledge that the "nonsense" isn't so nonsensical at all. There's no longer a way for a prominent comedian with Seinfeld's level of influence to be so glib about the issue — especially given that of his 26 guests, only two have been women and another two have been nonwhite. (There have been no minority women guests so far.)

Jews have traditionally been overrepresented in comedy in America. In 1979, for example, *Time* estimated that whereas Jews made up only 3 percent of the American population, fully 80 percent of professional comedians were Jewish. It probably stems from the Jewish habit of dealing with misery and adverse circumstances by making jokes. I thought that was a great contribution to American culture; unfortunately, being funny is no longer the main criterion for being in a comedy, so ethnic groups that have dealt with adversity through violence rather than jokes now have an equal right to be represented in comedy as elsewhere. Poor Jerry, something has changed and he doesn't get it.

As a Canadian who must live with so-called human rights commissions adjudicating on diversity issues, I have seen the future that Seinfeld does not understand; it is not pretty.

Take a look at the second story, which comes from what I have called the "first front" in the Islamist war against Western values – Israel. With all its security problems in its very hostile neighborhood where Muslim children are incited in kindergarten against the Jewish State, one would think there would be little interest in the diversity obsession.

However, in the *Jerusalem Post*, reporter Lahav Harkov wrote about a controversy that arose when the Knesset's Labor, Health, and Welfare Committee was discussing a bill to give Arab Christians separate representation from Arab Muslims on the Advisory Committee for Equal Opportunity in Employment.

Arab Muslim Member of the Knesset Jamal Zahalka took offense and suggested that the bill's proponent, rather than seeking to promote diverse membership on the Committee, was intending to "wickedly divide the Arab public, which is oppressed anyway."

Christian IDF Officers Forum leader, Lt. (res.) Shadi Halul, however, said he is proud to be a Christian and that he wants and deserves to be recognized as such. Furthermore he called the Arab Muslim objectors "racists."

This was too much for Arab Muslim member Haneen Zoabi. This woman, who has a B.A. from Haifa University and an M.A. from Hebrew University (and who worked as a school inspector for the Israeli Ministry of Education), at the Knesset swearing-in ceremony on February 24, 2009, left the room because she objected to the singing of Hatikva, Israel's national anthem; she has voiced support for Iranian acquisition of nuclear weapons and participated in the Gaza flotilla, on board the MV Mavi Marmara.

Zoabi was ejected from the Knesset building by Committee chairman Haim Katz for implying the Christian Halul deserves violence, after she declared to him: "You are a coward! Go to the streets of Nazareth and Kafr Kana, say what you just said, and they'll give you the response you deserve."

The proposed legislation sought to expand the advisory committee by giving the 160,000 Christians in Israel their own representative and adding another Druze member. (Druze are an offshoot of Ismailism, a branch of Shia Islam, whose adherents participate in the Israeli army, and the Israeli Judiciary and Foreign Service.)

The panel would also have representation from the ultra-religious, new immigrants, reservists, older people, and women.

So we see that attempts at diversity, rather than implementing fairness and harmony, will become nothing more than alternate battlefields in the culture war that has befallen us. The left liberals who think that respect for diversity is the recipe for their tolerant paradise on earth will soon come up against the hard reality of the culture war where the Islamists merely *use* our tolerance, until they get power -and then will end all diversity representation just like they will end all tolerance.

And as Jerry Seinfeld would say, there is nothing funny about that, and it is, as he puts it, *"anti-comedy."*

Chapter 9:   The Sad Ideology of Inclusive Diversity

As the small New Brunswick Canada city of Fredericton has found out, it is problematic to take 19 and 20 year old Syrian refugees who might not have attended school for years, and have grown up in a culture of hate and sexual assault and place them in high schools to learn English, alongside local teenagers.

On July 1, 2016, David Akin, of the *Toronto Sun*, reported:

> Syrian refugees at a New Brunswick high school bullied young students, ignored teachers, and harassed a Jewish student, educators wrote this spring in a series of e-mail messages. One e-mail even detailed how a student enthusiastically shared his love for rocket-propelled grenades.

Akin reported that Fredericton has received about 450 Syrian refugees since Nov.4, 2015 and of those, 29 attended the high school primarily to learn English.

> One memo noted that many of these Syrians had not been in a school environment for years and that they needed special counselling as they were coming from a war zone where rape, murder, and other violent acts were common.
>
> A school vice-principal, Robyn Allaby, wrote to a colleague on March 3: "It would appear that the honeymoon is over with a few of the Syrian men – the 19 & 20 year olds. Things have been brewing for a few weeks now – the older males challenging (two other teachers) particularly when it comes to the girls in the class and also bullying others in the class. There was an incident today and things also got physical with a few students."
>
> After ISIS terrorists killed 32 people in Belgium on March 22, teacher Chantal Lafargue e-mailed several teachers and administrators that "in our wing for students of a certain culture ... there is a lot of energy and excitement ... we should be mindful of today."

In another e-mail, a teacher details how an older Syrian student bullied a younger Jewish student. "Obviously this is a cultural and political scenario that runs deep and while I like to think we can transcend it all in our classrooms, so far it doesn't look good,'"teacher Neil Brewer wrote on March 3 to several colleagues.

... School vice principal Robyn Allaby wrote on March 22 regarding the school's "English as an Additional Language" class, where students range in age from 15-20. "Just last week we had an incident where 19- and 20-year-olds were making racist comments to young students and intimidating them. We had to bring in a translator for a full day to help us smooth the waters and get back on track."

But it seems one priority is to give the new Muslim students the special privilege of their own "prayer rooms." David McTimoney, the superintendent of the Anglophone West School District, first downplayed the emails by saying that the selected e-mails "painted an inaccurate picture," and "were taken completely out of context and sensationalized." He then confirmed a prayer room had been created within the school and said it was a symbol of the school's commitment "to recognize and value the diversity among those that we serve."

Tolerating racism and violence; valuing the diversity brought by the bullies; submitting by giving up separation of religion and education through giving the bullies their own prayer room. Unbelievable.

Just as puzzling was the hasty retraction of a Halifax Nova Scotia school to allegations of Muslims bullying children in an elementary school. The story was reported in *The Globe and Mail*, on April 11, 2016, just a couple of months before the New Brunswick story. (Nova Scotia and New Brunswick are adjoining provinces on Canada's east coast, with modest economies and have never been the destination of choice for Asian immigrants, who tend to prefer the larger cities of Ontario or elsewhere in Canada.)

From *The Globe and Mail*:

The publisher of Nova Scotia's largest newspaper apologized on Monday after one of its stories ignited a firestorm with unverified allegations that young Syrian refugees had attacked fellow students at a Halifax elementary school.

The *Halifax Chronicle Herald* story, which alleged numerous acts of playground abuse at Chebucto Heights Elementary School – including an incident in which one "refugee boy" choked a girl in Grade 3 with a chain while yelling "Muslims rule the world," and another in which "refugee students" threatened others on the soccer field – was published online late Friday and in the paper's Saturday edition. It suggested school administrators had responded weakly to the alleged abuse.

After criticism on social media, editors removed some details from the online story, including the religious reference and the mention of the chain, and softened the original headline, prompting some critics to complain the paper was bowing to "political correctness." But on Monday the entire article was removed from the site and replaced with a lengthy editor's note, which also ran in the paper, saying the piece had "needed more work."

"Bullying is a sensitive subject. So is the integration of newcomers, particularly those who have faced challenges, even trauma, on their way here," the note read.

Canada's *National Post* on April 17, 2015, reported that the province's human rights tribunal ruled that:

A Calgary private school unlawfully discriminated against two Muslim students by refusing to allow them to pray on campus.

The Alberta Human Rights Commission fined Webber Academy a total of $26,000 for distress and loss of dignity after the boys were forced to hide at the school or leave the property during the city's chilly winter to fulfill their faith's obligations.

Neil Webber, the facility's founder and president, said he was disappointed with the ruling released Thursday and said an appeal with Alberta's Court of Queen's Bench will be filed.

"A key pillar of our founding principles is that the school be a non-denominational environment in which children can thrive and focus on their academic success," Webber said.

"This remains our goal."

This, in my opinion, is a case where a private school was developed in an era where non-denominational meant no religion on site. But in the new Canada with its human rights tribunals, schools or employers must accommodate religious people who want to pray on site.

Where this ideology gets a little bizarre is when the school itself is a religion-based school, such as the publicly supported Roman Catholic schools in Canada. The *Toronto Sun* reported in September, 2012, that in London Ontario:

> Mother Teresa Catholic secondary school is turning a second-floor office into an Islamic prayer room -- the first high school in the city, private or public, to do so.
>
> Carpet will soon cover the tile flooring, speakers will be installed and prayer mats purchased to provide the school's Muslim students, estimated at around two dozen, with a quiet and private place to pray.
>
> The idea has been in the works since the end of the last school year after a group of Muslim students lobbied administration to create the space.
>
> "They're members of our school community. We want to ensure that all our students feel welcome, that they feel that they belong," said Principal Ana Paula Fernandes.
>
> The prayer room, expected to be completed by the end of September, is located on a busy stretch on the second floor, just metres from the school's large chapel.
>
> "That was very important to ensure that it was included in the main building, and not tucked away somewhere," Fernandes said.

I do not understand why a Roman Catholic school that has as a significant part of its mission the teaching of the Catholic religion and makes Catholic religious instruction part of its curriculum, should need to make Muslim students feel that they "belong" and feel "welcome." Again, it looks a lot like *submission* to me.

It is of interest in this discussion that in the 1988 case of Zylberberg v. Sudbury Board of Education the use of the Lord's Prayer in opening exercises in public schools in Ontario was challenged. The Ontario Court of Appeals ruled that the recitation of the Lord's Prayer ultimately "infringes the Charter freedom of conscience and religion," even in cases where the students were allowed to opt out.

The prayer was "removed" insofar as it could not be used to pressure religious minorities to conform to the practices of the Christian majority. I can accept this in the case of public schools, but I do not agree that a religious Christian school must provide facilities for those practicing another religion or that a private school built on the foundation of non-denominationalism or separation of religion and education must allow for prayers; it seems that parents who want their children to practice religion in schools, now have the right within the public system to do so; to me, these cases carry "inclusive diversity" too far.

In an opinion piece on January 12, 2017, Canadian writer and television host, Christine Williams, entitled "Canada: School board allows Muslim sermons in schools", noted that:

> Despite the foundations and long tradition of Christianity in Canada, any accommodation of it — even at Christmas time — is largely rejected in the public school system, which supposedly adheres to secularism. But there is a single exception to the rule, as one religion seems to stand supreme: Muslim students in the province of Ontario are entitled to hold weekly prayer meetings, held on Friday. These "Jumm'ah" prayer and sermon sessions have been the focus of intense criticism as the provincial public school system is not supposed to be promoting any religion or hosting any religious instruction.

Williams queries why The Peel School Board in Mississauga (near Toronto) is not only allowing Islamic sermons, but it is also refusing to monitor the *contents* of those sermons.

Williams is concerned that this might lead to the spread of Islamism. Back in November 2016, she reported that the Board heard from a large delegation of Muslims that Muslim students feel 'stigmatized and targeted' because their Friday prayers were restricted to pre-approved sermons, whereas previously, Muslim students were free to use any sermon they chose that was approved by an administrator. The complaints from the Muslim community led to the reversal of the policy: the practice of allowing Muslim students to choose sermons was resumed.

She notes that "Muslim Friday prayer is the only group-prayer activity that is allowed by the Peel District School Board."

Says Williams: "Peel board members justified the policy reversal not to monitor the Islamic sermons by insisting it represented a commitment to inclusiveness."

Yet she argues that "its singling out of Muslims for preferred treatment above all other faiths was not an exercise in inclusivity, but rather a demonstration of the appalling exclusion of all other faiths."

This sort of thing has even entered American schools where the constitutional prohibitions should be clear. In an article entitled "Prayer Room At Public High School Raises Legal Concerns," by Mary Lou Lang-Byrd, *Daily Caller*, March 17, 2017, she writes:

> A prayer room at a Texas high school is raising legal concerns and the state's attorney general's office in a letter on Friday to school district's superintendent indicated the school's policy should be neutral toward religion.
>
> Liberty High School's prayer room, which is reportedly dedicated to students who practice Islam, allows the students to pray at the school on Fridays instead of leaving to say their required prayers. The letter cites the school's own news site, which focused on the prayer room.
>
> In a letter Friday to the Frisco Independent School District, the Texas attorney general's office outlined the legal concerns over the prayer room, indicating it may violate the First Amendment's protection of religious liberty.

The ideology of inclusive diversity erodes the center in our society and conduces to radicalism on both the Right and the Left.

Tabitha Korol, writing in the *New Media Journal*, on March 3, 2017, looks at how some Jewish left-center (non-Orthodox) day schools in the United States are departing from traditional values, and preparing their students for life in a globalist and "diverse" world.

I wonder if, in this diverse world, biblical values may eventually be considered part of a majority oppression of immigrant groups with Islamist values?

Korol says about some of these Jewish schools: "Their children are to be 'active students in the global world,' making them ideal subjects for a multicultural outreach program. They're being taught to abandon their own standards of morality while accepting the evils perpetrated by others."

She brings up an educational plan promoted by the Jewish organization, the *Anti-Defamation League*. The ADL, for many years, stuck to fighting anti-Semitism. But now under the new leadership of Jonathan Greenblatt, whose past includes working with George

Soros-sponsored organizations, the mission seems to have changed to one of propagandizing a leftist tolerist ideology and promoting it through the sponsorship of educational programs for schools.

The *No Place for Hate Workshop*, sponsored by the Anti-Defamation League claims to prepare students to support and assist in resolving peer conflicts and to uncritically accept all manner of belief systems, cultures, ethics, values, behaviors, and religions.

I researched some of the lesson plans being disseminated under this program and was shocked to come upon this example for high-school students:

Current Events Classroom—The 'Muslim Ban' and the Power of Protest

Topic: Social Justice

Grade Level: High School

Common Core Standards: Reading, Writing, Speaking and Listening

On January 27, 2017, President Trump signed an executive order called "Protecting the Nation from Foreign Terrorist Entry into the United States," which he says is to screen out "radical Islamic terrorists." The executive order is quite controversial and many of its critics refer to it as a "Muslim ban" because it temporarily bars the entry of even visitors from seven majority Muslim countries. Within 23 hours of the order being signed, immigration agents began detaining travelers from designated countries. Word spread through social media and protestors gathered at airports across the country to demand the detainees' release and the rescinding of the ban; these protests continued the next day in airports and other locations nationwide. In addition, hundreds of attorneys showed up at U.S. airports to offer free legal help to the travelers and family members of loved ones detained under the executive order. The American Civil Liberties Union (ACLU), along with other organizations, immediately challenged the executive order in court and a stay was issued, temporarily blocking President Trump's policy from taking effect and preventing refugees and immigrants from being deported.

This lesson will provide an opportunity for students to learn more about the executive order and the actions immediately following the signing of it, reflect on trending hashtags to gain insight into people's thoughts about the

> executive order, read an op-ed critical of the executive order and write their own op-ed that represents their point of view on the topic.

One doesn't know where to start in objecting to this sort of stuff being foisted upon our children. One could note that teaching students to protest the results of a democratic election is of course problematic. Or one can just note that the teacher will give the students an op-ed *critical* of the executive order, but no corresponding op-ed in favor of the order. This is not education; it is indoctrination for submission.

Professor Salim Mansur of London Ontario's Western University (in private correspondence) put the issue very well, when he wrote:

> Discussing "diversity" in the abstract is more or less worthless. We need to know in what context we are discussing "diversity."
>
> The celebration of "diversity", for instance, in the high noon of the Victorian era of the British Empire meant one thing in contrast to its celebration in the circumstances of Britain sans empire, sans power, sans glory as now when a soldier-drummer boy can be decapitated with impunity on the streets of London by denizens of a very diverse city.
>
> When Victoria celebrated her Diamond Jubilee with full splendid display of the "diversity" of her Empire, the celebration of "diversity" was – if I may use this term as explanation – centripetal, wherein the Empire brought together people of diverse ethnicity, language, religion towards the centre and for its glory.
>
> In contrast today, the obsequiousness to "diversity" among the ruling elite in Britain, or here in Canada, is evidence of the centrifugal nature of the society where the centre has considerably weakened and the diverse elements of that society is pushing out further and further from the centre that has less and less commanding or assertive value, and those who once defended the centre are now given to undermining it as a display of some superior virtue.
>
> Multiculturalism is, of course, the lie told to sell the virtue of "diversity" in the evening hour of a society or state stricken by the paralysis of self-doubt.

"Diversity" or "inclusive diversity," together with illiberal notions of "social justice" have created within the post-modern universities a set of problems, discussed by Philip Carl Salzman, Professor of Anthropology at Canada's McGill University, writing on February 1, 2017 for the *Gatestone Institute*. (gatestoneinstitute.org/9604/social-justice). Says Salzman:

> Many have established "equity and inclusiveness" committees to oversee "just practice," to disseminate "correct" views through literature, posters, and re-education workshops, in some cases mandatory. They also sanction faculty members who express unacceptable views. Schools of education ensure that their graduates will be inculcating their school pupils in the principles of "social justice," and in identifying the deplorable "multiphobes" in their families and communities. American schoolchildren have been taught by teachers determined to discredit America, that slavery was an American invention and existed exclusively in America -- a staggeringly counter-factual account.

Making diversity a moral end in itself, making capitalism into the cause of inequality, and "hurt feelings" the criteria for permitted speech, the young totalitarians learn all that opposition to their social justice opinions are evil or racist or fascist.

Anthropologist Salzman states:

> The illiberal social justice movement strikes at several important liberal values: First, it undermines individual autonomy and freedom by reducing individuals to being a member of one or another ethnic, racial, gender, sexual, national, or religious "category." Second, it strives to undermine individual autonomy and freedom by restricting outcomes of activity through imposing arbitrary criteria of equality of result. Third, it undermines basic human rights, such as freedom of speech, by forbidding any speech that "offends" anyone. Fourth, it undermines the right to assemble peaceably, because social justice warriors try to shut down any assembly where incorrect views might be expressed. Fifth, it undermines understanding by reducing all people to victims and oppressors, good versus bad, a gross oversimplification of the complexities of history and human life.

Salzman sees the social justice ideology in the universities as a movement of intolerant authoritarianism, in complete opposition to the tradition of open-minded, inquiring, liberal university.

The Islamists have taken advantage by portraying themselves as the ultimate victims, and the Jewish State as the ultimate oppressor. What we see in the universities is a failure to understand that if truth is not a truth for everyone, it is not truth but ideology. If the students think that they alone possess the truth, they are the enemies of freedom, and they should be known as totalitarians. The universities are giving their students ideological blinders as they make good candidates for submission at a very crucial time.

In the chapter entitled "Beyond Tolerance", I discuss Canadian Prime Minister Justin Trudeau and his reliance on the idea of "inclusive diversity" being his idea of the most important Canadian value. I ask, "Should we welcome evil ideologies as part of our inclusive diversity? Do we still believe that some things are good and some are evil? Do we think that a nice Canadian welcome, together with conduct and words not just tolerant, but *beyond* tolerant, will turn intolerant jihadists into tolerant Canadians?"

Perhaps Trudeau is not aware that giving "rights and choices" to some illiberal people may deprive existing liberal citizens of *their* rights and choices. Trudeau has supported something he calls "inclusive diversity" which I suppose is based on the flawed concept in multiculturalism that all cultures are equal. He believes that *diversity is a goal in itself*, and like Hillary Clinton and Barack Obama, we must respect and admire our enemies, the Islamists. Prime Minister Trudeau now seemingly believes, that tolerating those with illiberal opinions, is not enough; we must give them "understanding" and a *special place* for their choices in our public realm. We examine Trudeau's thinking more in the next chapter. Unfortunately, inclusive diversity does not distinguish, at least in Trudeau's mind, between Islam and Islamism. Inclusion of the Islamists is a bad idea, and one only possible when the prevailing ideology is a tolerism heading to a submission. Our governments, our universities, and our school boards must come to this understanding and soon.

Chapter 10: Trudeau at Auschwitz

The Achilles Heel of Multiculturalism

In November, 2015, Canada's new Prime Minister Justin Trudeau made a speech in London England, setting out his view of Canada's values:

> Compassion, acceptance, and trust; diversity and inclusion— these are the things that have made Canada strong and free," he noted, and continued: "We have a responsibility— to ourselves and to the world—to show that inclusive diversity is a strength, and a force that can vanquish intolerance, radicalism and hate.

Trudeau, then, emphasizes something he calls "inclusive diversity." His father, former Prime Minister Pierre Trudeau, was responsible for the concept of multiculturalism finding its way into Section 27 of the *Canadian Charter of Rights and Freedoms* in 1982. This section of the Charter was part of a range of provisions that helps to determine how rights in other sections of the Charter should be interpreted and applied by the courts. It is believed that section 27 "officially recognized" a Canadian value, namely multiculturalism.

The section reads,

> · 27. This Charter shall be interpreted in a manner consistent with the preservation and enhancement of the multicultural heritage of Canadians.

Then in 1988, the Mulroney Government completed the institution of "multicultural" values by enacting The *Canadian Multiculturalism Act*, with two fundamental principles:

> All citizens are equal and have the freedom to preserve, enhance and share their cultural heritage.
>
> Multiculturalism promotes the full and equitable participation of individuals and communities of all origins in all aspects of Canadian society.

It pains me to think that it is the law in Canada that illiberal cultural heritages should be enhanced.

Ezra Levant, writing in the *Toronto Sun*, pointed out that Justin Trudeau criticized the new citizenship guide for new immigrants, called *Discover Canada*. One passage in that guide book said, "Canada's openness and generosity do not extend to barbaric cultural practices that tolerate spousal abuse, 'honor killings,' female genital mutilation, forced marriage or other gender-based violence."

Note carefully Trudeau's immoral response to what should be morally obvious: "There needs to be a little bit of an attempt at responsible neutrality" by the Canadian government. Honor killings shouldn't be called "barbaric," he said. Amazing.

His brother Alexandre is a filmmaker who made a film called *The New Great Game*, about Iran's "courageous" decision to defy America and Israel. Sacha made it in co-operation with *Press TV*, the state-run propaganda agency of Iran.

At Auschwitz, Trudeau spent nearly three hours touring the infamous death camp that used industrial techniques to murder in gas chambers about a million people, mostly Jews, including my paternal grandparents and then eight year old sister of my father. In the last six months of the war, when the world had clear knowledge of this attempt to destroy every Jew in the world, the pace of executions sped up, so that about 600,000 were killed in that period. The Jews were brought into the concentration camp in packed cattle cars. A few bombs dropped by the Allies on the tracks leading to the camp could have saved the lives of tens of thousands. In total, six million Jews were murdered.

Racism is one thing; exterminationist racism is another thing. In the world today, proponents of exterminationist racism still exist and still aim to destroy another 6 million Jews, now living in the homeland of the indigenous Jews, Israel. Iran is the leader of the movement to destroy Israel and exterminate its Jews. Justin Trudeau's brother (by implication), Iranian-sponsored terrorist and political groups like Hamas and Hezbollah, and even the Palestinian Authority share the wish to destroy the Jews of Israel; that they cannot do so, is the work of Israel in building a strong military and high tech weapons, and not any great support lately of Israel by the very European nations that handed over their Jews willingly to the Nazis.

Previous Prime Minister Stephen Harper took a sometimes unpopular moral stand on Canadian foreign policy, which resulted in his strong support for Israel. Back in 2003 Mr. Harper said Canada's conservatives needed to "rediscover" the traditional conservatism of political philosopher Edmund Burke, which valued "social order," custom and religious traditions. President Trump is not one to analyze the nature of conservatism, but his thinking ends up somewhat similar to Harper.

Trudeau was guided through Auschwitz by 88-year-old Nate Leipciger, now of Toronto, who survived Auschwitz. The prime minister couldn't hold back the tears as he stood before the ruined gas chamber where Leipciger's mother and sister were killed 70 years ago.

Leipciger was effusive in his praise of Trudeau: "He cried with me. That's what happened. He shed tears with me," Leipciger said of the words and emotions he shared with the prime minister when they embraced. "It proved he is a fine human being who understood what I was trying to convey about why we were there."

Trudeau signed the memorial book in this way:

> Tolerance is never sufficient. Humanity must learn to love our differences.
>
> Today we bear witness to humanity's capacity for deliberate cruelty and evil. May we ever remember this painful truth about ourselves, and may it strengthen our commitment to never allow such darkness to prevail.

Auschwitz defines Evil, except to those Islamists in Britain and elsewhere who petition local school boards to drop it from their children's curricula because they find it offensive, do not believe it happened, at least not to the extent accepted by others, and believe that it was some kind of lie made up to gain advantage for the Jews in the attempted partition by the United Nations, (which was not accepted by the Arabs who attempted to end it by war in 1948, 1956, 1967 and 1973 and by constant terrorism since the 1920s.)

"Inclusive diversity" does not know how to deal with "humanity's capacity for deliberate cruelty and evil." Trudeau's compassion, trust and inclusive diversity are no equal to deliberate cruelty and evil, nor is it a force that can "vanquish intolerance, radicalism and hate."

Trudeau cried, in my opinion, not only because of the stories of life and death in Auschwitz told to him by his guide, the survivor Mr. Leipciger. He cried because deep down, he began to realize, that diversity, respect for all communities, whether good or evil, is not a moral policy. It is a component of moral and cultural relativism – the belief that there is no good and evil and that all truth and morality is relative, and no cultures are better than any other cultures, so we should include them all, and respect them equally and import them into our country; and interpret our laws to accord respect for any and all evil communities that wish to join our country, not for the purpose of accepting traditional values, but the new inclusive values of the *Multiculturalism Act* that says that "All citizens are equal and have the freedom to preserve, enhance and share their cultural heritage."

Perhaps Justin Trudeau cried too because his celebrated father did not see fit to help stop Hitler and the Nazi atrocities by opposing conscription and not serving with the army during the Second World War. In his Memoirs (1993), the elder Trudeau wrote: "So there was a war? Tough … if you were a French Canadian in Montreal in the early 1940s, you did not automatically believe that this was a just war … we tended to think of this war as a settling of scores among the superpowers."

This moral confusion of the father was surely passed down to the son, who advocates for loving differences without any moral judgment on those differences. For if a cultural heritage is anti-Semitic, anti-woman, anti-gay, anti-child, how do we celebrate cultural diversity in the aftermath of Auschwitz? Evil exists. The lesson of Auschwitz is that we must eradicate evil and recognize that some nations become evil and we should not want their people in our communities enhancing and sharing their cultural heritage and asserting "group rights" over the individual rights that should be the bedrock of our civilization.

There are some differences that I do not love and will not love and will not tolerate. Trudeau's tears at Auschwitz demonstrate that official Multiculturalism has an Achilles Heel – when you grow up, you understand that there is Evil and unless you can articulate better values than inclusive diversity, you may start to cry when confronted with such overwhelming evidence of evil. Better that one adopts the values of Stephen Harper – that there is no room for moral relativism in foreign policy and that the 6 million Jews of Israel today face a new Auschwitz – the soon to be nuclear Iran and the terrorist groups who kill Israeli children in their beds and school buses.

I cry too, when our prime minister can't seem to understand the contradiction in his policy of enhancing all cultures—when not all cultures are good or liberal. Moreover, he is keen to admit into the country some cultures despite their cultural celebration of the murder of Jews, gays, Yazidis, and Christians together with a culture of rape towards women who do not follow their dictates.

For the definitive liberal critique of multiculturalism, see Salim Mansur's *Delectable Lie: a liberal repudiation of multiculturalism.*

After Auschwitz, multiculturalism and moral relativism, are obscene. Moral values in domestic and international matters must reflect our traditional Judeo-Christian ethics of the Bible. Inclusive diversity is a weak substitute, and sometimes it takes a visit to Auschwitz to understand why.

Although I support the rights of Muslims who are not Islamist, I contend that morality dictates that they must accept the moral foundations of our traditional values and make their religious observance fit into that moral framework; if Trudeau's vision prevails, we shall all have a lot to cry about.

CHAPTER 11: BANNING AND BOYCOTTING IN THE AGE OF TOLERISM

The Moral Darkness Behind the Left's Targeting of Israel

In an age where so many of our elites assert that tolerance, pacifism and dialogue are the foundation of the moral life, we are certainly seeing a lot of intolerant banning, shunning and boycotting. This notion of tolerance for the intolerant Islamofascists (who, when they take power, ban all tolerance) is the main concern of my previous book, *Tolerism: The Ideology Revealed* (Mantua Books).

For the current ideology of tolerism is in fact only tolerant towards evil and is very intolerant of the traditional Judeo-Christian ethic.

In my book, I outline how cultural and moral relativism and moral equivalency act to twist the value of tolerance into a value that replaces traditional values like justice and individual liberty with some kind of multicultural appeasement, where the appeasers see nothing in American values that are more admirable than the Islamist values rooted in 6th century jihad.

We know that the tolerists do not really act in a tolerant way when it comes to the country in the forefront of identifying the evil and taking concrete steps against it. Instead, we see:

· Banning of Israelis speakers or professors from American campuses.

· Boycotting Israeli companies (except apparently when they make the essentials of the computer you are using or the medical device that will save your life) in the so-called BDS (Boycott, Divestment and Sanctions) movement.

· Banning by a cultural group of artists in Britain of 100 actors, musicians, artists and writers, of performances anywhere in Israel.

Dennis Prager, writing soon after Netanyahu's speech to Congress, in *National Review*, makes an interesting point:

"Those who do not confront evil resent those who do."

And so in the eight years of the Obama administration America minimized the Islamofascist war declared against it. Obama wouldn't say the words "Islamic terrorism" together, and saw his mission as reconciling America to Islam, in all its varieties, whether or not that hurt traditional American values. Obama, schooled by Bill Ayers, Frank Marshall Davis and Reverend Wright, could hardly be expected to reflect traditional values.

We should all realize that Israel is the first front in the Islamist war against liberal modernity. Europe seems to think that by sacrificing Israel's security interests it can buy time -- but appeasement of evil does not slow that evil, it speeds it up. And so Prager says:

> It only makes sense, then, that no other country feels the need to warn the world about Iran and Islamic terror as much as does Israel ... Virtually everyone listening knows he (Israeli Prime Minister Benjamin Netanyahu) is telling the truth. And most dislike him for it. Appeasers hate those who confront evil. Given that this president (Obama) is the least likely of any president in American history to confront evil — or even identify it — while Benjamin Netanyahu is particularly vocal and eloquent about both identifying and confronting evil, it is inevitable that the former will resent the latter.

"Resentment," however may be too weak a word for what we are seeing from some Democrats and left-liberal media people. As a student of anti-Semitism throughout history, I know that resentment by immoral people (like Hitler, whose policies breached most of the Ten Commandments) is especially acute in the case of the Jews who stand for the morality of the Torah. So yes, this resentment has a certain kinship to classical anti-Semitism.

Although some Democrats who boycotted Netanyahu's speech to Congress in 2015 were honestly concerned about certain breaches of protocol with respect to Boehner's invitation, that concern does not justify the boycotting. It did not justify Nancy Pelosi turning her back on Netanyahu when he said,

> For the first time in 100 generations, we, the Jewish people, can defend ourselves.

> This is why – this is why, as a prime minister of Israel, I can promise you one more thing: Even if Israel has to stand alone, Israel will stand.

The Left, including the Jewish left, hate a proud and strong Jew. In *Tolerism*, I wrote about the bizarre nature of Holocaust commemorations and museums that ban any reference to contemporary Israel's problems out of some misguided notion of tolerance for Israel's enemies.

Boycotting speeches, turning your back on the speaker who is a prime minister of the one state that is surrounded by Islamist mischief on a daily basis, is not just rude, it amounts to a delegitimization of that speaker and of that country. And, we know from the great human rights activist, Natan Sharansky that demonization, delegitimization and double standards constitute the "3 D" test for anti-Semitism.

Our enemies do not just boycott people and products; they boycott the *truth*. The average person now believes that Jews came to Israel from Europe and stole land from an indigenous people called the Palestinians. The truth is completely the opposite: the Jews were indigenous and were expelled from Israel a number of times, but always returned. When expelled, Jews went to various areas of the world, including Europe, but a lot lived in Arab lands. Most of the Arabs who resided in Jewish lands refused to share and various international bodies who sought to divide the land found that the Arabs would not accept the division. Moreover, they even expelled the Jews living in Arab lands, so great was their hatred of Jews and ideology that all of the Jews' Holy Land was in fact their holy land.

The Jews who lived in various European countries, often being expelled from one to another, were just part of the story: the other part was the 850,000 Sephardic Jews expelled from Arab lands, from the '30s to the '70s. It is necessary to fight back against the boycotting of the truth. In this regard it was interesting to read in *hasbarafellowships.com* about siblings Ariella and Noam Sibony, passionate student leaders of Moroccan Jewish heritage. The Sibony siblings recently participated in Arab Culture Day at York University in Toronto—a university with significant anti-Israel activity. They presented a musical performance highlighting Moroccan Jewry in front of a packed audience of almost entirely non-Jewish students.

One of the biggest lies that is spread against Israel states that Israel is populated with Jews who arrived from Eastern Europe in 1948, and says nothing about the history and the diversity of Israel and its people. We must continue, like these brave students, to work against the boycott of truth. Otherwise, the Arabs are not ashamed to make the most outlandish claims, whether those claims are about the Jewish Temple in Jerusalem or about the Holocaust. These lies must be challenged by making clear to anyone who will listen that the first victim of the BDS (boycott, divest and sanction) movement is the TRUTH.

I am not impressed with the way some pacifists portray themselves as taking the moral high road. They do not; the Bible makes clear that sometimes you have to go to war to protect your civilians against the Hitlers of this world.

A good example of the problem is leftist Senator Bernie Sanders who ran for the Democratic nomination for president. In an interview with CNN immediately after the 2015 speech by Netanyahu, which he boycotted but watched on television, he clearly demonstrated the moral equivalency and cultural relativism that is at the heart of Israel-hatred.

The interviewer asked him to comment on Netanyahu in the past calling Iran an "apocalyptic death cult." Sanders at first tried to say he didn't want to "go there," which is a typical response from an Israel hater to solid facts that might expose the seriousness of the threat from Iran. But then Sanders started his non-answer by alleging that Israel helped push America into the War in Iraq, and so he adopted the "Israel as warmonger" argument. Nevermind that Israel took years of rocket attacks from Gaza before it started a war, and that no other country would try so hard to give diplomacy a chance, as it did with the Oslo Process.

The interviewer tried to bring Sanders back on topic and asked him, "Do you think the people running Iran are rational actors?" With the ultimate in moral equivalency, Sanders answered, "Let's not say that these people are not rational actors. Are we the only rational people in the world?"

How very troubling it must be to people like Sanders to have to hear the truth: That Iran is a terrorist-sponsoring, apocalyptic, anti-gay, anti-Semitic, anti-woman, anti-child, anti-freedom of expression aggressor. No wonder he responds with venom and moral equivalency between Iran and America. And he reflects the anti-tolerance totalitarian tactic of boycotting, banning and shunning.

For the tolerists, the ones like Sanders who wrap themselves in the cloak of anti-war and pacifism and protection of social programs that might be cut in wartime, do not comment on the horrible history of Iran after the Islamist Revolution.

They should read some history about the Iranian-sponsored terrorist group, Hezbollah. It killed hundreds of American troops and dozens of French troops participating in a peace-keeping operation in Lebanon in 1983. When then Secretary of Defense Caspar Weinberger talked Ronald Reagan out of firing a missile at the terrorist headquarters America missed the opportunity to destroy an organization of truly evil nature.

Then study the 1994 Iranian-backed Hezbollah bombing of the Buenos Aires Jewish Community Center, killing 85 and injuring 300. Argentina, like Sanders, wanted to keep out of war, so it tolerated what happened and no serious criminal investigations were launched until a decade ago when a brave young Argentinean prosecutor, Alberto Nisman, got to the bottom of the matter, and issued indictments, based on fact, that the Iranians had organized the attack with Hezbollah perpetrators and corrupt Argentinean enablers. This story is well chronicled in the important book by Gustavo Perednik, *To Kill Without a Trace: A Prequel to 9/11.*

Then, as a result of the Argentinean government in its highest offices trying to waive the criminal indictments in return for an oil-for-wheat deal, we saw Iran's response. As outlined recently in the security magazine *Debkafile*, an Iranian double agent, a supposed defector who got Nisman's trust, murdered Nisman hours before he was to testify about the new evidence of obstruction of justice by the president and the foreign minister.

The Obama administration openly interfered with money and personnel for Netanyahu's opponents in a coming Israeli election, but at the same time complained that Netanyahu, whose country faces an *existential enemy* in Iran, should not be allowed to meddle in American foreign policy. A double standard, indeed.

Of course, Obama, early in his administration, pledged to support the Arab "Spring" and democratic rights, but did nothing to help Iranian protesters against their awful regime. Accordingly, Obama himself is a tolerist and appeaser of the Iranian Ayatollahs and their puppet governments. Obama thinks that the Israelis are "occupiers" of land that was historically Jewish and that Israel gained back in a defensive war against Arab nations who were trying to kill all of Israel's Jews and make it Islamist. The land may be "disputed" and Israel may give some back in the context of a peace agreement should the Arabs finally agree to accept a Jewish state in the Jew's ancestral homeland (which existed far before Islam was invented) but in no way is it a matter of occupation of land belonging to someone else.

The Obama crowd tell Israel what to do. But look at Obama's foreign policy towards the end of his second term. He gave the Saudis help (with targeting intelligence and fuel) in their bombing campaigns against civilians in Yemen, which targeted *hospitals and schools*: See the article in the *New York Times* by Mark Mazzetti and Shuaib Almosawa (nytimes.com/2016/08/25/world/middleeast/yemen-saudi-arabia-hospital-bombing.html)

Says this report:

> It is now 17 months into a military campaign that began after Shiite rebels, known as the Houthis, overran the Yemeni capital, forced the government into exile and began positioning missile batteries close to Saudi Arabia's southern border. Saudi Arabia and its Gulf allies have portrayed the Houthis as puppets of Iran, a charge that American officials view with deep skepticism, even though they say Tehran has provided the militia with some arms and money.

In other words, Obama and John Kerry, always critical of Israel, first helped the Iranians get hundreds of millions of dollars that the United States was withholding, and then once the Iranians had the money and helped the Houthis, Obama and Kerry felt obligated to help the Saudis in their war crimes. And Obama won a Nobel Peace Prize?

It obviously was not a prize for real peace, but a prize given by leftist Scandinavians in the hope that Obama would carry through on anti-Israel pro-Islamist sentiments. They have named war "peace" and given a peace prize for war. When your ideology contains a large dose of anti-Semitism, this is the kind of ideological confusion that happens; Israel has to deal with it.

See Ezekiel, Chapter 13, verse 10: "Because, indeed because they misled My people, saying, 'Peace,' when there is no peace, and it is building a flimsy wall, and behold they are plastering it with daub." (daub-earth is a substance that does not resist the rains).

I predict that the banning and boycotting and shunning of Israeli politicians and supporters will soon pass over to banning Israeli books. This is the inevitable result of what is going on at universities today, where Israeli speakers or professors are banned and the lies of Israel Apartheid Week, the short snappy slogans of hate, are welcomed.

This *mis-education* is surely being accompanied by an *un-education*, where students are failing to read the great books of the great thinkers. This was of course one of the main points of the late Professor Allan Bloom's, *The Closing of the American Mind*. But even Bloom, I dare think, would be surprised to read the following rant by a current pop star named Kanye West: *"Sometimes people write novel and they just be so wordy and so self-absorbed. I am not a fan of book. I would never want a book's autograph. I am a proud non-reader of books."*

The world has turned upside down: The more hateful and simplistic the message, the more it is acceptable; the more intellectual and complex is the message, the more it is hated. The hatred of Jews has been extended to the hatred of truth, morality and goodness and a tolerance for evil. Netanyahu is hated for his truth; Obama got elected for his slogans. It is no longer important to say good and do good, but like Obama you have to be a symbol, and then you collect your Nobel Prize without doing anything at all.

That is the truth the liberals cannot see. It is far worse than what American liberal Jews understand. There is no reasoning with those who will not reason, will not read. They will stand by while your grandchildren are beheaded by Islamists and preach tolerance of the executioners because they are driven by poverty, supposedly.

The tolerists don't understand that they should study Israel as the template for what might be happening here in ten years. In other words, Israel should be the model for how to maintain a liberal democracy and a rule of law when you are surrounded by Islamist genocidal terrorists. The fact that Israel remains a joyful, positive, freedom loving, place, honoring the religious and the secular, with music and dance and patriotism should be studied by us to convince ourselves not to submit but to fight on. Israel shows us that it is possible for a tiny country hated by all its neighbors to avoid a fate of losing hope and submitting to demands to place it in an untenable security situation. Yes, there are some suicidal leftist parties wishing to appease the Arabs, but after the tragic failure of the Arabs refusing to respond with peace and recognition in return for Israel's steps in the Oslo Process, support for the leftists has declined. It has had numerous wars fought against it, its young people have to interrupt their studies and "fun" years to serve in the army, and yet they do not give in. Families have lost members to terrorism, but they live on. It is a lesson for all of us.

Dr. Stephen Malnick, a British-born resident of Ashkelon, Israel, made a simple rebuttal of the cultural boycotters in a recent *Guardian* letters page:

> As a citizen of Ashkelon who was nearly killed when a missile missed my car by a few meters, I have a message for artists with a selective communal conscience. I do not want you to visit my city and insult 120,000 people who were daily attacked in violation of international law. There are no military targets in Ashkelon, but lots of Jews.
>
> After you make a stand against the extrajudicial killing of people in Gaza, and the whipping of a blogger in Saudi Arabia, and you apologize to the citizens of Ashkelon, I will consider extending you hospitality. I will continue my daily tasks, including treating Gazans who are brought to the medical center I work in. Odd, isn't it, that they visit but you won't?

In fact, it is only under President Trump that there is a chance for peace between Israel and the Palestinians and the other Arabs. All the other plans have been unrealistic in terms of giving a terrorist Islamist group prime land of historical Israel close to Israeli population centers and airport (which is a security nightmare) and too close to Jordan which already has a large Palestinian population; the Hashemite rulers of Jordan fear that a Palestinian state would lead to revolutionary violence by its own Palestinians.

Obama was an ideologue; Trump is a practical deal maker. There is an opportunity to implement a deal as described by Lawrence Solomon in Canada's *National Post*.

Solomon quotes Ayoub Kara, a minister in the Israeli government who has a history of spilling the beans on internal deliberations, and who spoke to Netanyahu prior to the Israeli prime minister's departure for Washington: "Trump and Netanyahu will adopt the plan of Egypt's Sisi. A Palestinian state in Gaza and Sinai. Instead of Judea and Samaria (the historic name for the disputed West Bank)." Solomon reports that Kara claimed that Egyptian President Abdel Fattah el-Sisi's proposal, which first surfaced in 2014, will be part of a regional peace deal involving Saudi Arabia and other Sunni Arab nations. "This is how we will pave a path to peace, including with the Sunni coalition," he enthused.

Trump and Netanyahu have made reference to a regional deal involving the Sunni countries, one Trump described as "a much more important deal in a sense. It would take in many, many countries and it would cover a very large territory."

Trump sees the situation much more clearly than the tolerist crowd. He sees that the Middle East is in disarray with wars in Iraq, Syria and Yemen, complicated by the split between the Iranian-backed Shiite groups and the Saudi-backed Sunni groups. He sees that Egypt's Sisi is not a captive of the Islamists and could be persuaded to give up some desert to implement the deal.

Moreover he knows this deal may be the only long term hope for Jordan's avoidance of an Islamist-Palestinian revolution. 70% of Jordan's population is Palestinian but is ruled by the Hashemite King Abdullah, a U.S. ally. The Palestinians claim to represent Jordan's Palestinians and this poses a threat to King Abdullah. We need only look at history, back to 1970 when the Palestinians did try to overthrow the monarchy in 1970 in the bloody Black September civil war. Solomon points out that while they were unsuccessful then, it might be a different story for Jordan if the Palestinians acquire the military advantages that would come with being a state.

Solomon writes:

> A Palestinian state in the West Bank would also be unstable because of its geography — it wouldn't be contiguous with its sister Palestinian territory of Gaza, the statelet created after Israel vacated the strip along Egypt's Sinai border. The Sinai, on the other hand, is not only contiguous with Gaza, its border city, Rafah, was split during the 1967 Six-Day War into an Egyptian and Palestinian half, separating families and businesses. Carving out part of Sinai to create a home for Palestinians adjacent to Gaza would reunify Rafah and its surrounding Palestinian communities, restoring not only families but a significant crossroads city.
>
> Westerners are told that Jerusalem and other Holy Lands in the West Bank have monumental religious significance to Muslims. That religious claim is belied by history. Under Muslim control over most of the last 1,000 years, the Holy Lands — which had been prosperous and politically vital under Jewish and Christian rule — became a backwater, poor and derelict, warranting little investment in their upkeep. Jerusalem was never a Muslim capital and unlike cities that are considered by Islam as truly holy, it was neither an important cultural nor scholarly center for Muslims.

Solomon argues correctly that with the present variety of Mid-East conflicts, the situation has changed and he quotes the respected Saudi weekly Asharq al-Awsat, "Due to the destruction and displacement that has affected the Middle East in Iraq, Syria and Lebanon, the Palestinian cause is no longer central."

It is very much a brilliant deal, and should be accepted by everyone except the most twisted Israel-haters. Unfortunately, these Arab and Iranian Israel-haters and their leftist and European backers will construe the plan as a "submission" and submission is only for the infidels. This is where Europe needs to step up, put its Jew-hatred away forever, and promote a Palestinian state, where it can be established without cursing the following generations to a continuation of the violent past.

The Sunni Arab states and Israel both share the common enemy of Iran and this is an important factor to bringing them together to cast aside Islamist ideology and accept a deal to cut the power of both Iran and ISIS. The better minds across the world are getting tired of Palestinian rejectionism and terrorism and tired of the massive funds that to go to the West Bank, much siphoned off due to corruption and terrorism, making the Palestinians, the world's largest per capita recipients of foreign aid. Says Solomon: "The offer of a state in nearby Sinai, just 80 kilometres away, coupled with promises of massive development aid by the West and the Saudis, would be an offer they could not refuse."

This should be the goal of the West: to defeat the Islamists everywhere, starting in Israel. The money spent on war should be spent to relocate whatever Arabs living in the West Bank or Israel proper, who identify as Palestinian, to a Palestinian state that Egypt would want to see run differently than the terror state of Gaza. It should be demilitarized and both Israel and Egypt would work together to ensure its success. The Israelis could help make this future state a center of high tech and other products produced nowhere else in the Arab world. The Israelis would, I believe, rebuild the greenhouses that the Palestinians destroyed when Gaza was given to them. Palestinian Arabs who presently have Israeli citizenship could stay in Israel as a minority with full liberal democratic rights if they do not feel like moving.

This would be a triumph of morality over Islamist ideology and would hopefully spread all around the world.

CHAPTER 12: TOLERISM AND WELCOME OF REFUGEES' CULTURE OF ATROCITIES

As a retired lawyer who practiced law for twenty years, and now writes about political culture, I am sensitive to legal issues. After many days of reading about the widespread support to give admission to Canada to young Muslim men who may or may not have been involved in war crimes in Syria, Iraq, Somalia or Afghanistan, I began to think about exactly what this means for Canadian women. And as a retired lawyer, I know that foreign women who are at risk of rape in their native lands, can sometimes be protected by being accepted as a convention refugee to Canada. If we assume that importing potential rapists to Canada is a threat to the safety of Canadian women, and that we protect refugee women from such rapists in their lands, then perhaps we are favoring non-Canadian women's rights over Canadian women's rights. This is the kind of conundrum that tolerism creates in our political culture.

Professors and journalists who profess this tolerism, evidence a self-hatred of Western liberties, a refusal to study real negative cultural differences, and the embrace of the doctrine of Multiculturalism, which Professor Salim Mansur of Western University has aptly called a "delectable lie" in his liberal repudiation of this ideology – which often dismisses our historical *individual* rights in favor of some concept of *"group* rights."

First, let us look at Canadian Immigration Law, which allows a female refugee certain rights to claim to be a "convention refugee."

According to the Immigration and Refugee Board of Canada web site:

> The definition of a Convention refugee states that a claimant's fear of persecution must be "by reason of" one of the five enumerated grounds—that is race, religion, nationality, membership in a particular social group and political opinion. There must be a link between the fear of persecution and one of the five grounds.

It is for the Refugee Division to determine the ground, if any, applicable to the claimant's fear of persecution. This is consistent with the overall obligation of the Refugee Division to determine whether the claimant is a Convention refugee. If a claimant identifies the ground(s) which he or she thinks are applicable to the claim, the Refugee Division is not limited to considering only those grounds and must consider the grounds of the definition as raised by the evidence in making their determination. However, once the Refugee Division has found that the claimant's fear of persecution is by reason of one of the grounds it is not necessary to go on to consider all of the other grounds.

When determining the applicable grounds, the relevant consideration is the perception of the persecutor. The persecutor may perceive that the claimant is a member of a certain race, nationality, religion, or particular social group or holds a certain political opinion and the claimant may face a reasonable chance of persecution because of that perception. This perception may not conform with the real situation.

Reference should be made to the Guidelines on *Women Refugee Claimants Fearing Gender-Related Persecution*: Update issued by the Chairperson pursuant to section 65(3) of the *Immigration Act* on November 25, 1996, for an analysis of the grounds as they relate to gender-related persecution.

In two federal court cases in Canada, *Dezameau* and *Josile*, two Haitian women claimed a fear of persecution in the form of sexual violence. In these cases, the court cited the principle in *Ward* that "gender" can provide the basis for a particular social group. The court also cited jurisprudence from the Supreme Court of Canada in support of the proposition that rape and other forms of sexual assault are crimes grounded in the status of women in society.

In *Dezameau*, the court found that a widespread risk of violence in Haitian society does not rebut the assertion that there is a nexus between the applicant's social group and the risk of rape. Based on a review of Canadian law and the documentary evidence, the court in *Josile* concluded that the notion that rape is an act of violence faced *generally* by all Haitians is untenable; rather the risk of rape was grounded in the applicant's membership in a *particular social group, that of Haitian women*. Accordingly, Convention Refugee status applied.

Now let us turn to how we are dealing or not dealing with the threat of rape culture to Canadian women.

We must recognize in this endeavor that many who assert historical or current facts in their criticism of certain cultures are dismissed as racists and are shunned and often banned from university campuses and newspaper op-ed pages.

To call the ideology of tolerism a form of "political correctness" is to underestimate its threat to our freedoms, which ideology is more akin to repressive totalitarianism than to some gentle doctrine of correctness. I am unafraid to blow the whistle, on behalf of Canadian women, on the tolerist rush to welcome to the West tens, if not hundreds of thousands of predominantly Muslim refugees from Iraq, Syria, Pakistan, Afghanistan and Somalia. It is my contention that it is the tolerist ideology, followed by the other ideologies discussed in this book, that see these refugees as good candidates for western citizenship and values, despite the fact that more than a few are guilty of war crimes, including rape and that nastiest of nasties, group rape. Why are we so concerned about foreign women's rights and not Canadian women's rights to be protected from immigrants who may or may not have committed rape but are surely immersed in the culture of rape?

To recite the facts is to risk being called "racist"— but any male proponent of feminism as a respect for women's rights should place an extremely high value on women's right not to be raped. One must be brave enough to point out that certain cultures blame the victim for her rape, suggesting that immodest dress or religious unorthodoxy justify rape, often group rape. The Islamist jihad and desire for a world-dominating caliphate, and their apologists, sometimes justify rape as just a typical weapon of war, a war crime but not unique to Muslims.

Yet, in an article published by the *Gatestone Institute*, Ingrid Carlqvist and Lars Hedegaard, who look at rape statistics in Sweden, hardly a country at war, note that there is an obscene increase in rapes by immigrants, especially by those unknown to their victims (and hence differentiated from so called "date rape"). They report that forty years after the Swedish parliament unanimously decided to change the formerly homogenous Sweden into a multicultural country, violent crime has increased by 300% and rapes by 1,472%. Sweden is now number two on the list of rape countries, surpassed only by Lesotho in Southern Africa.

Tolerist empathetic judges or "human rights" tribunals have taken to charging writers, who seek to investigate these matters, with new crimes such as Sweden's "denigration of ethnic groups." Carlqvist and Hedegaard note that despite the attempts by the Swedish establishment to convince the population that everyone setting foot on Swedish soil becomes exactly like those who have lived there for dozens of generations, the facts are otherwise. But political correctness, or tolerism, whatever one calls it, makes the facts hard to come by and harder still to report: Carlqvist and Hedegaard note that the latest statistical survey of immigrant criminality compared to that of Swedes was done in 2005. The results are practically never mentioned. And anyone who dares refer to them, for example on social media, is viciously attacked or threatened with violence or state-sanctioned criminal proceedings.

A study done before 2005, showed men from North Africa were 23 times more likely to commit rape than Swedish born men, and the explosion of gang rapes by Muslim men is not likely to be the subject of any studies by the tolerist academy in Sweden.

In Oslo, Norway in 2011 a Police report stated that every single rape with violence in the past year was committed by men of non-western backgrounds and that Muslims who at that time only comprised 1.5% of the total population in Norway, were responsible for 50% of the entire country's rape statistics.

Western nations seem to be trying to outdo each other in accepting Muslim refugees that have been pouring into Southern Europe and seeking entry to the more prosperous European nations.

Most of the migrants seem to be from the highly dysfunctional artificial states of Iraq and Syria (artificial because they were not historical states but were created in the modern era, and still manifest tribal conflict, violence against minorities like Kurds, Yazidis and Christians, and conflict between Shias and Sunnis). Some are also coming from other Muslim nations such as Afghanistan and Somalia and Sudan.

Lost in the rush of humanitarian sentiment is the nature of the culture that these migrants may be bringing with them. In particular how many bring with them the "culture of rape"?

Most reports estimate that around 75% of the total migrants are young single men, not families, and this is the demographic that may have committed rapes against Christian and Yzedi women; without appropriate marriage-aged Muslim young women, these single young men might undergo a conflict between their conservative Muslim values and the open societies of the West, such a conflict being a stressor for rape, one would think. The important issue, and so little discussed in the media, is whether these men have been immersed in a culture of rape, as well as being immersed in a culture of antagonism towards "infidels" be they Christian, Jewish, Yzedi or Hindus.

If so, and if we still feel the humanitarian impulse to take them in, do not our women deserve the security of knowing that all of these young men will first attend an intensive instruction in western liberal values, religious freedom, and women's rights, including, most basically, the right not to be raped. Shouldn't we impose on prospective immigrants a type of Marshall Plan, which helped turn around Germany and Japan, to turn around the illiberal attitudes of many, if not most, of the migrants? Wouldn't that make it clear from the beginning that we reject a culture of violence and sexual assaults? Shouldn't we finally acknowledge that our culture of women's rights is to be cherished and enhanced, not by the importation of thousands of men whose culture legitimizes rape?

Leo Hohmann, writing in *WND.com*, cites a report in German provided by Pamela Geller, on the mounting evidence of rape in the refugee camps recently set up in Germany: Raping of female refugees has become epidemic at the Muslim-dominated refugee centers in Germany.

According to this document, women are "assigned a subordinate role" and unaccompanied females are treated as "fair game." Many of these women, according to the document, are fleeing "forced marriage" and/or "female genital mutilation." The consequences are numerous rapes and sexual assaults.

There is ample evidence of Muslim refugees throwing Christian refugees overboard from the small boats used by the traffickers of refugees. Anti-Christian and anti-Yzedi violence by Syrians has been so prevalent and so vicious, that one cannot fathom why the media promotes massive and quick Muslim immigration to the West. Do they even understand the prevalence of the Islamist culture of rape, or has cultural relativism blinded them to all cultural differences, when those cultural differences endanger our wives and daughters and even Muslim daughters who are deemed to dishonor their families by being the *objects* of sexual assault?

The media must start to report on some of the horrible cultures that surround certain immigrant refugees. It is not only Donald Trump that thinks the media are "crooked" in their selective reporting and non-reporting. The media must prod the governments to somehow ascertain which of the refugees have the ability to rise up against their culture, repudiate their culture and come to the West for a "fresh start." Or are we simply importing such problems as the culture of rape into our countries? Where is the discussion of this culture and the discussion of how we can take steps to prevent the immigration of this sick culture along with the refugees? Or are we so stupid to believe that all cultures are equal and that any criticism of other cultures is somehow "racist"? If we do not stand up for a culture of liberal democracy and a culture that gives fundamental individual rights to women, gays, and ethnic and religious minorities, and water it down with people who not only have participated in war crimes but seek to impose their illiberal culture on us, we shall breach an important obligation to our children and grandchildren to pass along the same rights that were passed on to us.

For the purpose of this chapter, I do not want to get into the contentious issue of the reason for the culture of rape, so endemic in Muslim countries. Suffice it to say it is far more prevalent among Arab Muslims and Islamists or radical Muslims in Pakistan, Afghanistan and Somalia, than in countries like Indonesia and Malaysia (yet note the gang rapes of Chinese women in the Jakarta riots of 1998 and that *FreeMalaysiaToday* reports one rape every 35 minutes in Muslim Malaysia). There is a raging debate underway now between those like Daniel Pipes, Zuhdi Jasser, and Salim Mansur who hold that it is only radical ideological Islam or "Islamism" that is the problem and that moderate Islam is the solution, on the one side, and others like David Solway, Andrew Bostom, Robert Spencer, Bill Warner, Bat Ye'or and Hirsi Ali, on the other, who argue that violence, rape, conquest, and enmity to other religions are inherent in the Koran and other religious writings, and therefore endemic to Islam.

I like to think that I have a realistic understanding of this debate. I believe that the main problem is with the Islamists, but I also think that Islam must undergo some reform and liberalization in the way it is practiced now if it wants to co-exist with Western rights-based cultures. Of course that reform is not up to me, it is up to Muslims who want to prove to me that they can reside in peace in liberal countries based on an understanding of human rights and freedoms that are different than what they have learned. I insist that I am not Islamophobic with such a position but that I know where the line should be for our tolerance and where we must take positions that the Islamist immigrants do not like. But it is up to them. As a Jew, I am more than a little sensitive to the *real* neo-Nazis, not the ineffective skinhead types, but the highly organized, financially strong, leftist supported, Nazis of our time, the Islamists, especially the Iranians and the non-people calling themselves Palestinians who have adopted the genocidal goals of Nazis themselves. The delegitimization, demonization and double standards applied to the one Jewish state, a beacon of liberal rights, minority rights, and innovative capitalism, without equal in the Middle East, reflect an anti-Semitism that has been well explained in the writings of Phyllis Chesler, Melanie Phillips and many others.

It is undeniable however, that there is a contemporary culture of rape in many Muslim countries, and the refugees, who are reported to be over 70% single men of military age, must necessarily have come from a Culture which treats rape very, very differently than we do.

Germany seems to have abandoned any standards for weeding out young single men until they can be properly vetted. The United States and especially Canada do make a greater effort to import families. However, in Edmonton Canada in February, 2017, a Muslim refugee, who is a father of six, was charged with sexual assault of numerous teenage girls in a public swimming pool.

The great American conservative writer Daniel Greenfield, of *Frontpage Magazine*, argues that:

> Their advocates talk about "human rights", but in Muslim culture there is no such thing as human rights. Their cultures are tribal. There are no universal rights, only responsibilities to members of kin groups. When those kin groups remain intact, then members will prey exclusively on outsiders. When they fall apart, as they do during immigration and migration, then mass rapes and murders take place.

Query whether Greenfield paints with too broad a brush, and is he concentrating on *Arab* Muslim culture?

CBS reporter Lara Logan, who as a foreign woman dressed in "immodest clothing" was gang raped by those in Tahrir Square, who Obama says were there for an "Arab spring," surely knows that Egypt has a rape culture. In Muslim Egypt, 99.3% of women and girls have been sexually harassed. Says Greenfield:

> When Australia's Grand Mufti Sheikh Hilaly justified a notorious series of gang rapes by comparing women to uncovered meat left out in the presence of a cat, he laid out the basis of Muslim rape culture. Women are always the guilty party, because they are women. If they refuse to defeminize themselves by putting on a Burka and becoming just another dark ghost haunting the streets of Cairo or Sydney with their lack of selfhood, then they are automatically guilty of their own rape.

Greenfield has argued that increasingly, in the West, Muslim rapists, pedophiles and the like are being given light sentences based on "misunderstandings" based on "cultural differences" with respect to women and the signals given off by women who are "immodest."

As the father of a daughter and three granddaughters, I worry about our tolerism of the culture of rape, in that we seem to be prepared to accept as refugees, men whose culture makes them a serious threat to those daughters and granddaughters. To those who advocate the wholesale immigration of such men, what do you plan to do to cure them of the culture of rape?

And why should our immigration system give rights of protection to foreign women facing a culture of rape in their homeland but not protect Canadian women from importation of that culture of rape into Canada?

David Goldman, writing at *Asia Times*, (atimes.com/more-horrible-than-rape/), makes a good case that we are dealing with more than a culture of rape, but a culture of atrocities, on display almost daily as Muslims attack other Muslim civilians in addition to non-Muslims. When we confront a large part of the world which embraces atrocities and when we invite people with that culture into our cultures, we can feel trapped in a dying civilization. He writes:

> (I)n a dying civilization, (r)ationality ceases to have meaning. Upon learning that you have an inoperable malignant brain tumor, you might cash in your insurance policy and go on a spree—but not if everyone who speaks your language and shares your memories already is extinct. In that case there is nothing to do with your money. You can sit at the bar by yourself and drink Chateau Petrus. Or you can go out and stab the next Israeli you run into.

> The death of Muslim civilization is too horrible for the Germans to contemplate, because the bell tolls for them, too. And it is particularly painful for Germans to consider the possibility that the source of the terrible events that have driven millions to Germany is the character of the people themselves. Syria has torn itself to pieces not only because of the malfeasance of its leaders but rather because of the character of its people. Once the Sunni revolt against Shia-majority government in Iraq enlisted elements of Saddam Hussein's army as well as the "Sunni Awakening" funded by Gen. Petraeus during the 2007-2008 "surge," sectarian war to the death became inevitable in Syria, with both sides inflicting the most revolting atrocities imaginable.

> The Assad regime has killed more people because it has the aircraft to attack Sunni civilians, but the Sunni opposition – including the "moderate," American-backed Sunni opposition–has committed mass murder and bragged about it. *Human Rights Watch* states in October 2013 that in one operation near Latakia in the Alawite heartland, Sunni "fighters killed 190 civilians. Residents and hospital staff in Latakia, the nearest city, spoke of burned bodies, beheaded corpses and graves being dug in backyards. Two hundred people from the area remain hostage." Free Syrian Army chief of staff Salim Idriss, the poster-boy for "moderate opposition," praised the operation in a video and took partial responsibility. ISIS has captured the world's imagination and turned its stomach with public executions

and the destruction of archaeological treasures, but that is how Muslims have fought wars for 1,500 years. Just ask the Christians of the Balkans or the Armenians of Anatolia about the Turks.

Very large parts of the Syrian population are complicit in the civil war's atrocities, almost certainly by intent. Mass complicity in war crimes has two functions–first, to destroy the enemy's will, and second, to make entire populations complicit in the atrocities. The Nazis made sure that the German population knew about the Holocaust in order to bind them closer to their leaders.

And yet judging by the opinion of the Canadian media, welcoming Syrian refugees, including those who are inadequately vetted for participation in war crimes, is a good, actually holy, endeavor. For those who sit by, having the knowledge of the character of the Syrian people, we not only contemplate the death of a civilization based on liberal justice, we endanger ourselves should we speak out against the culture of atrocities we are importing. That should be a scary thought to those whose morality has not been corrupted by the ideologies we have been discussing.

CHAPTER 13: AM I A RACIST?

In the United States, there was by the year 2015 considerable opposition, especially on the state level, to high numbers of Syrian and other Middle Eastern migrants entering the country. Then Donald Trump made it clear as he ran for president that he would, if elected, pause further immigration from certain countries until the immigrants would pass a severe vetting to ascertain that they were not Islamists but would accept basic American values. However, the mainstream media, acted as if no president had ever instituted such an approach and instead portrayed Trump as a racist and a xenophobe. Court challenges to his executive orders and shrill opposition from left-liberals, as of the time of writing, may deprive the president from his usual powers over National Security. That would be bizarre, if you agree, as I do, that there is a war going on against America by the Islamists and that care must be taken not to admit hostile enemy aliens into the country. Yet, looking at American media, my position might well be in the minority in America; looking at the Canadian media, it is certain that my position is in the minority in Canada.

In Canada, when Justin Trudeau and his Liberals defeated Stephen Harper and his Conservatives in 2015, a "Tolerist" defeated a "Conservative."

Day after day, most of our Canadian media broadcast a message that anyone opposing the hurried entry into Canada of 25,000 migrants by the end of February from Syria and other dysfunctional Muslim Islamo-totalitarian states is clearly "racist." (Prime Minister Trudeau first promised to get all 25,000 into the country by Christmas, 2015, but then slowed that down to the end of February.)

The United States has nine times the population of Canada, so 25,000 immigrants to Canada would be the equivalent of 225,000 to the United States. The Democrats might well have been expected to allow in some 300,000 Muslim immigrants.

My local newspaper, *The Hamilton Spectator*, in November, 2015, carried the view of the Chair of its Editorial Board who made this clear: "Will we welcome [the migrants], as our better natures would suggest? Or will we see the darker nature of some citizens come through?" Yet, I must ask: Is an opposing viewpoint evidence of a "darker nature"? Do I have a "darker nature"?

The editorial asked us to not just "tolerate" the immigrants but do so "in a welcoming way." In talking about their needs once they arrive, the editorialist listed affordable housing, language training, education, learning Canadian "customs" and geography.

But nowhere was mentioned *Canada's needs* that these immigrants be taught before they arrive that Canada's political culture is based on individual rights and freedoms, including the rights of women, gays, children, ethnic and religious minorities and dissenting political and culture viewpoints, and the right to be free from violence.

Do the migrants have anything to fear from me? Is it "racist" to ask of our government to at least take the necessary months it must take to properly vet these people? Is it racist to query whether these immigrants supported ISIS and other Islamists with their records of war crimes and murder of ethnic and religious minorities, rapes, beheadings, etc.?

I have written that countries like Sweden and Norway have seen tragic levels of rapes after Muslim immigration whereas, prior to that, rape numbers were almost negligible. Is that enquiry "racist," or do I, as the father of one daughter and grandfather of three girls, have the right to be concerned if migrants are coming from a culture that absolves them from the responsibility of rape if the victim was immodestly dressed, or is an "infidel"? Do we not have an obligation to our women to make sure we do not create the tragedy that is ongoing in Sweden and Norway, and in fact within the very refugee camps set up in Europe. After the Second World War, the Marshall Plan and some decent politicians helped to ensure that the German people were completely re-educated so that they could understand, repudiate and apologize for Nazism.

Initially, it was thought that Nazism had been *imposed* by an evil dictator and a small group of psychopaths. Gradually, it became the understanding of many historians, with the groundbreaking work of Daniel Goldhagen's work, *Hitler's Willing Executioners: Ordinary Germans and the Holocaust*, that a culture of anti-Semitism had long roots in the general German population, and over time this became "eliminationist" in character, so that nothing less than the elimination of all Jews would suffice.

Obviously, then, in Syrian culture, and in practically every Arab country, there is history of anti-Semitism, which resulted in the expulsion of all Jews from Syria and all other Arab Muslim countries, and it is mainstream in these countries to call for the "destruction" of the state of Israel and to support terrorist organizations that are "eliminationist" in character. Even in so-called "moderate" non-Arab Muslim countries, Jews and Judaism are ostracized. One lesson of history is that not everyone now fleeing Syria can be presumed to be an innocent party in a country where totalitarian and racist abuses have been endemic. What about the "vetting" process? All I can do is quote FBI Assistant Director Michael Steinbach who has admitted that in a "failed state" like Syria, "all of the data sets — the police, the intel services — that normally you would go to seek information don't exist."

How can we be sure the "vetting" of prospective immigrants is successful? In this book, we have looked at the suggestions of Daniel Pipes. Americans have in the past made terrible mistakes: The FBI received multiple warnings from Russia about one of the Boston Marathon bombers, Tamerlan Tsarnaev, but after a single interview with him, they concluded he posed no threat. The American government ignored numerous warnings about the increasing radicalization of Fort Hood shooter, military psychiatrist Nidal Hasan, and then Obama had the nerve to call the obscene attack "workplace violence" rather than terrorism.

I am more than a little concerned about the culture of the people we are inviting to Canada. In fact, I don't recall anything near the emotional love-in by the press of the Muslims with respect to any other group of immigrants. This book is an attempt to bring some light to the submission inherent in this love-in.

The migrants shall probably get their news from Arabic language cable TV and social media, perpetuating their anti-Western culture.

Like the Lebanese immigrants to Canada who fly frequently back and forth to Lebanon, despite the terror created by Iranian-backed Hezbollah, these migrants, once they have money saved up, will spend as much time as they can afford back in the Middle East, allowing their children to be radicalized while visiting there.

Some of the young people, like the duo from London Ontario who attacked the Algerian gas plant, will become "radicalized" in local mosques whose imams did not study in Canadian universities but are emissaries of the Wahabbist Saudi regime. Those that go to university are likely to join the innocent-sounding Muslim Students Association, which is actually an arm of the radical Muslim Brotherhood with funding from Qatar.

Anthony Faiola and Souad Mekhennet, writing in *The Washington Post*, and carried by *The Vancouver Sun* on February 18, 2017 explore the Islamist tactic, supervised by ISIS, of teaching Muslim schoolchildren in European countries to hate and commit acts of terror. *Schoolchildren!* Once again, the failure to sufficiently condemn child terrorists against the Jews of Israel is coming back to haunt Germans. If they showed more empathy to Israel's struggle against child terrorism, instead of empathy towards terrorist Arabs, perhaps the Germans would have seen this coming. What starts with the Jews does not end with the Jews.

They write of the terrorist attack against a Sikh Temple in Essen Germany in April 2016, committed by three 16-year old boys, who had been supervised online. They write: "Even as it suffers setbacks on the battlefield in Iraq and Syria, the Islamic State is cultivating adolescents in the West, who are being asked (not to come to ISIS battles in the Middle East) but to stay in their home countries and strike targets with whatever weapons are available, such as knives and crude bombs."

They quote Daniel Kohler, director of the German Institute on Radicalization and Deradicalization Studies who states, "The amount of Islamic State videos and propaganda aimed at children has really jumped in recent months."

Their article shows, often using encrypted internet messaging apps, how ISIS handlers target young Muslims in Germany, resulting in 10 minors being involved in five terrorist plots in the year previous to their writing. Most of these minors were "second generation" born in Germany to Muslim immigrants. It is difficult to track child potential threats in the same way security officials track adults, due to lack of legal authority, especially for children under 14; however intelligence agencies in Germany believe that at least 120 minors have been radicalized as terror threats. The Islamists will find a way to exploit legal protections in the West.

The authors contend that, as Turkey has made it more difficult for the thousands of young European Muslims to cross the country to join and fight for ISIS, that means the country faces more domestic terrorism by young people. And yet, says Hans-George Maassen, head of Germany's domestic intelligence agency, "What is really worrying is that people frequently look the other way. They say it is just a phase of adolescence and surely they will grow out of it. Often parents don't really know what their children are doing in their rooms."

It seems to me then, that vetting adult refugees may be inadequate if their children bear any substantial risk of ideological loyalty to the Islamists. Perhaps the parents make a choice to come to the West and their children make a choice to not only damage the West but to commit atrocities. That is the kind of thought that drives Europeans crazy and divides the nations of Europe between tolerists, on the one hand, and reactionaries in nationalist parties, on the other.

Saudi Arabia has facilities to take up to 3 million Muslims in the 100,000 air-conditioned tents used by Muslim pilgrims to Mecca, yet refuses to take even a single refugee. Shouldn't we insist that wealthy Muslim oil countries take their share? What is the reason they don't? Are we allowed to discuss the notion, spearheaded by ISIS, but clearly tolerated by the Saudis, that they are working towards the creation of a world-wide caliphate? And ISIS is far from the only jihadist radical Islamist group, whether you look to the Palestinians' Hamas, the Lebanese Shiite Hezbollah, the Pakistani Lashkar-e-Taiba (which was behind the 12 coordinated bombings and shootings in 2008 in Mumbai killing more than 250 people), the Taliban, Boko Haram based in northeastern Nigeria, the Moro National Liberation Front in the Philippines, and dozens, if not hundreds, of splinter groups all with Islamist aims.

How many of the migrants will be young single men with no records available of whether they participated in war crimes? Any serious student of the Syrian civil war knows that especially when it comes to dealing with Syrian Christians and Yazidis there were many war crimes, but there is also sectarian violence between Sunnis and Shiites. Only the Christians and Yazidis are actually persecuted refugees. The Sunni Muslims can go to Sunni areas of Turkey, Jordan, and Lebanon and the Shiite Muslims can go to Iran or Shiite areas of Lebanon. Daniel Greenfield has argued convincingly in *Frontpage Magazine* that the so-called refugees, other than Yazidis and Christians, are actually economic migrants, trying to get into those countries like Germany and Canada that have the most generous welfare systems.

Am I racist for writing all of this?

CHAPTER 14: TRUTH OR CONSEQUENCES

For over 30 years on American television, and before that on radio, the premier game show was called "Truth or Consequences." For about 20 years, it was hosted by the ever-popular Bob Barker.

On the show, contestants received roughly two seconds to answer a trivia question correctly (usually an off-the-wall question that no one would be able to answer correctly, or a bad joke) before "Beulah the Buzzer" sounded. If, as was almost always the case, the contestant could not complete the "Truth" portion, there would be "Consequences," usually a zany and embarrassing stunt. From the start, most contestants preferred to answer the question wrong in order to perform the stunt. Said the show's producer Ralph Edwards, "Most of the American people are darned good sports."

In many broadcasts, the stunts on *Truth or Consequences* included a segment with a popular, but emotional, heart-rending surprise for a contestant, that being the reunion with a long-lost relative or with an enlisted son or daughter returning from military duty overseas, particularly Vietnam.

Bob Barker would sign off the show by saying "I hope all your consequences are happy ones."

It is my contention that in this sad era of Islamist terrorism, jihadism and attempts to form a "world-wide caliphate," (starting with a desire to remove the Jews from Israel, followed by a gradual demographic/migratory take-over of Europe and a myriad of mini-wars in Africa, the Philippines and other Asian countries where Muslims seek the submission of their neighbors), the idea of accepting hundreds of thousands of Muslim migrants to Canada and the United States, has some consequences, and these should be discussed, frankly and honestly.

And to understand this topic, there is no better way than to use Truth or Consequences, the television show, as a metaphor.

The contestants were only given a few seconds to come up with a factual answer to an obscure question, and no one really expected the contestants to come up with an answer. In fact, when on a rare question, someone had the answer, the host would turn it into a two or three part question, virtually guaranteeing that the contestant couldn't answer the whole question.

The "consequences" were accepted; even though the game was stacked against the contestant. The fun or glory of being a contestant meant that the embarrassment suffered by the contestant in the "consequences" part, was of course accepted. And the producer said that most Americans are "darned good sports." We might also say that they are darned tolerant. In some extreme cases they could be considered downright masochistic.

The questions and their answers, then, the knowledge of obscure facts required to fairly play the game, were all irrelevant. For the entertainment of the public, contestants were only too happy to play a game that they could not win, that would embarrass them, but might bring on some emotional prize of being reunited with a family member that usually happened once a show.

As I have argued in my book, *Tolerism: The Ideology Revealed*, when tolerance becomes a culture's preeminent virtue, it can morph into masochism all too easily.

Americans are such "good sports" that their tolerance of a president, whose background and values were inadequately vetted by the mainstream media, continued for eight years. Their president repudiated most traditional values and twisted world events so that Islamist goals were obfuscated and most problems of the world were accepted as being the fault of the Americans, not the jihadists.

In fact the mere attempt to discuss the real problem, the real "truth" is something the media only allows for a few seconds, as most investigation of the problems are prevented by the adoption of verbal barriers – when the real contestants of real life talk, they are forbidden to talk about the real truth, by the adoption of words in our vile political correctness like "racist," "intolerant," "occupier," etc. Just as Mr. Barker gave the contestants only a few seconds to answer the question, which was not possible, we today have consented to a world promoted by the media and the universities, where facts cannot be discussed, nor the opinions based on the veracity of those facts. We cannot critique any other culture for fear of being shunned and marginalized as "racists", even though our very heritage requires that we demand liberal values like the protection of individual rights and our liberal justice system should be paramount always, and that we oppose cultures that are anti-liberal, anti-Jewish, anti-Christian, anti-Yazidis, anti-gay, or anti-woman, etc. We are ready to be embarrassed by the consequences and don't see that we are abused by the very rules of the game.

Donald Trump was dissed as a "racist bigot" by most of the media for daring to question Muslim immigration, until we can get a better handle on the consequences, even though a Canadian Muslim professor (Salim Mansur) made that very argument in testimony on immigration policy to the Canadian Parliament. Hardly anyone even entered into the discussion because it was labeled politically incorrect.

We are not even allowed, it seems, to discuss the facts and the consequences, even though not all of our consequences "are happy ones." Moreover, we just don't seem to understand that the consequences stem from failing to know the truth.

Here is the truth:

· Not all cultures are equal
· Muslim terrorists, unlike random killers, have a transnational movement now based in the ISIS state.
· Terrorism is not just violence, but violence to strike such fear into a society that people submit to certain politico-cultural demands.
· War was declared on 9/11 and our problem is that we don't take that seriously enough.
· As I have written in an earlier chapter, many Muslim young men come from a culture of rape.
· As Daniel Greenfield wrote, 13% of the (mostly) Syrian refugees/ migrants support the aims of ISIS, the greatest evil of our times.
· Many of the migrants have turned down Canada's offer of refuge. They are more attracted by the generous welfare systems of Germany and Scandinavia.

· Syria and Iraq both expelled their Jewish populations. The migrants are very anti-Jewish.

· Canada has in part delegated the vetting of refugees to the United Nations (UN). The UN does not espouse western liberal values.

· Some of the migrants traveled on small boats from which Christians and Yazidis were thrown into the sea to die. Do we know how many and who did this? Do we care? Doris Epstein has recently argued that western governments are "ignoring the most-at-risk refugees: the non-Muslims targeted for genocide by the Islamic State (ISIS). At the top of the threatened and persecuted list are the Yazidis, and then the Chaldo-Assyrian Christians. But all of the non-Muslim minorities, such as the Mandaens, the Bahai and the Assyrians, are targeted."

Too few people in the United States and Canada actually care about the facts and have re-imagined the migrants into refugees deserving of the billions of dollars we shall spend on them. Moreover, the consequences of not wanting to know the facts are that all opinions are suspect without knowledge of the facts.

Shouldn't Muslim migrants be trained to overcome the dangerous ideas taught to them in the dysfunctional, illiberal countries from which they come?

The most important point is that real life is not a game show, where lack of knowledge of the facts results in silly, sometimes embarrassing consequences. In real life, the failure to know fact from fiction may result in deadly consequences. Look up the Wikipedia entry for "List of Islamist terrorist attacks" for a rather complete history of major attacks from 1980 to the present, which show approximately 395 major Islamist terrorist attacks.

How many of them can you name? Oops, your two seconds are up; you now have to live with the consequences.

CHAPTER 15: MUNICH 1972 AND 2016

German Ideology and Incompetence
in the Face of Islamist Terrorism

We all know about Germany under Angela Merkel deciding to admit about a million immigrants from lands where jihadism, Sharia law, terrorism and hatred of women, Jews and gays are endemic.

Most of us know that on New Years' Eve, December 31, 2015, some 1000 of the recent immigrants, predominantly young males from a culture of rape, began sexually assaulting hundreds of German young women in Cologne.

Fewer know that German police took days to acknowledge the extent of the mass rapes and sexual attacks and in this they and the German media have been following the lead of Sweden whose police and media, according to an article in Britain's *The Spectator*, have been actively *covering up* the facts on the nature and extent of Muslim sexual attacks on their women.

German police declared within one day that the German-Iranian shooter who killed 9, including children, in the Munich mall attack in July, 2016, acted alone, and inferred that this was mental illness not terrorism.

This happened during a period where police and security services were on "high alert" due to information about a possible terrorist attack. Unlike most shooters who are killed on site as they continue to shoot, this shooter was found a kilometer away from the mall, and police quickly said that not only did he act alone but that it was suicide. He had been walking around with a Glock 17 semi-automatic handgun and 300 rounds of ammunition in his rucksack. I ask whether it is reasonable to accept such a fast conclusion from police that it was suicide and not terrorism.

I do not understand why the country that makes Mercedes cars that can drive themselves cannot, during a period of high alert, protect public gatherings, or find a shooter in a dense urban environment and must rely on the killer committing suicide a kilometer away—unless of course your ideology says all Muslims are culturally equal to all Western Europeans and that it is appropriate to accept a million mostly unvetted, mostly Muslim, migrants during *wartime* (radical Islam has declared war, and Hollande accepts this, but not Obama, and it would seem that Merkel does not accept it either). The ideology of tolerance—"tolerism"—says that tolerance and compassion and empathy, and yes, "submission" to a million demographic soldiers of the Islamic retaking of Europe, will somehow ease the problem.

The perpetrator shouted, "Allahu Akbar"—the terrorist battle-cry. Munich police chief Hubertus Andrae, however, told a news conference there were no indications the gunman had links with ISIS, identifying the attack as a "classic shooting rampage" and not terrorism. Why do we insist that we are only worried about links to ISIS and not links to cultural jihadism and conquest?

Police were quick to emphasize that the shooter also shouted that he was a "German," all but ignoring that he was, or perhaps his parents were, from Iran, the major terrorist-exporting nation in the world. Even if he was not *directed* by Iranian terrorists, one cannot say that he was not *inspired* by the constant anti-western propaganda and warlike statements coming out of Iran. One would think that Germany, in light of its crimes during the Nazi era, but also due to its role in selling chemicals to Iraq and Syria for its chemical weapons program, and as disclosed in a report by the World Nuclear Organization, providing 24% of the parts for the Iranian Busheir 1 nuclear plant, would be more diligent in pursuing world peace by stopping its tolerance for Islamic warmongers.

The purpose of this chapter is to re-examine the 1972 terrorist attacks in Munich and reflect on the Munich mall Islamist terrorist attack. For it is my contention that a review of the facts will disclose that the undue tolerance and political correctness sweeping Europe has made it very difficult to protect Germans, as well as their visitors, from Islamist violence. It is no coincidence that this sort of submission to Islamism inherent in incompetent responses to terrorism in both 1972 and 2016, comes out of the European nation that seeks to obviate some of its guilt for the Nazi era by its masochism of importing young unvetted male immigrants, some of whom undoubtedly are Islamist in orientation.

Let us examine the historical context of the murder of the Israeli athletes at the 1972 Munich Olympics. Eight Palestinians from a terrorist organization called Black September, a group within Yasser Arafat's Fatah and PLO, took Israeli athletes hostage at the Munich Olympics, and, in the course of the attack, 11 Israelis and one German police officer were killed.

While terrorist attacks have become very common, we must remember that the Munich massacre was something much more unique at the time. Author Steven Reeve, who did a 2001 study of the attack and its aftermath, writes that Munich was one of the most significant terror attacks of recent times, in that it "thrust the Palestinian cause into the world spotlight, set the tone for decades of conflict in the Middle East, and launched a new era of international terrorism." And as Arab Muslims continued to find terrorism useful to attain the support of Europeans and the United Nations, then it was sure to follow that terrorism would be used against the West.

Accordingly, it must be understood how incompetent was the response of the German authorities and how mild was the response of the International Olympic movement.

Two of the Israelis were killed immediately upon the hostage-taking. The hostage-takers then demanded the release and transfer to Egypt of a large number of Palestinians and others jailed in Israel. Israel's response was absolute – no negotiations with terrorist murderers. Israel offered to send a special forces unit to Germany to try to free the hostages, but Germany refused. Instead Germany undertook an operation which was so incompetent that it would be laughable if the consequences hadn't been so tragic. (We must credit the Germans, however, with the moral step of offering to the Palestinians a substitution of some high-ranking Germans in place of the Israelis, which the Palestinians refused.)

First, the Germans dispatched to the Olympic village some members of the border-police, completely untrained in any sort of counter-terrorist response, and without any plan of attack. They took up positions, awaiting orders that never came. Second, German television camera crews starting filming the police squad on the roof of a building, and once the terrorists saw the footage on television, and showed they knew where the police were, the operation was abandoned.

The German authorities pretended to give in to the terrorists' demand for transportation to Cairo; but instead of taking them to the international airport, the Germans transported them to a military airbase, where they planned to attack them.

The Germans selected five snipers, but none of them had any special training and were only chosen because they shot competitively on weekends. A Boeing jet was positioned on the tarmac, and the Germans placed five or six armed police, dressed as flight crew, in the plane. They were to overpower the terrorists who would be inspecting the plane, and the other snipers were to kill the remainder of the terrorists who would be in the helicopters which delivered them from the Olympic site. The armed police, however, again had no counter-terrorism training, and at the last moment just as the helicopters arrived, the police panicked and voted among themselves to abandon their mission, which they did, without even contacting their central command. When the terrorist leaders inspected the empty jet, they knew they had been duped, and a chaotic scene ensued. But the German snipers, who had no radio contact with each other, and hence no coordination of their efforts, were not even equipped with steel helmets or bullet-proof vests. In the end all of the hostages were killed, and all but three of the terrorists.

After a one-day suspension, the Games continued. At a memorial service, IOC President Avery Brundage spoke about the strength of the Olympic movement, but chose not to refer to the slain Israeli athletes! And the Arab nations objected to a plan to fly flags at half mast!

The bodies of the five Palestinians who were killed were, for some reason, delivered to Libya, where they received heroes' funerals with full military honors. The three surviving terrorists were jailed, but less than two months later, a German Lufthansa jet was hijacked and the Germans quickly traded two of the terrorists for release of the hijacked plane.

We should understand that 9/11 and the various terrorist attacks in Europe are part of the same problem that Israel faces. Sadly, the European Left (and increasingly the American Left) seeks to distinguish the two and continues to work to sacrifice Israel to the Islamist beast, in the hopes it will be sated, and not come after them.

The tolerant elites of Europe have ignored all history, and welcomed some one million migrants into Germany alone, from Syria, Afghanistan, Somalia and other dysfunctional Muslim countries. Britain's *Express* newspaper (consisting of the *Daily Express* and the *Sunday Express*) reported in February on a leaked government report that the refugees to Germany (numbering some one million people) committed some 200,000 crimes last year! Most were minor, but some were murders, assaults, thefts, sexual assaults, etc. It takes a special kind of ideology of naive faith in tolerance (*tolerism*) to destroy the safety of your own people in favor of some notion of "rights" of migrants, most of whom were inadequately vetted.

Significantly, German security forces were on high alert after a teenage migrant stabbed and injured five people on a train in Bavaria shortly before a larger terrorist attack claimed by so-called Islamic State: A terrorist in December 2016 driving a truck plowed into a Christmas market in Berlin, killing 12 people and injuring 48.

The authorities had warned of the danger of further incidents. Yet, to the best of my knowledge, German authorities are not implementing what Israel did way back in 2001, where those entering malls are checked for weapons by highly trained security guards. Not checking, not understanding the difference between mental illness and cultural incitement, 24 hour conclusions ruling out "terrorism," are all signs of incompetence: Incompetence to save Israeli athletes in 1972 and incompetence to save their own people in 2016. And the reason for the incompetence is the foolish ideology adopted by the children and grandchildren of Nazi murderers, that the problem of terrorism was a deserved problem of the Israeli Jews, and that it *wasn't **their** problem.*

CHAPTER 16: 'BEYOND TOLERANCE'

The Delusional Ideologies of
Obama, Clinton and Trudeau

In a press conference in December, 2016, Canadian Prime Minister Justin Trudeau told the media that Canada, having been tolerant enough to admit many Muslim immigrants, including some 25,000 Syrians in the past year, should now go "beyond tolerance."

I like press conferences and also debates because at such times it is hard for our politicians to be "scripted" and therefore they tend to say what they are really thinking, not what their PR people tell them to say. And so, Trudeau, whose response to Islamism seems to involve something he and others call "inclusive diversity," avoids the gist of the issue, which is to determine to what extent radical Islam and its political ideologies of jihad and Sharia law are threats to Canadian values and rights. This politician, who never finished university, seemed rather uneducated in the matter of ideology. Should we welcome evil ideologies as part of our inclusive diversity? Do we still believe that some things are good and some are evil? Do we think that a nice Canadian welcome, together with conduct and words not just tolerant, but *beyond* tolerant, will turn intolerant jihadists into tolerant Canadians?

The problems we are facing are legion. A recent report was issued on the extremist literature found in Canadian mosques. In *The Lovers of Death? Islamist Extremism in our Mosques, Schools and Libraries*, a former RCMP security analyst and an Egyptian-born expert on Muslim extremism concluded: "It is not the presence of extremist literature in the mosque libraries that is worrisome," the new report contends. "The problem is that there was nothing but extremist literature in the mosque libraries."

If our prime minister thinks the solution to jihadist pro-Sharia law extremism and terrorism is to be more and more "inclusive" and "beyond tolerant," we may have a problem.

Let's bring into the discussion the views of former American President Barack Obama and presidential candidate Hillary Clinton.

The term "Islam" literally means "submission," and whether that submission is confined to the personal realm of man-God relations or it extends to acceptance of not only a system of law (Sharia) but an entire political ideology of outer-directed jihad, is a matter of much contention.

Those who seek to conquer, and restore a caliphate and force submission to this entire political ideology and system of law, are generally called Islamists. Whether President Obama admits it or not, reasonable people will conclude that Islamists and their terrorist minions have in fact declared war on liberal democracies -- starting with countries close by, such as Israel, and now undeniably extended to Europe, America and Canada.

Islamism confuses the diversity-minded West, for it forces us to question whether there are significant numbers of Muslims who publicly renounce Islamism and take steps to limit the threat to liberal freedoms posed by it. Those willing to confront the radical, totalitarian, expansionist, jihadist, terrorist menace are unfortunately in a minority. Absent a significant number of true "moderates" willing to leave Sharia law and any illiberal ideology at our borders when they are given permission to immigrate here, it is difficult to see any clear divisions among prospective Muslim immigrants. To the extent that everyday Muslims feel unwilling or unable to challenge the Islamist hegemony within Islamic centers of power, the problem of assimilating Islamic immigrants or working with Islamic nations is a problem stemming from Islam and its tolerance of Islamism, not from Western lack of tolerance.

And so, to decry as "racists" proponents of liberal democracy who want Islam to clarify its compatibility with Western liberal traditions of human rights and justice, including rights for women, gays, children, ethnic and religious minorities and those who choose to leave their religions, is foolish, notwithstanding it is standard practice among cultural relativists and the politically correct. Moreover, the allegation that someone is "racist" is meant to cause shunning and censorship, and is unfortunately an effective weapon. It should not be a weapon but a conclusion reached only after a lengthy dialogue and weighing of values and arguments rather than a knee-jerk response to any criticism of Islamism.

Of course, Barack Hussein Obama grew up in one of the largest Muslim nations in the world – Indonesia -- and it is seldom mentioned that his stepfather, Lolo Soetoro, worked for the Indonesian military during Indonesia's genocide against ethnic Chinese and Communists. Obama, in the opinion of many, has become infamous for that mainstay of cultural relativism – the notion of "tolerance." Tolerism is the full-blown ideology holding tolerance to be just as important, if not more so, than the traditional Western biblical values of justice, liberty, and human rights and responsibilities.

Obama, for his first foreign trip as president, chose to go to illiberal Egypt to propound America's new Middle Eastern doctrine of giving more "respect" to the Muslim world in word and in deed. He stated:

> I have come here to seek a new beginning between the United States and Muslims around the world; one based upon mutual interest and mutual respect; and one based upon the truth that America and Islam are not exclusive, and need not be in competition. Instead, they overlap, and share common principles – principles of justice and progress; tolerance and the dignity of all human beings.

To any student of the Middle East, where most Islamic countries do not allow the residence or citizenship of Jews, and do not extend to Christians or Jews full rights, this talk of "mutual respect" made no sense at all. Then, Obama's equivalency between American notions of justice, tolerance and human dignity to that found in Muslim countries was quite simply shocking. So was his invitation to several members of the Muslim Brotherhood, widely viewed as a terrorist-supporting Islamist organization, to attend his speech.

But Hillary Clinton took the matter even further. Clinton, whose close friend and top aide is the Saudi-raised, Muslim Brotherhood-allied Huma Abedin, has some very odd opinions, which she expressed at a speech at Georgetown University. She claimed in her speech that women are superior to men in diplomacy and security and, strangely, gave as an example a couple of female Philippine Muslims who were instrumental in negotiating (submitting to?)

Muslim rule over an area of the Philippines. She cited their feminine skills as part of something she called "Smart Power" and then claimed that Smart Power would use "every possible tool … leaving no one on the sidelines, showing **respect** even for one's enemies, trying to understand, and insofar as is psychologically possible, **empathize** with their perspective and point of view, helping to define the problems (and) determine a solution" [emphasis added].

So Hillary Clinton wanted to show "respect" even for one's enemies. We can't be sure what Hillary meant in her own mind, but the Oxford Dictionary defines "respect" as "a feeling of deep admiration for someone or something elicited by their abilities, qualities or achievements." But to me, Islamists who use beheading, rape and sexual assault, torture, persecution of ethnic and religious minorities and gays, and disregard most human rights, do not deserve our "deep admiration" and do not show any great "qualities or achievements." The fact that Hillary argued otherwise validated the concern of Trump supporters who did not want to place in her hands the responsibility for war and peace and the fulfillment of American values for liberty and human rights, and did not fees admiration for our enemies.

Would a confused young second generation Muslim young woman attracted to the romance of a mission with ISIS become more or less interested in leaving for the Islamic State after listening to Hillary's speech? Did Hillary take us "beyond tolerance" into admiration and submission to the enemy's values?

Beware of the tolerists preaching compassion and *empathy* for our enemies, because once you commit to empathy, that constitutes entering the other's perceptual world; once you learn to feel what he or she feels, and unless one has a firm grasp of your own values, you may never return from your empathetic journey into the mind of the enemy. Ask Patty Hearst.

Let us return to the press conference of the young Canadian Prime Minister Justin Trudeau. A reporter from Quebec asked Trudeau about his recent trip to Toronto to visit some of the 25,000 Syrian refugees that his government admitted into Canada, and whether his feelings are the same about the ability to assimilate them into Canadian values. His response (translated from the French) was as follows:

> There are countries in the world where tolerance is essential. You have to be tolerant towards your neighbors.
>
> I think in Canada we should go *beyond tolerance*, being tolerant is accepting some people, but you don't want to be too bothered, but you have to have an openness, comprehension, understanding, and this is what we are aiming for; this is what we see every day when we see diverse communities enriched by their communities. This is what they have to aim for.

Perhaps Trudeau is not aware that giving "rights and choices" to some illiberal people may deprive existing liberal citizens of *their* rights and choices. Trudeau has supported something he calls "inclusive diversity" which I suppose is based on the flawed concept in multiculturalism that all cultures are equal. He believes that *diversity is a goal in itself*, and like Hillary Clinton and Barack Obama, we must respect and admire our enemies, the Islamists. Prime Minister Trudeau now seemingly believes, that tolerating those with illiberal opinions, is not enough; we must give them "understanding" and a *special place* for their choices in our public realm.

Going "beyond tolerance" is dangerous indeed. Anything beyond tolerance is *submission*. Respect for our enemies is to admire Evil. If terrorism furthers our tolerance so that we become "beyond tolerant," then terrorism is successful indeed and these leaders are therefore paving the way for more terrorism. What is wrong with these people, and what is wrong with us for electing them?

CHAPTER 17: ISLAMIFICATION IN SOUTHERN ONTARIO, CANADA

Watching the Cultural Imperialism of Islamism

Islamism is not just an ideology of enforcing submission to Islam through terrorism, lawfare, and the like. It can also be seen as the ideology behind spreading Islam by any means possible to the West, to prepare for a world-wide caliphate and the imposition of Sharia law.

Muslims who subscribe to the ideology of the caliphate and Sharia law, really do have views that are incompatible with liberal democracy and its individual rights regime.

Those who advocate tolerance for the caliphate and Sharia law, must realize that their tolerance is endangering the liberal freedoms of women, children, gays, and ethnic and religious minorities, protected by our existing justice system.

In my book, *Tolerism*, I gave many examples of how this is working in contemporary culture, and in media, universities, and the entertainment industry.

Aside from a number of years in Toronto and Vancouver, I have lived most of my life in smaller cities in Southern Ontario.

I wish to examine some ways in which the cultural imperialism of Islamism is working in a small Ontario city. I believe, that like Europe, we shall one day wake up to find that what I call *tolerism* has eroded our rights to liberal democracy, and most people will have no clue how it happened. So this essay shall help to show how it happens.

Brantford is a city of around 100,000 people, and was once a major manufacturing center, but many of the large industries closed. A good location near Hamilton, Toronto and other cities, however, has prevented population loss as low housing prices attract people to live locally and work regionally, and the local population requires the usual services and retail.

A city of magnificent churches dotting its older downtown area now is watching as declining church attendance is resulting in the closing of churches, especially among the traditional denominations, as opposed to Evangelical Christian congregations, which are growing. The Sikh Temple and Muslim Mosque are growing quickly. A Jewish Synagogue lasted from 1907 to 2001 before it closed as Jews gravitated towards bigger cities.

The local Mosque recently invited local politicians and media to an Iftar meal during Ramadan. Its imam stated to a local newspaper that Ramadan is the perfect time to explain the Muslim faith to others in the community.

"The Qur'an was revealed to the whole world. It is not just for Muslims," he said in an interview and to the gathering.

"We have invited everyone to share the message for all of humanity."

The newspaper article, however, did not see fit to make it clear what is the message of the Qur'an for non-Muslims and what exactly is its message beyond doing works of charity and praying the requisite number of times per day.

"We must thank Allah that we are in Canada," said a retired imam to the reporter. "I never forget what Canada stands for. Peace, love, harmony, tolerance."

Unfortunately, it is not correct that Canada stands for peace, love, harmony and tolerance, however much that formulation might appeal to aging hippies or those seeking to obfuscate the reality of our contemporary culture wars.

Traditionally, we in Canada are said to believe in "Peace, Order and Good Government." Peace is of course a goal, but, to further that goal, Canadians have served in the forefront of military operations or Wars where armed conflict was deemed necessary to defeat Nazis, or more recently, the Taliban or ISIS. To hope for Peace without acknowledging that Evil must sometimes be eradicated by War is simplistic nonsense.

Our "Order and Good Government" imply the use of a liberal justice system to enforce order and uphold liberal rights and freedoms. Nowhere is tolerance said to be the main goal, as it is surely assumed that tolerance without justice or tolerance of illiberal evil are not worthwhile goals.

"Islam is all about inclusiveness," said the imam to the reporter. "We have invited people to join us not just to eat, but to share in friendship so we can know each other better."

Knowing each other better is probably a worthwhile goal, as long as communication is a two-way street and offense is not taken when some of us state that Sharia law is not compatible with liberal democracy. And if Islam is "all about inclusiveness," are we allowed to ask why countries ruled under Islamic law and in the name of Islam are seldom inclusive, having banished all Jews and are increasingly persecuting and banishing Christians?

And must Islam continue to be "inclusive" to the radical elements that are driving it in a violent and illiberal way? In London, Ontario, an hour to the west of Brantford, two local teens, one a recent convert to Islam and one born Muslim, were somehow radicalized enough to help seize a natural gas plant in an Algerian desert with al-Qaeda. They died, along with 37 hostages and 27 other Islamist militants. No one in London, at the mosque they attended or elsewhere knew enough to raise a red flag about these terrorists in training.

The reporter was convinced that the sharing of food and invitation to hear the message of the Qu'ran constituted a "spirit of camaraderie" showing that the Muslim community "is prepared to do all the reaching out to belong to the wider city."

But is it "belong(ing)" to the "wider city" or is it public relations and proselytization?

The second event to be discussed happened during the war between Israel and the Hamas terrorists in Gaza. A local man, with medical qualifications in Gaza and not in Canada, decided, against Canadian government advice, to travel to Gaza, as he had to do sufficient medical work there to keep his medical license in force.

Despite the dangers there, he took his 8 year old daughter with him, and she stayed with relatives. When the war broke out, after years of Hamas sending rockets against Israeli civilian areas, the wife, a pharmacist at the local hospital was of course frantic. Canadian officials worked diligently and arranged for the girl's return to Brantford. Her father of course stayed on, whether it was to protect his medical license or whether it was because medical doctors were needed to treat casualties.

A local United Church minister partnered with the Islamic association and an association of Palestinians to organize a candlelight vigil, which was well-publicized in the local paper. This minister had a long record of criticizing Israel and siding with Palestinians.

In his church newsletter in 2010, he cited as a voice of "reconciliation, commons sense and moderation" the Supreme Leader of Iran Sayyed Ali Khamenei, because Khamenei in response to a Florida pastor threatening to burn the Koran, sought to equate both mainstream Christianity and Islam regarding supporting extremists. The Minister quoted approvingly Khamenei's boast that "We Muslims will never commit similar acts against what are held to be sacred by other religions." Of course, Iranian-backed ISIS has committed against Christians, Jews, Hindus, Yazidis and others a lot worse than threatening book burnings – ISIS has been seeking to remove the Christian presence from Iraq and Syria, and Iranian-backed Hamas desecrated Jewish synagogues left behind when Israel sought peace by giving up control of Gaza. The terrorist group *Hezbollah* receives military training, weapons, and financial support from Iran. The local minister of course has become a mouthpiece for Iranian propaganda.

He was held in high esteem by City Council and the local media, until sadly he was arrested for sexual exploitation and luring of a 17 year old girl in his congregation and then later for child pornography. Nobody except me comments on the link between his personal immorality and his hatred for Israel.

I have no problem wanting to support a young girl getting home, but Hamas is a terrorist organization with a Charter to murder Jews. Salma's father had no business taking her there, to let her watch Hamas television which incites children to murder Jews. Imagine, how I, a grandfather of four, and the son of a Holocaust survivor, feel when I see our government allowing the immigration of people who have been trained by their totalitarian country to hate Jews, and who are not coming here to get away from their Islamofascist leaders, but maintain frequent contacts and travel back to these hateful places, like the girl's father does.

I wouldn't have a problem with the father going on some humanitarian mission but when he went there it was for the purpose of keeping up his medical credentials there. In other words, once Hamas murders all the Jews and takes over Israel, he will be in a position to go back there and practice medicine.

Also, Brantford was the home for 25 years of Mahmoud Issa Mohammad, a convicted terrorist murderer of Jews on a hijacked El Al flight at an airport in Greece in 1968.

Part of the Popular Front for the Liberation of Palestine, he and another man hurled grenades and sprayed the plane with machine-gun fire, killing a 50-year-old Israeli maritime engineer.

In 1970, Mohammad was convicted in Greece and sentenced to 17 years in jail. However, he was freed a few months later after another Palestinian terrorist group hijacked a Greek plane and threatened to kill the passengers unless the Greek government released Mohammad, which of course it did.

In 1987, he applied for residency in Canada while failing to disclose his membership in the PFLP and his criminal history.

Although on Dec. 15, 1988, an immigration adjudicator ruled Mohammad should be expelled from the country because he had concealed his role in the 1968 attack in Greece, before he could be deported, he filed a refugee claim and was able to avoid deportation for more than **25 years** due to appeals and legal maneuvering by his lawyer. The legal case is estimated to have cost Canadian taxpayers over $3 million.

Mohammad denied he was a terrorist, stating in 1988 that he was "a freedom fighter."

Upon his deportation, our immigration minister was quoted as saying, "Mr. Mohammad flagrantly violated Canada's fair immigration laws and this country's generosity. He made a mockery of our legal system." A mockery indeed. Later the Canadian Government, by a close vote of 149 to 130, passed legislation making it easier to deport foreign criminals.

What always stays with me, when I hear of an open house at the mosque or a candlelight vigil for the daughter of a Hamas supporter, is that the local Muslim community did not to my knowledge speak out against this terrorist murderer in our midst. They do not speak out against Hamas. Our Muslim neighbors minimize the value of justice and instead assert the value of tolerance. We have been tolerant enough, in my opinion.

As I walk down the street in Brantford, I fear this new world of tolerance and appeasement that has reached my town and is changing it; I am one of the few who even cares.

The local newspaper will not run any opinion piece that I have written. When I grew up here in the '50s and '60s, there were over 80 families in the local synagogue. Today there is no synagogue and only 3 or 4 Jewish families. The newspaper knows to avoid me; people like me are the past not the future. As Leonard Cohen wrote in his song, "The Future":

> *You don't know me from the wind*
> *you never will, you never did*
> *I'm the little Jew*
> *who wrote the Bible*
> *I've seen the nations rise and fall*
> *I've heard their stories, heard them all*
> *but love's the only engine of survival*
> *Your servant here, he has been told*
> *to say it clear, to say it cold:*
> *It's over, it ain't going*
> *any further*
> *And now the wheels of heaven stop*
> *you feel the devil's riding crop*
> *Get ready for the future:*
> *it is murder*

Left and Right

Every "populist" politician in the West who voices concerns about Islamism or unvetted immigration, will undoubtedly be called "Islamophobic" or "racist" by the popular leftist media. This media will insult such politicians by calling them "right wing bigots" or such other terms. Unfortunately, the more such populists win elections, whether in Britain, America or the Netherlands, the less likely will the media be to compliment them on their desire to preserve Western "freedoms" in the face of Islamist fundamentalism and intolerance of free speech. But there are some serious thinkers who have written on the subject, from cultural to political to psychological perspectives.

The Canadian writer David Solway, in an article entitled "The Right Stuff" in the August 6, 2009 issue of Montreal's *The Metropolitain*, formulated a distinct challenge to those of the historical Left.

The problem, according to Solway?:

> (T)he Left-oriented European Union will increasingly find itself trapped in a pincer movement launched by two aggressive far-Right-wing forces that will spell the end of its dream of multicultural beatitude. The Islamic theocratic Right is gathering strength with every passing day, intent on imposing sharia law through incremental advances and, ultimately, to acquire hegemony across the long historical haul, creating an Islamic brutopia on European soil ... (T)he resentment animating large segments of the European public, which feels it has been betrayed by its leaders, is being co-opted by the indigenous parties of the hard Right. And in country after country, they are making important electoral gains.
>
> In the absence of common sense, adherence to the principle of civic stewardship and the consequent protection of core liberties, excessive tolerance has a way of ushering

in the spectre of social repression. This is the lesson of the Weimar Republic we do not seem to have learned. It is no better today. Self-abasement, political correctness and the mantra of universal brotherhood—the European project— constitute a social pathology that can lead only to misfortune and collapse. Living in a multicultural rhapsody with its formulaic notion of the sacred equivalence of all cultural values, Europe now confronts a double danger: the invasion of radical Islam with its blood-hatred of its Western host, and the resurgence of the reactionary Right with its blood-hatred of its non-Western guests.

And the solution, according to Solway?:

(I)t is vital to distinguish between the two Rights. There is the rational Right—as embodied in the Danish Freedom Party and Geert Wilders' Party of Freedom in the Netherlands which, as political analyst Soeren Kern writes, have "called for stronger sanctions against totalitarian regimes and dictatorships, especially those in the Islamic world," (*Pajamas Media*, June 12, 2009), and which struggle to preserve the rights and obligations of citizenship against the multicultural fragmentation of national unity—and the irrational Right which finds its home in racist and intolerant organizations like the Freedom Party in Austria, Jobbik in Hungary, the National Alliance in the United States, the Front national in France and the British National Party and its associated National Front, to mention only a few.

But if the rational Right fails to consolidate its base in the European political landscape, then the European Left will have brought its own eventual demise upon itself in the form of militant, illiberal and xenophobic parties of the extreme Right. It will, in fact, find itself squeezed between the jaws of an ideological vise of its own making, as two competing fascisms, one Islamic and the other indigenous, engage in a battle to the finish. Absenting the rebirth of a hardy and vigorous conservative movement, which does not shrink from instituting stringent immigration policies and enacting rules for the deportation of those who undermine the common peace, the long-term prospect for Europe doesn't look encouraging.

And Solway, a reformed leftist himself, addresses the issues in terms of tolerance. He writes:

There is only one way to defeat the extreme Right as it rises to its own depraved version of the defence of the

West, and that is to disarm the common enemy and, by so doing, deprive a nascent fascism of its populist fuel. Which is another way of saying that immigration policies currently in place will need to be rethought and rendered more appropriate to the nation's requirements, as is the case, for example, in Switzerland, the sole western European country that attaches a high value to citizenship. And unpleasant as this may sound, we will also have to become less tolerant of the intolerant Other which refuses to recognize our values if we are to avoid the pendulum swing toward a vicious intolerance of all perceived outsiders.

We will, in short, have to embrace the conservative tradition of the moderate Right, based on the liberty of the individual, the duties of responsible citizenship, a coherent pluralism that respects the customs of the majority culture rather than a fractious multiculturalism that corrodes them, and the robust defence of the homeland against the threats, both domestic and external, that mobilize against it.

Accordingly, to the extent that the American media, during the Obama years, made the moderate Republican Party their enemy in its promotion of the incompetent, law-breaking tolerist Hillary Clinton, they made it more likely for the Republicans to choose the more populist Donald Trump. Not having learned the lesson that Mr. Solway suggests above, the media has helped destroy the American center by its failure to properly criticize the immoral Clintons and their foundation and Islamist friends. Having caused the election of a candidate that this media never stops from calling incompetent, bigoted, Islamophobic, xenophobic, misogynist, etc., America faces future choices between the tolerist left and the populist right, a rather dramatic reversal of the stability of American political history.

Writing this after the first 100 days of the Trump administration where the media seems to be at war with the presidency (and vice versa), and where protests financed through George Soros and well organized by the organizations he funds, we are seeing a rather startling resistance to the results of a democratic election. A "women's march" where some women marched in obscene get-ups, and which had as one of its organizers, the disreputable Islamist Linda Sarsour, was held to protest what the American people voted for, only one day after Trump's inauguration. The American people were being told, in effect, that Trump's election was "illegitimate" and the power of the president was going to be countered by people in the streets. This hardly serves the cause of reconciliation and working together and certainly promotes a future of left-right acrimony beyond what America has ever witnessed, aside from the secessionist pro-slavery southern Democrats fighting a Civil War in protest of the Republican Abraham Lincoln's emancipation of the black slaves.

Somewhat similar to Solway's are the views of columnist Mark Steyn. In a June 22nd, 2009 cover story for Canada's newsmagazine, *Maclean's*, entitled "Why the Fascists are Winning in Europe", Steyn distinguishes the quasi-fascist nationalist parties in places like Bulgaria, which is only two decades removed from one-party totalitarianism, with such parties in Western Europe. Steyn makes an interesting allegation on the effect of tolerist political correctness on the masses:

> (I)n the western half of Continental Europe, politics evolved to the point where almost any issue worth talking about was ruled beyond the bounds of polite society. In good times, it doesn't matter so much. But in bad times, if the political culture forbids respectable politicians from raising certain issues, then the electorate will turn to unrespectable ones.

And what of the historically free mainstream media? As Lee Smith, writing in *Tablet* magazine on February 22, 2017, puts it in his essay entitled, "Wayne Barrett, Donald Trump, and the Death of the American Press":

> Trump adviser Steve Bannon calls the media the opposition party, but that's misleading. Everyone knows that the press typically tilts left, and no one is surprised, for instance, that the New York Times has not endorsed a Republican candidate since 1956. But that's not what we're seeing now—rather, the media has become an instrument in a campaign of political warfare. What was once an American political institution and a central part of the public sphere became something more like state-owned media used to advance the ruling party's agenda and bully the opposition into silence. Russia's RT network, the emir of Qatar's Al Jazeera network—indeed, all of the Arab press—and media typically furnished by Third World regimes became the American press' new paradigm; not journalism, but information operation.

Another way of looking at these issues is through the framework of moral psychology and studies of globalism versus authoritarian nationalism. Jonathan Haidt, of New York University wrote an essay in *National Interest* in the summer of 2016 entitled "When and Why Nationalism Beats Globalism: And how moral psychology can help explain and reduce tensions between the two." Haidt is the author of *The Righteous Mind* (2012) and deals with the psychological foundations of ideology. Although I am more interested in the world of ideas than psychological predispositions, I like Professor Haidt's work because he earnestly wants to bring understanding and moderation to the Left and Right.

Haidt makes use of the work in psychology by political scientist Karen Stenner and her 2005 book called *The Authoritarian Dynamic*. Although I think that ideology is only in a small part psychologically determined, it is worthwhile to review Haight's perspective on Stenner's work and see how he seeks to mitigate some of the current hostility between left and right.

Her core finding is that nationalist authoritarianism is not a stable personality trait, says Haidt. It is rather a *"psychological predisposition* to become intolerant when the person perceives a certain kind of threat." The answer to understanding right wing nationalism, says Haidt,

> cannot be found just by looking at the nationalists and pointing to their economic conditions and the racism that some of them do indeed display. One must first look at the globalists, and at how their changing values may drive many of their fellow citizens to support right-wing political leaders. In particular, globalists often support high levels of immigration and reductions in national sovereignty; they tend to see transnational entities such as the European Union as being morally superior to nation-states; and they vilify the nationalists and their patriotism as "racism pure and simple." These actions press the "normative threat" button in the minds of those who are predisposed to authoritarianism, and these actions can drive status quo conservatives to join authoritarians in fighting back against the globalists and their universalistic projects.

As they grow wealthier and more citizens move into the service sector, nations move away from "survival values" emphasizing the economic and physical security found in one's family, tribe, and other parochial groups, toward "self-expression" or "emancipative values" that emphasize individual rights and protections—not just for oneself, but as a matter of principle, for everyone. The word "cosmopolitan" comes from Greek roots meaning, literally, "citizen of the world." Cosmopolitans embrace diversity and welcome immigration, often turning those topics into litmus tests for moral respectability.

What Stenner terms a "normative threat," is a threat to the integrity of the moral order (as they perceive it). It is the perception that "we" are coming apart, as globalism undermines traditional societies and causes a lack of consensus in group values and beliefs. The perception that diversity and freedom have gone too far should activate the predisposition to right wing nationalism. Haidt says, "authoritarians are not being selfish. They are not trying to protect their wallets or even their families. They are trying to protect their group or society." So, says Haidt,

> whether you are a "status quo conservative" concerned about rapid change or an authoritarian who is hypersensitive to normative threat, high levels of Muslim immigration into your Western nation are likely to threaten your core moral concerns. But as soon as you speak up to voice those concerns, globalists will scorn you as a racist and a rube. When the globalists—even those who run the center-right parties in your country—come down on you like that, where can you turn? The answer, increasingly, is to the far right-wing nationalist parties in Europe, and to Donald Trump, who just engineered a hostile takeover of the Republican Party in America.

Stenner contrasts her theory with those who see an unstoppable tide of history moving away from traditions and "toward greater respect for individual freedom and difference," and who expect people to continue evolving "into more perfect liberal democratic citizens." Haidt says that if Stenner is correct,

> then it leads to a clear set of policy prescriptions for globalists. First and foremost: Think carefully about the way your country handles immigration and try to manage it in a way that is less likely to provoke an authoritarian reaction. Pay attention to three key variables: the percentage of foreign-born residents at any given time, the degree of moral difference of each incoming group, and the

degree of assimilation being achieved by each group's children.

Haidt argues that,

> Legal immigration from morally different cultures is not problematic even with low levels of assimilation if the numbers are kept low; small ethnic enclaves are not a normative threat to any sizable body politic. Moderate levels of immigration by morally different ethnic groups are fine, too, as long as the immigrants are seen as successfully assimilating to the host culture. When immigrants seem eager to embrace the language, values, and customs of their new land, it affirms nationalists' sense of pride that their nation is good, valuable, and attractive to foreigners. But whenever a country has historically high levels of immigration, from countries with very different moralities, and without a strong and successful assimilationist program, it is virtually certain that there will be an authoritarian counter-reaction, and you can expect many status quo conservatives to support it.

And so, Haidt provides the globalists with a warning not to overplay their hand. The election of Trump in America and the challenge to the prevailing globalist elites in the European elections of 2017, seem to show what happens when globalists go too far. Finally, it is interesting how a political theorist like David Solway, who we have read above, comes to similar conclusions as a social psychologist like Jonathan Haidt.

Another topic worth looking at is how Islam is being promoted through leftist influences in the American army. During a time that Islamists are at war with that military, we must take a lot of care when it comes to religious affairs and educate soldiers on the crucial differences between Islam and Islamism; that is a matter of national security, not religious freedom. Jonah Bennett writing in *Daily Caller* reports that Army Lt. Col. Khallid Shabazz, a Muslim chaplain, has accepted the job of handling the spiritual affairs of 14,000 mostly Christian soldiers in the United States.

> Out of 1,400 chaplains in the Army, only five are Muslim. And across all the services, there are only ten Muslim chaplains total. Shabazz, a black man, formerly known as Michael Barnes, was born Lutheran in Louisiana. He later joined the Army at 23 and was stationed in Germany,

where he worked with a Muslim soldier. He says he quickly grew tired of the Muslim soldier bragging about Islam, so he challenged him to a public debate.

The ensuing debate while on base caused Shabazz to reevaluate his religion. He subsequently converted and changed his name, before encountering struggle after struggle in the Army and later joining on with the Chaplain Corps.

He's now served as a chaplain for 18 years and has deployed to Iraq, Kosovo and Guantanamo Bay.

Shabazz said he is not interested in converting anyone to Islam, but some soldiers do end up converting. "My job is not to convert anybody to Islam," Shabazz said. "God guides people. My only goal is to have people leave my office stronger than when they came in."

Most of the time, Shabazz spends his hours advocating for Islam, so as to prevent "anti-Muslim" incidents at bases.

I don't quite understand why a military base would allow a public debate between proponents of Islam and Christianity.

It would be interesting to know how many American blacks convert to Islam while serving in the military (and how many convert while being incarcerated). In any case, we have to make sure that what the soldiers are converting to is a form of Islam reconcilable with their military duties and their oath to serve their country not their ummah (i.e. the whole community of Muslims bound together by ties of religion)

We are entitled to examine them, just like new immigrants, for evidence of Islamist ideology that is a threat to our countries.

Whether we listen to political theorists like Solway and Steyn or psychologists like Haidt, we should understand that ideological excesses will help no one, and we must ask both Left and Right to work together. What we hope to do here is to explain where some of these ideologies lead us, in the hope that understanding will lead to goodwill and prevent submission.

CHAPTER 19: HILLARY AT GEORGETOWN: TOLERANCE, EMPATHY AND SUBMISSION

What it Really Means to "Empathize" with One's Enemies

Tolerism consists often of psychological denial, and it accepts United Nations Human Rights Councils led by Iran, Syria and other leading human rights abusers. Tolerism reflects a moral equivalency between terrorists and victims, and even a seeming masochism where we seek out painful retribution as a kind of catharsis for our supposed misdeeds. Tolerist "compassion," especially in the work of Karen Armstrong, assumes that there is equivalency in compassion between the "frequently unkind West" and Islam – which unfortunately in its present state is not at all compassionate to Coptic Christians, Yazidis, Jews, gays, women who seek freedoms, or even minority Muslim groups like the Ahmadis.

I believe that the ideology I call tolerism is expanding ever more rapidly beyond mere tolerance and unilateral compassion. It is now becoming an excessive *empathy* where the quest to share some other group's feelings is beginning to cause our liberals to accept the false facts and illiberal values of our enemies and in fact sometimes to convert or submit to Islam. We are seeing some young people convert to Islam and go so far as to join the forces of ISIS. We are even seeing young Western women convert to Islam and marry men whose attitudes toward women are almost barbaric. Submission, indeed.

Ms. Clinton, of course, served as Secretary of State during the Obama administration's new Middle Eastern doctrine of giving more "respect" to the Muslim world in word and deed. As President Obama stated in Cairo during his first major overseas appearance:

> I have come here to seek a new beginning between the United States and Muslims around the world; one based upon mutual interest and mutual respect; and one based

> upon the truth that America and Islam are not exclusive, and need not be in competition. Instead, they overlap, and share common principles – principles of justice and progress; tolerance and the dignity of all human beings.

Hillary herself has had a close relationship with Huma Abedin, who is connected to the Muslim Brotherhood, as are her parents. Ties to the Muslim Brotherhood and allowing its operatives into the Obama administration would be seen as treasonous if the country was not so immersed in tolerism.

Clinton is not apologetic in the least over her relationship with Abedin. Clinton felt that she should be president at a time when Islamist threats all over the world increased during the Obama years, and she felt that her "feminine" skills gave her the special qualification to right the ship she helped to tip over during her tenure as secretary of state.

So, in a 2014 speech at Georgetown University, she contended that when women participate in peace processes, "often overlooked issues such as human rights, individual justice, national reconciliation, economic renewal are often brought to the forefront." We discussed this briefly in Chapter 16, however it is in my opinion such an important topic in our study of possible submission, that I wish to address it in more detail here.

Clinton's talk (for which she apparently was paid $300,000) was at the launch of the Action Plan Academy, an organization which aims to explore how countries can craft strategies to help women rise into leadership roles on security issues and provide training and workshops.

"Today marks a very important next step," Clinton told an audience of diplomats and other officials from all over the world, "shifting from saying the right things to doing the right things, putting into action the steps that are necessary not only to protect women and children but to find ways of utilizing women as makers and keepers of peace."

Of the hundreds of peace treaties signed since the early 1990s, between or within nations, she said, fewer than 10 percent had any female negotiators and fewer than 3 percent had women as signatories.

"Is it any wonder that many of these agreements fail in a few years?" Clinton asked, implying, without any evidence at all, that women produce better peace agreements than men. If I was paying part of the $300,000 I would really have expected a better discussion of past female leaders like Ms. Bhutto in Pakistan (who transferred nuclear technology to North Korea), Golda Meir in Israel, Margaret Thatcher in Britain, Cristina Kirchner in Argentina, and current leader Angela Merkel in Germany. America itself has seen women leaders in security matters – former Secretaries of State Madeleine Albright and Condoleeza Rice (and Hillary Clinton), National Security Adviser Susan Rice, and first female Ambassador to the United Nations, Jeane Kirkpatrick.

Instead of discussing any of them, she raised the idea that two women were involved at a high level in brokering peace in the 40-year struggle between the government of the Philippines and the Moro Islamic Liberation Front and other Islamic groups in the southern island of Bangsamoro (meaning Muslim land), which has killed hundreds of thousands and displaced more than a million.

Unfortunately, whether these two women were in fact instrumental or not, the issue of the Philippines submitting to Muslim rule over areas of its impoverished, yet potentially oil-rich, south, after 40 years of conflict and the deaths of hundreds of thousands and the displacement of over a million people, is factually quite complex. Some argue that it was external pressure that helped this second peace initiative on the same territory for which the first peace treaty failed; and most recognize that this second one is very much up in the air as to its sustainability.

Under the proposal, Islamic Sharia law would apply to Muslims in the region, but the country's justice system would (hopefully) continue to apply to non-Muslims. The Moro group has renounced the terrorist acts of extremist groups, but at least three smaller Muslim rebel groups oppose the autonomy deal and have vowed to continue fighting for a completely separate Muslim homeland.

And one wonders, once the Muslim groups are granted jurisdiction over limited areas of government, whether this is viewed by them as a first step to future demands for full Sharia law. But Hillary was not interested in waiting to see how it turns out before attributing it to the presence of some women working on the negotiations.

This is a complex problem that Ms. Clinton obviously simplified for partisan political purposes, i.e. the female vote in America. Some commentators feel that the potential natural resource riches available to foreign business concerns is what eventually pushed the Philippine Government into the deal, rather than any great feminine talents as Hillary contends. Moreover, some believe that the United States and other Western governments have backed the autonomy deal partly to prevent the insurgency from breeding extremists who could threaten their own countries.

But the topic of feminine talents for security and diplomacy and her preference to cite Muslims as examples rather than American female icons is not the main concern caused by Ms. Clinton's remarks. The really scandalous part of the speech is when she cited feminine skills as a component of something she called "Smart Power" as follows [emphasis added]:

> This is what we call Smart Power, using every possible tool ... leaving no one on the sidelines, **showing respect even for one's enemies**, trying to understand, and insofar as is psychologically possible, **empathize with their perspective and point of view**, helping to define the problems [and] determine a solution, that is what we believe in the 21st century will change the prospect for peace.

What does it mean for a possible future president to seek to show "respect" for one's enemies?

Respect, according to the *Oxford Dictionary* is defined as "a feeling of deep admiration for someone or something elicited by their abilities, qualities, or achievements."

And here is where we begin to climb down into a terrible ethical hole. Islamists, with their history of beheadings, other murders, torture, persecution of ethnic and religious minorities, and gays, and their forced genital mutilation of young girls, their abuse of women and their general disregard for individual human rights, do not deserve our "deep admiration" and do not show any great "qualities" or "achievements"—unless your idea of an achievement is grabbing vast areas of Iraq and Syria from under Obama's nose, without his bothering to object until it was too late.

Let's dig a little deeper also into the whole concept of "empathy" for one's enemy. The idea of empathizing with the enemy was first popularized by the film, *Fog of War*, about former defense secretary in the Johnson administration, Robert McNamara, who made it one of the eleven lessons he learned. The concept of empathy is also something that has received the study of humanist psychologists, who are well-meaning in their attempts to aid interpersonal relationships and help people understand and therefore overcome misunderstandings in difficult relationships.

Carl Rogers, an important American academic psychologist of the twentieth century promoted the concept of empathy, or being empathetic as a process leading one to:

> Perceive the internal frame of reference of another with accuracy and with the emotional components and meanings which pertain thereto as if one were the person, but without ever losing the "as if" condition. Thus it means to sense the hurt or the pleasure of another as he senses it and to perceive the causes thereof as he perceives them, but without ever losing the recognition that it is as if I were hurt or pleased and so forth. If this "as if" quality is lost, then the state is one of identification.

Rogers reasoned that:

> An empathic way of being with another person means entering the private perceptual world of the other and becoming thoroughly at home in it. It involves being sensitive, moment by moment, to the changing felt meanings which flow in this other person, to the fear or rage or tenderness or confusion or whatever that he or she is experiencing. It means temporarily living in the other's life, moving about in it delicately without making judgements; ... It means frequently checking with the person as to the accuracy of your sensings, and being guided by the responses you receive. You are a confident companion to the person in his or her inner world.
>
> To be with another in this way means that for the time being, you lay aside your own views and values in order to enter another's world without prejudice. In some sense it means that you lay aside your self; this can only be done by persons who are secure enough in themselves that they know they will not get lost in what may turn out to be the strange or bizarre world of the other, and that they can comfortably return to their own world when they wish.

One can only conclude that real "political" empathy is for only the strongest, most intelligent intellectuals and politicians of our time, who are most secure in their liberal values and their constitutional limits and duties. If the person is not so strong, this journey into what can be "a strange or bizarre world" may result in the person feeling more comfortable in **that** world or identifying with that world.

Feeling more comfortable in that world may result in something way more than tolerant empathy, and may result in conversion or submission. This is not a job for postmodernists, but only for those with the clearest and most certain confidence in American values. Without clear values, and a fixed sense of right and wrong, and good versus evil, postmodernist empathy will make it harder and harder for the empathizer to return to his own world, especially if his president has said that America is no more tolerant than Islam, that American standards of justice are no better than Islam's and that countries that have banished all Jews and most Christians share the same view of dignity of all persons.

And so, when the president stated that America and the Muslim world share mutual respect (i.e. admiration); and that they share the same principles of justice and progress; tolerance and the dignity of all human beings; then one wonders if empathy will more likely lead to submission.

Because Hillary Clinton called for more respect and empathy for the enemy, she was a poor choice to lead a country as important as America is to the notion of individual freedoms and human rights based on Judeo-Christian values.

After the election of Obama, we had a very large problem on our hands. The moral and cultural relativism and postmodernism of our university campuses then entered the White House. Hopefully, the election of Donald Trump means the end of the corruption of American public policy by postmodern relativism. Hopefully, the new Trump Administration will prevent America, like some European countries, to submit to Islamist values, with acceptance of Sharia law as an alternative to its Constitution, Muslim religious teachings in public schools, and tolerance for "no-go" areas? America failed its young by failing to properly vet Obama's background and associations before electing him; the media did not do its duty to report on the ideological positions of Obama and Clinton. Hopefully under Trump the ideologies of tolerism, empathy and submission will be swept away. Hopefully, the mainstream media will see that they should report on values and ideologies in a fairer way that rejects relativism for the danger it is to American political culture. Submission to evil is not an option.

CHAPTER 20: NICE BURKA, NICE KEFFIYEH

Islamism as Fashion

Besides Christmas, what is the most popular holiday among children, in America? I would have to say it is Halloween, a pagan holiday, where children (and some adults) get to dress up in a costume and pretend that they are somebody else. For some reason, which is never discussed much, they get to go door to door and get candy, so this hiding of identity goes hand in hand with getting treats. No one seems too interested in discussing with their children anymore the actual meanings of various holidays like this one.

As we discuss in this book, one aspect of attraction to Islamism is having the ability to hide your own identity and assume a different identity. This is especially attractive to people who are less than satisfied with their own identities and overcome that with a new costume. Islamism can bring with it a new "costume" or a new "fashion."

In the context of Islamist attitudes to women and rape, the burka takes on a special function, which has never occurred to those who ridiculed former Canadian Prime Minister Harper's policy that no woman hiding her face behind a burka or niqab should be able to take the oath of citizenship. Daniel Greenfield, writing for *Frontpage Magazine*, explains:

> Muslim apologists insist that the Burka has something to do with female modesty. But the Koran spells out clearly the reason for it. "Tell your wives and your daughters and the women of the believers to draw their cloaks (veils) all over their bodies that they may thus be distinguished and not molested." The hijab was invented for similar reasons in 1970's Lebanon to mark out Shiite women so they wouldn't be molested by Muslim terrorists. The purpose of the Burka was closer to a cattle brand, separating women married to Muslim husbands, from slave women who were captured in

war. The former were the property of their husbands and untouchable, the latter were fair game for everyone. To a Muslim, the Burka is a sign that says, "only my husband may rape me" and the lack of a Burka means, "everyone can rape me." ... The Burka placed responsibility on women to defeminize themselves and mark themselves as property. Centuries of Islamic jurisprudence put the burden of responsibility for any assault on a woman as the object that tempts men to sin ... That femininity is inherently an object of temptation. The burka and the hijab began as a way of defeminizing women for their protection, but then became an indictment of women. Women were no longer being defeminized to protect them, but to protect men from them.

And so, by December, 2016, bearing in mind the upcoming elections, tolerist German Chancellor Angela Merkel said the wearing of full-faced veils should be prohibited in the country "wherever it is legally possible." At a meeting of her CDU party, she backed a burka ban in schools, courts and other state buildings. Most experts believe that a total ban would violate Germany's constitution.

"The full veil must be banned, wherever legally possible. Showing your face is part of our way of life," she said.

"Our laws take precedence over honour codes, tribal customs and sharia."

Rana Abdulla, writing in peacealliancewinnipeg.ca/2016/06/all-about-the-palestinian-keffiyeh/, discusses the Islamist view of the keffiyeh scarf:

The keffiyeh is one of Palestine's (sic) most iconic symbols. It is incredibly important; it is Palestinians' daily reminder of the repression they face on a daily basis and its cultural appropriation. The keffiyeh is the hope that's been passed down with every worn-out keffiyeh, generation after generation. Keffiyeh reminds all Palestinians of their right to resist. Keffiyeh reminds all Palestinians of their right to live in their land without any occupation. It is important, therefore, that non-Arabs, wear it only out of respect for the wishes of Palestinians themselves.

In late 2000, the keffiyeh became political when the fashion world collided with the political world. All of a sudden, the traditional Arabic head dress became a fashion statement. In 2007, it even made it to the major couture houses including Balenciaga and stores across the United States including Urban Outfitters as they began selling the keffiyeh as a fashion symbol scarf. The idea offended just about everyone. Those who understand the history of the Palestinian Arab's attempt to evict indigenous Jews from Israel, were appalled that it was suddenly fashionable to wear the terrorist's choice of scarf; those who were Islamist dissed those who used fashion to "culturally appropriate" the Islamist symbol of solidarity with the Palestinians.

Radhika Sanghani, writing in *The Telegraph* (telegraph.co.uk/ women/womens-life/11120588/Muslim-women-reveal-why-they-wear-the-veil-burqa-school-debate.html) about one 16-year-old pupil who was barred from her school in England for wearing a niqab – a veil that shows only her eyes. She canvassed thoughts from Muslim young women by taking the following from *Reddit* website. It seems to me that in a world where women must submit to men then the slightest choice in fashion becomes liberating. It is so sad.

One young lady writes:

> I like to use it to promote feminism, however it is very hard to express it because of how people view it. There ARE a lot of women who are forced to wear it, and I think that's really wrong, no matter how religious or what country.

Another says

> The hijab is forced in some places in the world, or by certain people—especially men in many cases. I will not deny this. This is not feminism. I want to take this hijab and make it my own. First choose if I even want to cover or not. Define WHY and HOW. I will choose what colors I will wear. What materials. Not just black and white.

Says one:

> I control if I want to use hijab pins, rhinestones, lace, or brooches. When I will wear it, how I will tie it. When I choose to take it off. It is my right. Also I will choose WHY I wear it. NOT wear it because someone told me to. These points combined promote feminism within women.
>
> If women can choose WHY and HOW, they are exercising basic rights. You decide if you want to, decide why, decide how.

Another says she started wearing a hijab five years ago in her secondary school, and writes:

I genuinely like wearing it. It makes me feel put together and confident in a weird way. Maybe because it does take a certain level of courage to visibly separate yourself from normal society. To start wearing a hijab I had to stop caring about what other people thought and now I can be proud of that.

It definitely doesn't stop street harassment, but men do treat you with a bit more respect. I don't think it's right to treat a girl differently because of how she's dressed but it does happen. When I'm wearing a hijab it's much easier not to care when I'm getting leered at because what exactly is he looking at? My face?

Another writes:

I wear the hijab because it is part of being a Muslim. It is a choice at the end of the day, but I prefer to wear it and identify myself as a Muslim. It's also a sign of modesty that I wear it, like I can't wear short or tight clothes with the headscarf. It definitely keeps away the male attention where they won't approach you to flirt etc.

It's a choice at the end. If you don't wear it, it doesn't make you a bad person or [a bad] Muslim. It is something that has its merits and its advantages but it is a choice.

Another is quite honest:

I was forced to start wearing a hijab at the age of 13 and now find it hard and very uncomfortable to take it off in public. Having said that, I do not take it as seriously as I should, in the sense that sometimes in places where there aren't a lot of men around, I take it off because it gets all sweaty in around my head.

Regarding the niqab, which covers the face ... I don't like it, but that's just my opinion. Firstly, because it isn't an obligation to cover your face in Islam and second, I want to be able to breathe ... ? It's suffocating as I've seen a lot of people I know who do wear a niqab. I'm not forced to wear a niqab/burqa. The only times I wear a burqa—the black robe thing, is when I don't feel like changing so I just throw it on when going somewhere.

A young woman who says she is a lawyer, writes:

The biggest benefit that I enjoy by wearing [the hijab] is that people deal with me as an individual and not just according to my looks. Yes, I've faced a significant amount of xenophobia, but I'm over it. I'm confident and happy with my decision.

I, as well as most Muslims I know in the West, am not fond of the burka or niqab here, because it could expose an individual to unnecessary harm and harassment. Since there are strong religious opinions that permit just the hijab without covering the face, I personally feel that it is a better choice. In the end, however, as long as that individual has made the decision independently and knows why she is doing something, I respect her decision.

Finally, we have this:

Personally, I love wearing the hijab. Nobody could pay me enough to take it off. It honestly liberates me because I get to choose how much of myself I reveal to the public. It's awesome. I have drawers full of a variety of vibrant colors and prints. I match them with my outfits and wear a different style every day. It's kind of like a beautiful, religious fashion statement.

Michael Lumish, PhD, has argued that the *hijab* is a symbol of Muslim supremacism, not liberal diversity. (israel-thrives.blogspot.ca/2017/03/hijab-cool.html) He states:

It could recently have *become* a symbol of liberal diversity in the United States if people like *faux*-feminist icon, Linda Sarsour, had made it so, but they did not. There is nothing essentially anti-feminist about any style of headscarf, so long as it is worn voluntarily, but unfortunately that is not the case for hundreds of millions of women throughout the Muslim world.

If Sarsour, and those westerners unironically adopting an Islamic patriarchal style of women's apparel in the name of feminism, had made it clear that they oppose the rise of political Islam things might be different. If they had stood up for the 1,200 women victimized by the mass rapes in Cologne on New Years Eve, 2016, things might be different.

"But they did not," points out Lumish, in an essay entitled *Hijab Cool*. He argues:

By embracing the *hijab* western feminism drains itself of ideological content. It stands for everything and nothing, which is precisely why the recent Women's Marches held aloft no specific demands even as they reduced women to their sexual organs and wore pink "pussy hats." Thus, whatever anyone might say about Sarsour, she is not liberal and neither is contemporary feminism.

> For most of us from the various abused ethnic minorities who lived for thirteen centuries under the boot of Arab-Muslim imperial rule, the *hijab* is not a cool western fashionable accessory representative of "hip" culture.

I have noticed lately that every television commercial or media advertisement showing more than 3 women at one time, will have one or more women wearing a hijab. Lumish explains why:

"The corporate embrace of the *hijab*, much like the now-and-again corporate embrace of hip socialist iconography, is a way of co-opting *cool* for the purpose of making a buck."

And so corporate America is enlisted in promoting an anti-American ideology for the purpose of making money.

We, in the West, must ask ourselves, "are so many men mistreating women, sexualizing them, using them for sex and then leaving them, that women may soon reject the halter tops and other revealing garments that make them feel that their purpose in life is to arouse men?" Will these women start to conclude, as much of Islam does, that men are beasts, incapable of controlling their sexual urges, and need to be "protected" from "slutty" women, being defined as those who show more skin than their face only? If we continue to see the increasing rate of rapes by Arab and other Muslim men against western women, might some western women finally conclude that if you can't beat them, join them, in putting on "protective clothing"?

It does not help when we have Judges do what a Canadian Judge did, as reported on March 2, 2017 by *National Post*, a young woman had drunk too much and called a cab to take her home.

"A judge acquitted a Halifax taxi driver of sexually assaulting a woman in the back seat of his cab because he could not conclude that she had not consented to the encounter despite being extremely intoxicated."

"Clearly, a drunk can consent," said Judge Gregory E. Lenehan in finding Bassam Al-Rawi not guilty on Wednesday of sexually assaulting the woman in May 2015. The comments have sparked a fierce backlash from experts in sexual violence and online.

The case itself began almost two years ago, when a police officer found the woman "naked from the breasts down" in the back seat of Al-Rawi's cab, according to court transcripts from the March 1 ruling.

"She was extremely intoxicated and unconscious in the backseat of the cab with her legs propped up on the front passenger seat. The officer said Al-Rawi's pants were down and he was holding the woman's urine-soaked tights and underwear."

The Crown prosecutor has already announced an appeal. But if the acquittal is not overruled, how long before any single woman who has been drinking and needs to take a cab will keep a burka in her bag to put on before she hails a cab? How long will women put up with such terrible court rulings before they decide to embrace the burka? Will some decide, as Mark Steyn analyzes it above, that it is safer to marry a Muslim, stay home, and wear a burka when she absolutely has to go out?

Fashion changes and culture changes. A lot of people forget that.

The most common definition of "fashion," according to the *Oxford Dictionaries*, is "A popular or the latest style of clothing, hair, decoration or behavior." However, we tend, in our usage of the word, to emphasize clothing or hair rather than "behavior." Perhaps we don't like to remind ourselves that our behavior is a mere "fashion" as that connotes that the ideologies in our environment might have more control over our behavior when we narcissistically think we are completely and individually in control.

So, while we start this chapter with the above introduction to Islamist clothing, we might emphasize that certain behaviors are no doubt in fashion and certain other behaviors are no longer in fashion. Young people, especially, like to adopt the latest way of dressing, talking, and behaving. That dress, talk and behavior can be seen as desirable for reasons of comfort or esthetics, but it can be adopted out of desire to appear "with it" or what we call "fashionable."

Accordingly, while the keffiyeh and the burka can be seen as fashionable in some circles, mainly Islamist, they can also be seen to be fashionable among those wanting to rebel against their own stagnant culture by embracing a new culture. And, since fashion applies to behavior, we must acknowledge that certain behaviors are a function of Islam becoming fashionable. To those followers of fashion who want to make the loudest statement of their dislike of their own culture, what can be more appealing than the culture of Islam? Islam, through its Islamist bosses, is being swept into media and the arts, as a tolerist way to welcome the others, even perhaps as being in the forefront of a perceived future. Even though I consider Islam*ism* as an evil, we acknowledge that Islam is a worldwide religion—even though we may want to see many aspects of it reformed to accord with our liberal values as it comes into the West through immigration policies.

By considering Islam as a "fashion" we may understand that those who want to be in the forefront of the latest "fashionable" ideology, may be drawn to it. It is not financially difficult, given that the Saudis are funding certain Islamic studies programs and other cultural events, and in fact funding the construction of mosques, while other religions make do with trying to fundraise among their members for decades until they can afford to build a structure.

When I attended university in the early 1970s, young men could fashion their rebellion away from their parents' culture by merely growing long hair and a beard. Some eastern religions, such as Hare Krishna, became fashionable for short periods of time. Later the "Moonies" came into fashion. But for those who tried them and later found them wanting, leaving the movement was of no consequence. In the fashion of Islam, as controlled by the Islamists, leaving the religion may be punishable by death. Leaving the conservative dress codes for women may result in sexual assault based on the Islamists' assumption that the victimized woman was asking for the assault by dressing immodestly. Young people who are drawn to the structure and opportunities in today's Islam must be taught that they are not dealing with the fashion of mere clothing, but a fashion that requires a life commitment. No fan of fashion should fail to understand this. Islamism as fashion is a serious business.

In November 2016, upon the death of longtime Cuban dictator, Fidel Castro, Canadian Prime Minister Justin Trudeau said he was mourning "a larger than life leader who served his people for almost half a century." It seems to me that a dictator who jails dissidents and gays according to his own whim rather than abiding by a liberal democratic "rule of law" based on justice, human rights and fairness that apply to everyone, leaves something to be desired when he "served his people."

"While a controversial figure," continued Trudeau, "both Mr. Castro's supporters and detractors recognized his tremendous dedication and love for the Cuban people who had a deep and lasting affection for 'el Comandante'."

To me, a brutal dictator who disallowed individual rights for his people is more than "controversial," I would call him "evil."

Digging himself deeper into his hole of moral relativism, Trudeau continued, "I know my father was very proud to call him a friend and I had the opportunity to meet Fidel when my father passed away. It was also a real honor to meet his three sons and his brother President Raúl Castro during my recent visit to Cuba."

The prime minister ended his statement by calling Castro a "remarkable leader." I think Justin Trudeau is also a "remarkable leader," but remarkable for his debased set of values, which this essay shall try to elucidate. A leader ought to be studied for his values and how well he implements the policy promises that got him or her elected. In Canada, at least up until Justin's father, Prime Minister Pierre Trudeau, embraced the value of "multiculturalism," we long defined ourselves by the notion of "Peace, Order and Good Government," based on traditional Judeo-Christian values of justice, human rights, individual rights and responsibilities.

It is sad that university students who seem to look under every stone to try to find evidence of racism against blacks and Muslims do not seem concerned about exterminationist racism. So many students had "hurt feelings" when Trump was elected that exams were deferred to let them recover. These "wimps" can hardly be expected to stand up against the exterminationist Islamists, as it is much easier to go to an anti-Israel or anti-Trump demonstration. They are cowards, both morally and physically.

Trudeau was instrumental in bringing into Canada some 30,000 Syrian immigrants without adopting solid criteria for entry based on whether these immigrants were oppressors of non-Muslims or otherwise undesirable. But our prime minister can't seem to understand the contradiction in his policy of enhancing all cultures when not all cultures are good or liberal. Moreover, he is keen to admit into the country some cultures despite their cultural celebration of the murder of Jews, gays, Yazidis, Christians, together with a culture of rape towards women who do not follow their dictates.

Once you make unconditional diversity your goal, you can easily descend further down the ethical hole you are digging. In a recent press conference, Trudeau told the media that Canada, having been tolerant enough to admit many Muslim immigrants, including some 25,000 Syrians between November 2015 and February 2016 and another 10,000 in the rest of 2016, should now go "beyond tolerance." "Beyond tolerance" sounds like "submission" and that really scares me; or perhaps he means active steps to test our tolerance by importing only the "intolerant." I don't like that either.

Trudeau, who never finished university, and before politics, worked as a part time drama teacher and ski instructor, seems rather uneducated in the matter of ideology. Should we welcome evil ideologies as part of our inclusive diversity? Do we still believe that some things are good and some are evil? Do we think that a nice Canadian welcome, together with conduct and words not just tolerant, but beyond tolerant, will turn intolerant jihadists into tolerant Canadians? What about their children who may not feel at home in either culture?

It is rather a large problem that Islamists under the protection afforded to religions are able to say the most hateful things in Canada, but those who object to such speech are threatened with being charged for hate crimes. Recently, in Toronto Canada, an imam at the Downtown Masjid prayed, "O Allah! Give us victory over the disbelieving people … slay them one by one and spare not one of them."

Canadian journalist Christine Williams reports that the downtown Masjid Toronto is affiliated with the Muslim Association of Canada—a self-described offshoot of the Muslim Brotherhood.

Jonathan D. Halevi February 18, 2017 *CIJ News* in Canada reports:

In 2016, the head imam … "at the mosque recited supplications to Allah in support of the 'mujahideen (those who engage in jihad) everywhere,' the total destruction of the enemies of Islam and the purification of Al-Aqsa Mosque from the 'filth of the Jews'."

The sermon was delivered by Dr. Wael Shihab on June 15, 2016 and published on *YouTube* on June 17, 2016.

> Dr. Wael Shihab was appointed in April 2014 to a full-time resident imam of the mosque Masjid Toronto.
>
> Shihab has a PhD in Islamic Studies from Al-Azhar University and he was the head of the Fatwa (Islamic opinion) Unit of IslamOnline.net (English website) and the Shari'ah (Islamic law) consultant of the Shari'ah department of Onislam.net.
>
> He is also a member of the International Union for Muslim Scholars (IUMS) headed by Sheikh Yusuf Qaradawi, who played a major role in launching both aforementioned websites.

This is but one example of a major mosque in Canada (actually it has grown to two branches now in Downtown Toronto) being led by Islamists preaching hate. In Montreal, similar prayers were also delivered in 2014 by Imam Sayed AlGhitawi at Al Andalous Islamic Center in Montreal, Quebec. At the end of his sermons AlGhitawi recited supplications to Allah to support the mujahideen in Palestine and to inflict total destruction on the Jews.

Williams also reports that a Toronto-area schoolteacher who called a jihadist—who crushed the skull of a four-year-old Israeli girl—a hero and martyr, is back in the classroom after receiving a mere rap on the knuckles for her abhorrently violent Facebook postings. She was not charged with a hate crime.

In the case of the Masjid Toronto, authorities need to be investigating the activities inside that mosque. We should be concerned about a tangible danger posed by an organized network of Islamic supremacists (aka stealth jihadists).

From the article, "Canadian Anti-Muslim Protesters Could Face Hate Crime Charges", by David Krayden, *Daily Caller*, February 19, 2017, we learn that Police in Toronto, Ontario might charge a group of anti-Muslim protesters for violating hate crime laws.

So, under our protections for freedom of religion, Islamists like Shihab are allowed to advocate for "mujahideen (those who engage in violent jihad) everywhere," the total destruction of the enemies of Islam and the purification of Al-Aqsa Mosque from the "filth of the Jews."

However, after a group with placards stating "Say No to Islam" was standing outside of Toronto's Masjid mosque on Friday, police said they received multiple complaints about the demonstration from some in the mosque and others who weren't present, and so are considering charges under Canadian hate crimes legislation.

My counsel to the protesters is that next time they should limit their objection to Islam*ism*, rather than *Islam*. As I have written throughout this book, freedom loving Canadians must be in the forefront of stripping Islamism away from Islam and ascertaining that our laws see the difference between Islamism and Islam, and only limit speech against what we shall need to determine are the non-Islamist parts of Islam, as duly reformed and limited by moderate Muslim groups living in the West, and understanding that the West can only host reformist Muslims and not supremacist hate-filled Islamists.

"You're used to seeing this kind of vitriol in the comments sections of newspapers or online. You don't necessarily see it in person. So that's what was surprising about yesterday," a police spokesman said of the protest. And then he mentioned the effect on the police of the recent killing of six Muslim worshipers in a mosque in Quebec City, by a lone dysfunctional young man with no known ties to any organizations. The Canadian public reacted to the Quebec City shootings with enormous support and goodwill for Muslims, so although the shootings were tragic, it cannot be said that all or even a large portion of Canadians are "Islamophobic" as we have studied the term earlier in this book.

The event came just days after a Toronto-area Liberal Member of Parliament (MP) officially tabled a motion in the Canadian House of Commons that has now passed and could potentially make "Islamophobia" another hate crime. Iqra Khalid's motion passed easily, with only the opposition Conservatives refusing to endorse the legislation because they said the definition of "Islamophobia" is too flexible and not even spelled-out in the motion.

Critics wondered why an Islamophobia motion was necessary if people could be charged with a hate crime for a simple protest under existing law. They wondered why there was a need to specifically mention Islamophobia as opposed to the hate of other groups, like Jews or Hindus, as that seems to give some primacy to Muslims – which of course was the goal behind the motion.

Virtually no press coverage was given to a frightening part of the motion. Even though a motion is something less than a law, this "anti-Islamophobia" blasphemy motion is dangerous because it called upon the government to "take note" of another "anti-Islamophobia" petition passed the previous year (Petition e-411), and that is where the danger lies. Otherwise, Petitions to the Parliament have no force of law and therefore do not bind the legislature or even the sponsoring Member of Parliament. So the issue is what the government's response was to the petition.

Petition e-411 said the following:

Whereas:

· Islam is a religion of over 1.5 billion people worldwide. Since its founding more than 1400 years ago, Muslims have contributed, and continue to contribute, to the positive development of human civilization. This encompasses all areas of human endeavors including the arts, culture, science, medicine, literature, and much more;

· Recently an infinitesimally small number of extremist individuals have conducted terrorist activities while claiming to speak for the religion of Islam. Their actions have been used as a pretext for a notable rise of anti-Muslim sentiments in Canada; and

· These violent individuals do not reflect in any way the values or the teachings of the religion of Islam. In fact, they misrepresent the religion. We categorically reject all their activities. They in no way represent the religion, the beliefs and the desire of Muslims to co-exist in peace with all peoples of the world.

We, the undersigned, **Citizens and residents of Canada**, call upon the **House of Commons** to join us in recognizing that extremist individuals do not represent the religion of Islam, and in condemning all forms of Islamophobia.

Here is the text of the motion M-103 and note the way it adopts the petition [my emphasis]:

That, **in the opinion of the House, the government should:** (a) recognize the need to quell the increasing public climate of hate and fear; (b) condemn Islamophobia and all forms of systemic racism and religious discrimination and **take note of House of Commons' petition e-411 and the issues raised by it;** and (c) request that the Standing Committee on Canadian Heritage undertake a study on how the government could (i) develop a whole-of-government approach to reducing or eliminating systemic racism and religious discrimination including Islamophobia, in Canada, while ensuring a community-centered focus with a holistic response through evidence-based policy-making, (ii) collect data to contextualize hate crime reports and to conduct needs assessments for impacted communities, and that the Committee should present its findings and recommendations to the House no later than 240 calendar days from the adoption of this motion, provided that in its report, the Committee should make recommendations that the government may use to better reflect the enshrined rights and freedoms in the Constitution Acts, including the Canadian Charter of Rights and Freedoms.

Score a very big victory for Canadian Islamists. The link between the motion and the petition was not, to my knowledge, ever explained in the media, which of course praised all of this as a feel-good story to defeat Islamophobia, whatever that is. If our prime minister thinks the solution to jihadist pro-Sharia law extremism and terrorism is to be more and more "inclusive" and "beyond tolerant," we may have a problem.

For the definitive liberal critique of multiculturalism, see Salim Mansur's *Delectable Lie: a liberal repudiation of multiculturalism*. For the definitive study of reclaiming Western values from relativists like

Trudeau, see Diane Weber Bederman's *Back to the Ethic: Reclaiming Western Values.*

After Auschwitz, multiculturalism and moral relativism are obscene. Moral values in domestic and international matters must reflect our traditional Judeo-Christian ethics of the Bible. "Inclusive diversity" and "beyond tolerant" are weak substitutes. Marco Rubio in hearing what Trudeau said about Castro's passing, stated that it was "shameful and embarrassing." According to my values, I agree with Marco. But how long will I, a pro-Israel Jew whose values come from our Bible, continue to be able to live in Justin Trudeau's multicultural, inclusive of diversity, and beyond tolerant, Canada?

CHAPTER 22: THE CONFUSION OF THE OBAMA YEARS

Not Understanding that Terrorism is
an Existential Threat

I have been writing about terrorism now for 13 years. Like many other writers, the tragic events of 9/11 in September, 2001 were one impetus for my inquiry into the goals and methods of terrorism. The other impetus is a growing recognition that terrorism often seems to work exactly as it is planned to do: it so strikes fear into the minds of otherwise good people that they begin to submit to the moral framework of the terrorists and begin to adopt the cause of the terrorists as they begin to see the world through empathy and the ideologies we have discussed here.

Unfortunately, during the Obama presidency, both politicians and left-leaning journalists scoffed at the proposition that terrorism poses any *existential* threat. That is because they define "existential" narrowly to mean anything that could defeat, destroy or wipe out America. They do not, as I do, define existential to include not just living but living "free" and having individual human rights, a fair justice system and the other Constitutional protections. For me, submission to the ideology of Islamists destroys bit by bit what I see as "free" existence. To the extent that we give in, submit to, respect, tolerate or empathize with the cause of the terrorists, we have lost our freedom and have gone down the road to submission, whether or not our militaries are defeated in "conventional war." We can look at opinions in the media and the universities to see this empathy, or look at how the Democratic Party has appointed a Muslim with contacts among Islamist terror supporting organizations to be the deputy chair of the DNC.

"Live Free or Die" is the official motto of the U.S. state of New Hampshire, adopted by the state in 1945. How things have changed in American political culture since 1945.

The Left and the Obama administration see an existential threat as one only coming from major nuclear powers. They ignore that Obama's Iran "deal" will allow Iran to give nuclear weapons to its terrorist proxies.

The Left seems to be mostly concerned that the government will, in response to terrorism, pass tough security laws that will inhibit the "rights" of Islamists and their supporters, or at least be offensive to them. Some naively think that the purpose of terrorism is only to wage an asymmetrical type of warfare against more military strong foes and hence to eventually defeat them, and anything short of that is not an existential threat.

Simonsen and Spindlove, in their textbook on terrorism, entitled *Terrorism Today: The Past, the Players, the Future*, say that terrorism, by its violence against civilians, brings awareness of the alleged grievance, uses the media to spread knowledge of the cause, and provokes fear, all of which attempt to secure policy changes and weaken government's resolve. *Attaining these policy changes occurs as a fearful people seek to feed the wild animal in their midst, hoping that its appetite for more random violence will be sated.*

Terrorism is the modus operandi of Islamists – the overtly violent jihadists seeking to spread Sharia law and a restoration of an Islamic caliphate. Obscene acts of violence, often involving suicide bombing are then followed inevitably by apologists and propagandists alleging that Islam is a "religion of peace" and that terrorism can best be fought by more understanding, tolerance, compassion and acceptance of political Islam's goals.

If the goals of terrorism are meant to support a submission to its radical ideology and Sharia law and induce tolerance for its illiberal policies and separatist illiberal communities within the liberal democracies, and eventually to bring Islam to the world, then tolerance, empathy, compassion, and acceptance are a *delusional* response to the problem. The successful way to stop terrorism is to convince the proponents of terrorism (including the passive supporters in much of mainstream Islam who fail to stand up in opposition to the jihadists) that the goals above-mentioned will *not* be achieved by their terrorist acts, and they will in fact be met with a strong resolve within Western nations to reject this attempt to diminish our fundamental human rights, individual freedoms and liberties and the hard-won rights of women, gays, children and ethnic and religious minorities.

The Americans, by allowing a UN Security Council resolution saying Israel illegally occupies the older part of the historical capital of Israel in Jerusalem, have shown terrorists the way to success.

In my book, *Tolerism: The Ideology Revealed*, I explore the ways in which our political culture has moved to change its policies as a reaction to the fear caused by catastrophic terrorism. It is my belief that the fear has caused us to become irrationally accepting and *tolerant* of many actions that are contrary to our most basic traditional values. In the book, I discuss:

· Our cultural Stockholm syndrome, based on the reaction of hostages who instead of hating their abductors, begin to not only sympathize with the grievances of their abusers but begin to advocate for them or even fall in love with them. Some readers will remember the Patty Hearst story and some will remember the bank hostages in Stockholm, two of whom married their captors when they were released from prison. Others will remember journalists who were held hostage by Hamas, face down on the floor in cells and forced to convert to Islam, but who nevertheless upon release praised their captors and their cause. I believe that Islamist terrorism with the relentless march of the Islamic demographic across Europe and now the rest of the West, is causing those who should be putting up red flags to curtail the immigration of those who might be at war with our values, to submit to the inevitable and use their energies to curry favors through their tolerism.

· The culture of denial that has arisen, where the West denies that the perpetrators are in fact seeking these very goals. Obama's negation of the phrase "Islamic terrorism" in favor of confused terminology like "workplace violence" or "man-made disasters" is meant to obfuscate the issue. When "diversity" becomes a higher goal than individual liberty, you start to include in your diverse society a number of people who oppose your traditional values and might even hate the very concept of freedom and individual rights.

· Our culture of *tolerism* hides the very definition of "tolerance" which is "a sympathy or indulgence for beliefs or practices differing from or conflicting with one's own." "Sympathy" is one thing, but how about "indulgence"? "Indulgence" is defined as "giving free reign, or taking unrestrained pleasure in, or treating with excessive leniency" some ideology or group or individual. Tolerance of course only relates to negative acts – we say that we tolerate pain, not pleasure. So tolerance as a value implies that we are taking some pleasure from, or giving some lenience to, groups of peoples and illiberal ideas that are threatening us.

· The indulgence inherent in "tolerism" relates to another little understood cultural reaction to jihadist Islamism, and that is the self-defeating concept of *masochism*. Through unresolved feelings of guilt or inadequacy, large groups of people take actions or adopt policies they know will cause pain to them or their children. To what extent did Germany's remaining guilt of the Nazi era atrocities influence Merkel and her ilk to allow a million unvetted Islamic migrants into the country including those who perpetrated mass sexual assaults in public places like in Cologne, and another who drove a truck into a Christmas market? The latter had already been ordered deported, but procedural issues had allowed him to walk the streets and kill people when he should have been in jail.

On March 26th, after the attack in Belgium, Gwynne Dyer, who is a London-based commentator carried in 45 countries, published an article headlined and subtitled in my local newspaper as follows: "Belgium and the true risk of deadly attack: Terrorists are not an existential threat, they are a lethal nuisance, no more than that."

Dyer took exception to a Belgian politician stating the terrorist attacks in Belgium meant that Belgium was now living through the darkest days since the end of the Second World War.

Most of us would have thought that statement to be unremarkable, but Dyer *minimized* these tragic events, (and their symbolic effects) by sarcastically stating, "Can any country be so lucky that the worst thing that has happened to it in the last 75 years is a couple of bombs that killed 34?"

Dyer minimizes terrorism by saying it is a "statistically insignificant risk – (people) are in much greater danger of dying from a fall in the bath than of dying in a terrorist attack." This of course misses the very essential nature of terrorism: bathtubs have no agenda and we can have hundreds of people slip and fall without any danger to our political culture and commitment to freedom. However, every major terrorist attack is followed by renewed calls for acceptance and tolerance of Muslims, including the radical ones who create "no-go" areas and seek to reverse the separation of church and state, or mosque and schools.

While the political and media "elites" dismiss the terrorism as insignificant, regular folks understand what is actually happening to their societies. According to a leaked government report carried last February by Britain's *The Express*, some 20% of the migrants have already been charged with some crime. The people sense this change, and sense the betrayal of the elites.

By July 30, 2016, Dyer argued that combating terrorism at home implied a war with Europe's own Muslim citizens. This, he then says is exactly what ISIS wants. Says Dyer: "they want to stimulate anti-Muslim hatred, turn the majority against this underprivileged minority and ensure the victory of … neo-fascist, anti-Muslim, anti-immigrant" parties.

"Why does Islamic State want an anti-Muslim backlash in European countries?" he asks. "Because it will radicalize many more European Muslims … Islamic State's ideology claims that the whole Muslim world is under attack by the evil West, and that only ISIL can defend it successfully."

I instead argue that terrorism is meant to result in *terror* which, in an overly tolerant, submissive West losing its loyalty to Judeo-Christian ethics, eases submission to the Islamist message—that the caliphate will be revived, that Europe will be taken back again as in the 12th century, as the rest of the world chooses between the embrace of Islam or dhimmi status, subject to Sharia law. Dyer's approach is meant to disarm the West from its resolve to stop the march of Islamism by falsely asserting it is just an attempt by one organization to gain power in the Arab world, rather than a world-wide problem. Dyer fails to see the difference in Islam and Islamism.

With the election of Trump, it is now time to challenge that agenda of minimizing the real effects of terrorism, and using words from an alternate leftist universe, such as calling Major Dr. Hassan's attack on the soldiers of Fort Hood "workplace violence" or calling terrorists "lone wolves" if the direct chain of command cannot be discovered. We hope to see a resurgent West understand the nature of this War and make a better effort to win this War. Writing from his home in England where separatist enclaves of intolerant Islamists are resulting in separatist "no go" areas and terrorist attacks, Dyer's approach does nothing to encourage Muslim immigrants who might be inclined to assimilate to British, Canadian, or American values; instead he parrots a rather discouraging anti-Western message that Islamism is partly the West's fault, that it must learn to live with it as it is not an *existential threat to our culture of freedom and human rights*, but a mere *nuisance*.

In the new era of a Trump presidency, I am hoping to see Americans join hands with Israel which has dealt with terrorism since the founding of the State. In Israel, of course, there is an existential physical threat, where tiny Israel is surrounded by hostile states and pseudo-states that make it clear they want to destroy the country and kill or deport most of its citizens. Hopefully, with an understanding of just how terrorism creates an existential ideological threat to America by its Islamist enemies, America will move forward as a strong, free, and proud nation.

CHAPTER 23: THE SWEDISH AND GERMAN MODEL OF PROGRESSIVE SUBMISSION

Losing Faith in Past, Present and Future

RT.com on March 1, 2017 did a story about one way that Sweden is attempting to deal with a massive number of Muslim immigrants, who have been admitted from countries like Somalia and Middle Eastern countries, where the immigrants do not have job skills relevant to a modern progressive country like Sweden. The report discusses that Sweden, which has a population of about 9.9 million people, hosted about 127,000 migrants in 2014, according to the EU statistical agency. Then, it received more than 163,000 asylum claims from people coming from the Middle East and North Africa since the summer of 2015 and took in one of the greatest numbers of refugees per capita along with Austria. The report states:

> The inflow of asylum seekers in Sweden, a country with one of the most liberal laws towards refugees, is putting an increasing strain on the country's police.
>
> The already uneasy situation with crime in several Swedish cities, including Malmo and Gothenburg, believed to be aggravated by an inflow of undocumented asylum seekers, prompted Swedish authorities to introduce so-called no-go zones.
>
> To be considered a no-go zone, the area usually has to be marked by a dangerous incidence of muggings, robberies, harassment, and sexual assault. In September 2016, the number reportedly rose to 55 areas.

Now, one would think that the appropriate response to finding out that Somalian and other refugees cannot find work because they have no skills relevant to a modern technological society, would be to invest in more training or perhaps stop the immigration if it is not working out.

But progressive, tolerist Sweden, has found a submissionist solution.

According to the *Goeteborgs Posten*, a local daily, as quoted by *RT.com*. (rt.com/news/377359-sweden-migrants-camel-park/):

> Sweden's second largest city of Gothenburg has invested in a Camel Park saying it will help integrate migrants and turn a depressed neighborhood into a tourist mecca despite strong criticism from politicians, businessmen, and locals. ... the major goal of the park would be to create jobs for migrants and ease their integration into Swedish society.
>
> The Camel Center is expected to be built in Gothenburg's north-eastern migrant-dominated suburb of [no kidding] Angered. ...
>
> Geza Nagy, the man behind the startup, said many migrants from the Middle East and Somalia have *"extensive knowledge"* of camels, which they will be able to apply in the park. ...
>
> "Tourism will become the largest source of income (for the park). There is a huge interest in camels both in Sweden and abroad. ..." Nagy told the Goeteborgs Posten.
>
> "They (the authorities) really believe in our idea of making Angered a tourist resort," he added. Nagy went on to say that he plans to build stables and a paddock and purchase camels and alpacas at the first stage of the center's creation, adding that visitors would be able to pet and ride the camels.
>
> The startup has been in the works for several years. In 2015 it received about a million Swedish kronas ($112,333) from various state agencies and in 2016, Gothenburg city authorities provided financial assistance amounting to 500,000 Swedish kronas ($56,166) from the city's integration fund.
>
> However, Nagy says that the project still needs more funds as the construction costs of the stables and the paddock amount to 2 million Swedish kronas ($224,666). The money received thus far has reportedly been spent on educational trips to Germany and Kazakhstan as well as producing souvenirs from alpaca wool, toys, and t-shirts. Nagy also imported 1,500 liters of camel milk from the Netherlands and sold it in Sweden.

This is being done at the same time as Police in the Swedish city appeal for public help amid "upward spiral of violence," which one would think might just scare away tourists.

> The project has already provoked a heated debate among local politicians and has been sharply criticized by some

commentators. Bert Karlsson, a businessman and a former Swedish MP, denounced the Camel Park idea by calling it *"stupid".*

"This must be a joke," he told the Goeteborgs Posten, adding that "it will never work in reality. ... You ride (a camel) once and then you will never come back," he added.

The project was also questioned by Maria Lexhagen, a tourism researcher at the Mid Sweden University, who said she *"does not see a great demand for camels – especially in Sweden." ...*

However, local officials, who decided to lend financial assistance to the project, insist the Camel Park could still become a major success. *"We thought it was an exciting integration project which could also attract visitors to Angered. It was also promising because it could lead to jobs,"* Marina Johansson, the Chairwoman of the Gothenburg Social Resource Committee, told the *Goeteborgs Posten*.

"If we grant money for something that does not succeed, it is still something we can learn from," she added, stressing that the municipality can always demand a refund from the project.

Somehow the Somalians are not that impressed with tolerist Sweden's efforts to create jobs looking after camels, which is something they definitely know how to do. The initiative was criticized by some migrant residents of the Angered neighborhood, who accused the authorities of *racial stereotyping*.

Ingrid Carlqvist and Lars Hedegaard writing for the *Gatestone Institute* on February 14, 2015, (gatestoneinstitute.org/5195/sweden-rape) summarize the effect of open immigration to Muslim migrants to Sweden. They state:

> · -Forty years after the Swedish parliament unanimously decided to change the formerly homogenous Sweden into a multicultural country, violent crime has increased by 300% and rapes by 1,472%. Sweden is now number two on the list of rape countries, surpassed only by Lesotho in Southern Africa.

> · -Significantly, the report does not touch on the background of the rapists. One should, however, keep in mind that in statistics, second-generation immigrants are counted as Swedes.

· -In an astounding number of cases, the Swedish courts have demonstrated sympathy for the rapists, and have acquitted suspects who have claimed that the girl wanted to have sex with six, seven or eight men.

· -The internet radio station *Granskning Sverige* called the mainstream newspapers *Aftonbladet* and *Expressen* to ask why they had described the perpetrators as "Swedish men" when they actually were Somalis without Swedish citizenship. They were hugely offended when asked if they felt any responsibility to warn Swedish women to stay away from certain men. One journalist asked why that should be their responsibility.

David Goldman writing in the *Asia Times*, October 2015 (atimes.com/more-horrible-than-rape/) shows that the Swedish death-wish has spread to Germany:

He writes that the body of a 20-year-old Syrian woman, "Rokstan M.," was unearthed from a shallow grave in the small Saxon town of Dessau last week. Her father and brothers stabbed her to death on her mother's orders, after she was gang-raped by three men.

In the Islamist opinion of her family, the rape left her 'unclean' and the mother allegedly demanded the killing to restore the family's honor. German police are seeking the father and brothers.

Goldman says:

That by itself is not newsworthy; what is newsworthy is the news itself, which appeared in not one of Germany's major daily newspapers or websites. The tabloid *Bild-Zeitung* ran the story, along with the regional press, while the arbiters of enlightened opinion buried it. *Der Spiegel*, the country's biggest news site, and the Frankfurter *Algemeine Zeitung*, the newspaper of record, made no mention.

Rokstan M. had found work in Germany as a translator for the government, but she knew her family would track her down and kill her. "I am awaiting death. But I am too young to die," she had written on a social media profile.

Says Goldman: "Her story deserves a line or two in the quality press. But it's one of many that German leaders want to ignore."

It is startling how the leadership of Germany, having admitted over a million migrants, could or would not respond to reports of a sex crime epidemic among newly-arrived Muslims. Interior Minister

Thomas de Maiziere urged Germans not to believe rumors of widespread rape at refugee centers, while Germany's police union chief Rainer Wendt warned, "There is a lot of glossing over going on. But this doesn't represent reality." Wendt added, "It is understandable that there is the desire to calm things down politically."

Germany's elite, argues Goldman,

> knew that the migrants could bring a sex crime epidemic because they watched it unfold in Scandinavia. Sweden now has the highest incidence of reported rape outside of a few African countries, and nearly ten times the rate of its European peers—and all this has happened in the past ten years. ... Sweden's political leaders not only refuse to take action, but have made it a criminal offense to talk about it.

We already know that the European Left is tolerist; and we know it is anti-Semitic in its delegitimization, demonization and double standards with respect to Israel. But it is astounding to witness a European intelligentsia giving up and submitting to the Islamist atrocities.

Goldman gets it when he writes of the Islamists,

> There have been many wars of extermination, but there is something uniquely horrifying about today's terrorism. Never in the history of warfare have tens of thousands of individuals stood ready to commit suicide in order to harm enemy civilians. Never for that matter, has one combatant (Hamas in the 2014 Gaza rocket war) sought to maximize civilian casualties on its *own* side. The Japanese killed over 20 million Chinese during the Second World War, but committed suicide in combat in the attempt to sink enemy warships, not kill enemy civilians. The Nazis did not ask their soldiers to kill themselves in order to kill Jews.

Sweden has long been seen by itself and others as a progressive, social welfare state, with adequate income support and housing policies showing its moral goodness. And now, the Swedes, and interested viewers, are seeing a self-destruction of epic proportions. The Swedes are near the top of the World Economic Forum's Gender Gap Index, yet it has become the most dangerous country for women outside of Africa. What is wrong with a feminist country that seems to not care about its women?

If, after decades of feminist accomplishments and social welfare progressivism, the Swedes are ready to submit to Islamist rapists, then something is a greater priority than feminism and social welfare programs. This is a frightening thought but we must address it.

Nima Gholam Ali Pour (gatestoneinstitute.org/8444/sweden-islamic-terrorism) writes that:

> The lack of understanding of violent extremism, combined with politicizing the problem, has been evident, for instance, in Malmö, Sweden's third largest city. After the November 2015 terrorist attacks in Paris, the city councillor responsible for safety and security in Malmö, Andreas Schönström, said that European right-wing extremism is a bigger threat than violent Islamism. And on June 5, 2016, Jonas Hult, Malmö's security manager, wrote: "The right-wing forces in Malmö are the biggest threat."
>
> With such statements, one would think that perhaps Malmö is a city filled with neo-Nazi gangs. Not so. Malmö is a city that usually ends up in the news because of Islamic anti-Semitism or extremist activists working to destroy Israel. There have been no reports of any neo-Nazi movements in Malmö in the recent past ... Of Malmö's residents, 43.2% were either born abroad or their parents were.

Magnus Norell, writing in *Huffington Post* (huffingtonpost. com/magnus-norell/the-muslim-brotherhood-in_1_b_10880432.html), provides some clear insights into how the Islamist Muslim Brotherhood became *the* voice for the entire Muslim community. The strategy in Sweden does not seem to be very different than other western countries but there is no doubt that Swedish tolerism has allowed Islamist influences to move farther and faster than elsewhere.

> The Brotherhood's strategy, developed since many years back, was to form, become part of (or in some cases, take over) educational institutions, social networks and so-called centers for dialogue. The goal was to establish itself politically and socially in the various European countries with existing Muslim communities, and thus gain influence over "their own" Muslim group. The basic idea was that "Muslims" form a collective with a certain specific definition of what constitutes Islam. This is still a core idea with Islamists; as Abirisak Waberi, former member of the Swedish Parliament (Moderate Party) and Omar Mustafa's

predecessor as president of the Islamic Association in Sweden (IFiS, see below), said: *"Islam has only one definition."* *It is a statement that Waberi shares with Islamists in general and sums up what is a fundamental idea with all Muslims who have not yet reconciled with Islamic history and privatized their religious tradition, i.e. who have not made religious beliefs a private matter.*

States Norell:

> The Brotherhood organization can be seen as a kind of loosely formed organization where an oath of loyalty is taken. By this oath, one is inducted into a spiritual world community. This is important, because inside this shared spiritual community, one is able to form any types of organizations, at any time, as long as there is support for the effort in question. This also means that when the question "are you the Muslim Brotherhood?" is posed, one can truthfully say "no" and refer to something else (such as "the Islamic Association" or the like). And it is absolutely correct since the Brotherhood is a widely spread spiritual network that can manifest itself in many different external organizations ... A key reason for this success story is the way in which the Brotherhood has constructed its networks in Europe (and elsewhere; the picture is similar in North America, for example).
>
> By promoting the importance of a unified ideology ("there is only one kind of Islam") while being open to different locally and regionally manifested organizational forms, they were able to effectively spread their message without forcing others into a pre-conceived framework. This allowed the Brotherhood to rapidly grow organically, without new or existing organizations needing to call themselves the Muslim Brotherhood. In this way, an apparently large variety of Muslim associations were able to emerge, all united by a common ideological belief.

It seems not to bother most Swedes, that although they value a tolerant society where freedom is paramount, that the fast-growing Muslim community is embracing the Islamist doctrine that Islam is a comprehensive system that covers all aspects of society and individual lives, being both religious ideology and political project. Swedes tolerate an ideology that everyone would benefit from Islam's divinely instituted Sharia law. The political project expressed is based on a strategy of identity politics that is well tolerated by the left-liberal

Social Democrats and the Left Party and significantly to the Green Party.

Having, out of tolerism or confusion, accepted the Muslim Brotherhood Islamists to be spokesmen for the fast-growing Muslim community in Sweden, and accordingly having accepted the idea that all Muslims are fundamentally the same, it is easy to see why Sweden and other countries then allow, even facilitate, a parallel Muslim civil society with its own institutions and schools. Allowing such apartheid damages social interaction and may eventually cause societal disintegration.

Concludes Norell:

> It is therefore critical that our politicians get themselves together, raise their gaze and broaden their horizons when it comes to Muslims in Sweden. As noted, most Muslims in Sweden are actually not members of any Muslim organization whatsoever. It is also about time to recall that in Sweden, religious identity is a private matter and that in our secular, religiously neutral country, we live in one common society, not several parallel ones.

Mr. Norell's analysis is fine as far as it goes. One is left with the desire to understand not just Swedish tolerance for the evil aspects of Islamism, but their actual **embrace** of evil. Toleration of evil is now the theme of Swedish government but as this book argues, it leads to submission. This submissive embrace of evil was on display in early 2017 when Sweden's trade minister made a pilgrimage to Tehran to beg approval from Iranian President Hassan Rouhani. The Swedish minister dressed her female delegation in long coats and head-scarves so as not to "offend" the extreme right-wing, theocratic hate-mongering Iranian regime. Facing criticism in the media for the veiling, she told the newspaper *Aftonbladet* that "she was not willing to break Iranian law," according to reports.

Shredding your values for fear of causing offense is submission. But there is a deeper reason for Sweden's willingness to submit.

In my view, Swedish values, including its emphasis on its supposed "neutrality" is not only based on fraud, but contains the seeds of a moral rot that has contributed to the submission to Islamism. Neutrality is not a constitutional imperative in Sweden but comes from a belief that being "neutral" will allow it to avoid war. This is not a pacifism, because Sweden has constructed an army strong enough to deter attacks from other countries. It is a policy of trying to avoid war. Instead, the Swedes try to occupy some moral high ground by fancying themselves skilled at peace-making and mediation.

I would like to avoid war too, but I believe that in the case of absolute evil, like the Nazis, morality dictates that we fight for our lives and those of our allies. Sweden does not believe in that, but it is an open secret that in fact Sweden favored the Nazis in World War 2—not because it was the right thing to do, but because it benefited Sweden to trade with Germany, especially when it came to selling iron ore to the Nazis for the war effort.

Once Germany attacked Denmark and Norway, Swedish neutrality was put to the test. Germany soon demanded to move military transports over Swedish territory to attack the defenders of Norway. At first, these demands were turned down in April and May of 1940, with only Red Cross transports to northern Norway being permitted transit. However, in June 1940, the Swedes caved in to the Nazis and permitted the transit of German military equipment and personnel on leave between Norway and Germany, via Sweden. Norway became one of the first countries to fall to the Nazis, aided by this Swedish assistance.

The Swedish Government and High Command portrayed their appeasement as simply a way to avoid a hopeless war with Germany. Imagine if every country would have taken a similar position. The Swedes then were guilty of appeasement and complicity both.

And then its moral position of neutrality became even more fraudulent. In connection with the German attack on Russia in June 1941, the transfer of a fully equipped German infantry division under the command of General Engelbrecht from Norway to Finland over Swedish territory was permitted.

While other such requests were refused, Sweden continued to trade with Germany during the war.

After the battle of Stalingrad, Sweden cut back on exports of iron ore to Germany.

It must be mentioned that during the war, some restrictions were placed on the press to placate the Germans!

Many cases of Swedish complicity with the Nazis only surfaced some 50 years after the War. For example, a 2012 book by journalist Espen Eidum, was written after three years of sifting through Norwegian, Swedish and German archives to discover how the Nazis had managed to get troops and supplies across Sweden to the front lines in Narvik, Norway in 1940, enabling the Nazis to turn a losing battle into a decisive victory that led to the conquest and brutal occupation of the whole country.

Sweden, although neutral, had in fact gone out of its way to aid the Germans, who would rely on the country for much of its iron ore during the war.

After the publication of the book, *Blodsporet, or The Blood Track*, Britain's *Daily Mail* newspaper quoted Mr. Eidum as saying: "The Germans used the Swedish rail network on a large scale during the fighting. The operation was much more extensive than historians have previously realised."

The book details how, in October 1940—four months after Narvik had turned into a crushing defeat for both the Norwegians and Winston Churchill, who had sent British forces there—Swedish diplomats in London lied to Norwegian government-in-exile representatives that it had not allowed any Nazi soldiers or weaponry to use its railway network to get to the front. Mr. Eidum said:

> The German foreign ministry had earlier summoned the Swedish ambassador in Berlin to inform him that Adolf Hitler had personally requested for the Nazis to be permitted to send three trains with 30 to 40 sealed carriages through Sweden to the far north of Norway.
>
> Hitler's representatives told the Swedes that the Germans had a number of wounded soldiers at the front and urgently needed to send in medical officers and food.
>
> The Germans also made no secret of the fact that winning the battle in Narvik was a matter of some pride for Hitler.

Once the permission was given, Germany sent in combat troops disguised as medical personnel. Mr Eidum said:

> For every actual medical officer or orderly, the trains carried 17 infantrymen.

> A report sent by a Swedish representative in Berlin, who watched the officers board the train, left little doubt that the Swedes knew the trains were being used for troop movements.

In addition, according to the book and the *Daily Mail* story about the book, the trains carried heavy artillery, anti-aircraft guns, ammo and a plethora of communications and supply equipment.

Mr Eidum said: "Sweden's railway network was used extensively to aid the German occupation of Norway. This included sending Norwegians to Germany, many of them bound for concentration camps."

And, once the swastika flew over Narvik in Norway, Sweden allowed German trains to go to the port—taking Swedish iron ore back to Germany, where it was used as an essential ingredient of the war effort.

Said Eidum: "And hundreds of thousands of Germans passed through Sweden on their way to the eastern front. This made a great deal of money for Swedish rail operator SJ over a three year period."

The book reproduces a letter from Norway's wartime prime minister, Johan Nygaardsvold—sent on New Year's Eve 1940 to his Stockholm-based envoy Anders Frihagen—showing Mr Nygaardsvold asking his government's Stockholm envoy to convey his anger to Swedish Prime Minister Per Albin Hansson.

The book shows that close to 100,000 railroad cars transported 1,004,158 military personnel on leave to Germany and 1,037,158 to Norway through Sweden by the time the transit agreement between the two nations was disbanded on August 15, 1943.

We should note that Norway lost around 10,000 people in the war, two thirds of them civilians.

There are other facts that have come out in recent years. In a February 2009 article by the *Daily Mail's* Allan Hall, it was shown that Sweden made secret loans to Nazi Germany during World War 2.

Hall reported that

> New documents show how the Swedish finance minister in wartime, Ernst Wigforss, approved bank credits to Berlin in 1941. The details were recently uncovered in a filing cabinet at the finance ministry.

> The loans served to increase Swedish exports to Nazi Germany, allowing it to prosecute its war on all fronts.

In summary then, Sweden's portrayal of itself as neutral in World War 2 is a lie. Swedes have been living a lie from early in the War for the 50 years it took for diligent reporters to find the real facts.

Sweden's submission to Islamism, by allowing nearly unrestricted Muslim immigration and by not vetting Muslims for Islamist sympathies or war crimes, is in fact an attempt at expurgating its guilt, the same way Germany's Angela Merkel has sought to reduce Germany's feelings of guilt by admitting a million migrants, often hostile to liberal values, from a culture of rape and other atrocities, and possessing anti-Semitic attitudes. Merkel, of course, comes from the former Communist East Germany which adopted an ideology that it was Communist more than Nazi; and so the East Germans went through less of an accounting and apology for Nazi conduct than those in West Germany. This somewhat unresolved guilt helps explain Merkel's bizarre acceptance of one million Islamic refugees including those who are now sexually assaulting German women. It also explains why German liberals fear most their own right-wing politicians and commentators, and less their own Islamists. For example, see Virginia Hale's article in *Breitbart* of February 21, 2017, "German Minister Pledges to Protect Families ... from Social Media Posts About Migrant Rapes."

After Sweden, the European nation that took in the most migrants per capita was Austria. Austria, the country that swiftly welcomed the Nazi annexation on March 12, 1938, also bears a collective guilt that is assuaged by its welcome of Muslims.

Newsweek magazine reported in 2016 that the number of anti-Semitic incidents in Austria nearly doubled in 2015, according to a Jewish watchdog in the country, with community leaders blaming an influx of Muslim immigrants from the Middle East and Africa.

"According to figures collated by the Austrian Forum Against Anti-Semitism and presented by the Jewish Communities of Austria (IKG), anti-Semitic incidents increased 82 percent from 255 incidents in 2014 to 465 last year." It seems that the desire to bring into the country massive numbers of anti-Semitic Muslim immigrants is both a cause and a result of the elevated figures for Austrian anti-Semitism.

We can now understand why Sweden, Germany and Austria have threatened their own citizens in a bizarre attempt to wipe out their guilt through appeasement of Muslims including Islamists.

To some extent we must acknowledge that certain western nations have self-identity issues resulting from the historical (and present day) treatment of Natives or other Aboriginals. Surely Australia, Canada and the United States have the historical guilt on how their indigenous peoples were treated and in the case of the United States, how its black people were treated. Is guilt over mistreatment of such indigenous people or black slaves in essence "washed away" by Islamophilia, love for Muslims? Is this guilt the equivalent of European guilt for colonialism and imperialism, then Nazism, which plays out as anti-nationalism? Is the successful nationalism of the Jewish people in Israel, another problem in the minds of those whose anti-nationalism encourages them to admit hundreds of thousands of Muslims whose loyalty is not to the State but to the Ummah?

Given France's record of surrender to the Nazis through the Vichy government, we understand why France too decided to open their beautiful country to less than desirable immigrants some of whom riot and steal and support terrorism.

With respect to my own country Canada, a 2015 report by *Human Rights Watch*, compiled government data for 191 water systems among First Nations in Ontario. "Tainted water and broken systems on Ontario's First Nations reserves are jeopardizing health, burdening parents and caregivers, and exacerbating problems on reserves," said Amanda Klasing, senior researcher at *Human Rights Watch* and author of the report. "First Nations people have the same human rights to adequate water and sanitation as all Canadians, but in practice cannot access them."

Across Canada today, there are 133 advisories in place in 89 First Nations reserves warning that the water is not safe to drink. Every university has protesters in place about the Palestinians, but few speak out about this national disgrace. Is there an inherent guilt that we bury by adopting Islamophilia?

We must face directly why in fact countries are submitting to Islamism. They have lost faith in their past, present and future. In years past, Christianity gave them a way to confess their guilt and atone for it and be forgiven. In their new secular world, they deal with their guilt through submission to the most evil group around, the jihadist Islamists promising world control.

I have argued that this submission is based on a certain masochism, as we are taking immigrants who are causing us pain. The immigration is completely contrary to a policy of preserving our hard-won individual rights and freedoms, which are not shared by many of the immigrants. Importing people who are unlikely to make a positive contribution to a country, based on established criteria for acceptance as an immigrant, reflects a masochism. If a person "hates" himself and his country's history, masochism, can become, in the words of Professor Roy Baumeister, from Case Western Reserve University, writing about sexual masochism, "*Escape from Self.*" (scribd.com/ document/341497554/Masochism-and-the-Self)

Not only have we lost faith in past, present and future, but we seek to escape from self by the masochistic desire to submit to Islamism. A popular reaction to this sad ideology is why Americans elected Donald Trump as president. They were tired of the self-hate of the elites, and chose someone who would lead a proud America. Trump's ideology brings hope to those like myself who are worried about America's submission. The Trumpers and the anti-Trumpers are now fighting the battle for America's future, and perhaps for the future of freedom in the entire West.

Two professors who study liberal democracy have written a report suggesting that the strength of liberal democracies is declining. While the number of "free" countries grew from the mid-1970s to the early 2000s, Freedom House, a watchdog organization, has seen a decline in global freedom each year since 2005.

Yascha Mounk, a lecturer in government at Harvard, and Roberto Stefan Foa, a political scientist at the University of Melbourne in Australia, report that in Australia, Britain, Sweden and the U.S., the percentage of people who say it is "essential" to live in a democracy has declined, with the figures especially low among younger people.

For example, they state, that the share of Americans who believe that army rule would be a "good" or "very good" thing has risen from 1 in 16 in 1995 to 1 in 6 in 2014.

What I found particularly distressing is the differences these researchers have found between older Americans and younger "millenials." For example, 43 percent of older Americans believed it was illegitimate for the military to take over if the government was incompetent or failing to do its job, while only 19 percent of millenials agreed that it would be illegitimate.

With this in mind, I have been worrying about some of the extremist speech and writing of leftist younger people in college and their professors in left-oriented groups, and certain journalists who are ranting and protesting about Donald Trump's election.

In California, a leftist professor of human sexuality studies, used class time to rant. *CBS Los Angeles* reported that Olga Perez Stable Cox, a human sexuality teacher at Orange Coast College in Costa Mesa, called Trump's election "an act of terrorism."

"Our nation is divided. We have been assaulted. It is an act of terrorism," she told the students.

Then in the *New York Times* (more about the *Times* below) a column by its columnist Charles M. Blow, alleging that it is pointless to wait and see how Trump actually does after he is sworn in as president, as what Mr. Blow has "already seen is so beyond the pale that it is *irrevocable.*" [my emphasis]

Blow charged that Trump

> has shown himself beyond doubt and with absolute certainty to be a demagogue and bigot and xenophobe.

Where he goes next with this opinion is what shocks me. Blow states:

> In that reality, resistance isn't about mindless obstruction by people blinded by the pain of ideological defeat or people gorging on sour grapes. *To the contrary, resistance then is an act of radical, even revolutionary, patriotism. Resistance isn't about damaging the country, but protecting it.* [my emphasis]

This sounds totalitarian to me.

Now, we all have seen politicians and pundits characterizing their opponents as liars and hiders of the truth, and frankly Obama and Hillary Clinton, have no moral superiority in these verbal taunts alleging that the others use lies and fake news. But what concerns me is that the *New York Times* has a columnist who states, "the emergence of Donald Trump as a political figure has threatened to kill many of the ideals that Americans hold dear: decency and decorum, inclusion and empathy" and ending his list, as might be expected, with "truth and facts themselves."

He titles this rant, *Agents of Idiocracy*, since to Blow, Trump's supporters are not merely wrong, but are idiots; only Blow knows what are the American "ideals that Americans hold dear," and he concludes: "We are not in an ordinary post-election period of national unity and rapprochement. We are facing the potential abrogation of fundamental American ideals. We stand at the precipice, staring into an abyss that grows darker by the day."

So, if the "idiots" choose a "demagogue" whose ideas of American traditional liberal values are not the same as Mr. Blow's, and are, clearly, in Mr. Blow's opinion, leading the country into the abyss, and professors give their students time off to mourn such a descent, how close are we really to a point where substantial portions of the population embrace "resistance" and are willing to break the rules of American liberal democracy in the service of this resistance?

You see, Mr. Blow's idea of American values is not the same as mine. Certainly, decency is a nice ideal, but "inclusion and empathy" are not really American constitutional values.

Rex Murphy, writing in *National Post* on February 3, 2017 has the perspective that we Canadians sometimes show as we view American political culture from outside the country but not too far. He writes:

> More and more those who are, as it were, genetically opposed to the results of the presidential election, make the assumption that the Republican victory handed them a license to violate all the codes of civil society and the understandings of democratic practice. That because their fellow citizens make a choice they find unpalatable they are thereby released to riot and violence and plaster their actions as heroic and noble. And of course the cringing authorities of the universities, instead of clarion denunciations of such actions, and absolute dissociation from all such charades, dance mildly down some imagined middle.

The reaction of the Left, the media, and the Democratic Party to the election of Trump was "over the top" to say the least.

Mr. Murphy, in another column dated March 11, 2017, made the case that Trump is a kind of populist, and that populism according to the great President Abe Lincoln, at Gettysburg, is "government of the people, for the people, by the people." Continues Murphy:

> Any leader that earns and enjoys a real connection with what we journalists unfailingly call "ordinary people" is a boon to democracy. In a time of deep cynicism about politics, a time when those who rule are seen and felt to be remote from their citizens, untouched by the tensions and burdens of everyday folks, a leader who—with the mysterious charisma that governs these things—owns an emotional identification of how the majority of citizens live, does much to shore up our democracies. Populism is just a short tag for another great rule of politics: never forget who put you there (meaning, in office).
>
> A system, American democracy, which has over time become the property of a class — credentialed, secure, highly but narrowly educated and financially insulated from all conceivable want — has "owned" politics for so long that

the demos, the people, no longer feel connection with their governors. Or trust them. Out of that discontent the people opted for a wild card, Donald Trump, and found, perhaps to their astonishment, that a New York tycoon, of flamboyant style and erratic manners, had more than a touch of the common man. That's the one element of Trump's rise that may be called populist. And far from being something to dread, it contains lessons to be learned.

Concludes Murphy in his rebuttal to the Trumpophobes:

Populism is not synonym for demagoguery, nor is it a step ladder to authoritarianism, or a shortcut (this is delusional) to fascism, as the more fevered of the Trumpophobics seem to believe. A strain of populism is good for all governments, and I would suggest that in any effective politician there has to be a touch of ... instinctive affinity for the little guy, and ... (an) ardent determination not to forget the people who elected him.

The Left and the Democrats have always painted the American Right as close-minded, bigoted, and have appropriated to themselves the notion of being fair and liberal. There is also the notion of right-wing closed-minded men versus more liberal more open-minded women. Now we know this isn't true. I came across a fact recently that accords with what Professor Bloom called *The Closing of the American Mind*.

Jeff John Roberts, writing in *Fortune.com* on Dec 19, 2016 reported:

This year's bitter presidential election has caused a rift in online relationships. According to a new survey, 13% of Americans reported blocking or unfriending a "friend" on social media because of their political postings.

But the results of the study, carried out by the non-partisan Public Religion Research Institute, show the impulse to block varies widely based on gender and political leanings.

The study shows Democrats were almost three times more likely than Republicans (24% vs. 9%) to have unfriended someone after the election. A similar disparity turned up for self-identified liberals versus conservatives (28% vs. 8%). Meanwhile, only 9% of independents reportedly booted someone out of their online social circles because of politics.

... the survey also identified "Democratic women" as the most likely of all groups to block someone on social media.

And young women are being propagandized at an early age, thanks to the new editorial direction of *Teen Vogue*. Sophie Gilbert, writing in *The Atlantic* in December 2016, notes that *Teen Vogue* published an op-ed by Lauren Duca titled *Donald Trump Is Gaslighting America* (teenvogue.com/story/donald-trump-is-gaslighting-america). The piece compared the ways in which the president-elect talks about his record to the ways abusive spouses psychologically manipulate their partners.

The hypercritical tone of Duca's piece was representative of a larger shift *Teen Vogue* has made over the last year. Gilbert notes that new editorial staff have moved the magazine more aggressively into covering politics, feminism, identity, and activism, including an interview exploring what it's like to be a Muslim woman facing a Trump presidency, a list of reasons why Mike Pence's record on women's rights and LGBTQ rights should trouble readers, and a video in which two Native American teenagers from the Standing Rock Sioux tribe discuss the Dakota Access Pipeline protests.

Not all parents are happy with their daughters reading what they thought was a fashion and wellness magazine dealing with the usual concerns of teenagers. Tabitha Korol in an essay published in *New Media Journal*, (newmediajournal.us/korolon) March 21, 2017, *Teen Vogue goes Rogue*, writes:

> *Teen Vogue* is an appalling anti-American propaganda rag, complete with disrespectful, insulting articles about the President of the United States, as well as one that puts the onus of failing peace talks on Israel's Prime Minister Benjamin Netanyahu. It serves as a Muslim Brotherhood façade in the way that it presents a heavily biased account of the Palestinian Arab war against the Jewish State of Israel, America's staunchest ally and the only country in the Middle East that shares our values. *Teen Vogue* Emma Sarran Webster's un-researched revised history, taken from selected leftist news sources, is an insult to their readers' intelligence and a betrayal of democracy. It is such writing that helps twist the minds of our youth, inciting them to participate in the charade marches that support un-American issues, such as the one led by anti-Semitic, faux-feminist Linda Sarsour, who is against police, mosque surveillance, and American ideals.

In its continuously hysterical coverage of Donald Trump, first as candidate, and now as president, let us examine the *New York Times*. I receive the International Weekly edition along with my local paper. I like to read it, painful as it might be, in order to see how the leftist press perceives events that I see so differently.

If the *New York Times* was a fair or moderate media, it would have done far more to cover former President Barack Obama's ideological positions. His speech to the Muslim world on June 9, 2013 stated that Americans and Muslims "share common principles – principles of justice and progress; tolerance and the dignity of all human beings." Any serious student of ideology knew then that cultural and moral relativism, moral equivalency and post-modernism were now in charge. His background as a congregant in the church of the anti-American Reverend Wright, his friendship with former domestic terrorist William Ayers and Bernadette Dohrn, and his upbringing in a Muslim family in Indonesia, all made for a president whose ideology had to be studied responsibly by the media, but which was seldom done.

And yet, the same media obsesses over every aspect of Trump's history, routinely calling him a misogynist, an Islamophobe, and a xenophobe, etc., and this was before the expiry of the 100 day period where it is traditional for media to allow a new president room to grow into the job. Those so "fearful" of what they think President Trump might do to America, should be reminded that in his first 100 days, the late great President John F. Kennedy ordered the very unsuccessful Bay of Pigs invasion in Cuba. And yet, with more experience and with a mental and political toughness well beyond what Obama has, that same President Kennedy stared down and overcame the Russian wish to place nuclear weapons in Cuba.

Here are problematic examples from the February 4, 2017 *New York Times International Weekly*:

The front page top headline claims America is "Torn in Two" and shows one protest sign calling Trump a "fascist" and another saying "Stop Trump/Pense." The article doesn't discuss that the protester calling for the "stopping" of a democratically elected Republican party president is the fascist. Then another front page story alleges that "A Ban (sic) Betrays Friends and Bolsters Enemies." The same folks who accuse Trump of Orwellian mis-use of language, routinely used political correctness to distort language and censor opposing views during the Obama era. The alleged "ban" on Muslim immigrants is blatantly false. From a campaign that promised "extreme vetting" of possible Islamist terrorists seeking entry into the United States, Trump followed through for what is actually not a "ban" but a "pause" from seven (later reduced to six) Muslim majority countries that have weak or barely functioning central governments and strong Islamist organizations. The lead editorial for this edition of the *Times* screams "Donald Trump's Cowardly Ban." Again language is mis-used.

And it goes on and on. Maureen Dowd calls Trump a "Wild Child," David Brooks alleges Trump's politics are "Built on Fear." One wonders how many breaches of human rights and how many rapes and terrorist attacks it would take on the part of Islamists for Mr. Brooks to understand that some people might be expressing fear for their children and a wish for government to protect the American people, given what is going on in Sweden, Norway, Germany and other European nations.

Roger Cohen in the same edition calls Trump "abnormal" but not in a good way. He writes that for a president, "impetuosity allied to cruelty combined with immense power equals trouble." Then, Thomas Friedman, having had most of his opinions rejected by the American people through their election of Trump, wants to override that democracy by "A Plea to America's Business Leaders" asking them "to do a job that you have never thought of doing before: saving the country from a leader with a truly distorted view of how the world works and role America should play in it." Now, to people who have actually studied fascism, it is immediately apparent that Friedman's call for big business to ally with leftists to overrule the wishes of the American people is about as fascist as one can get. Would that our university professors would teach that to their students, rather than the prevailing rot that everyone should be "safe" from anything "offensive" and not "politically correct."

All of President Trump's policies should of course be discussed, and Congress will play its role as will the justice system. It appears to be Trump's style to sometimes "float" ideas in his tweets and then take the criticisms and modify his positions as necessary. That may be a better idea for a corporate executive than for a president. But in my opinion the *Times* gave a free ride to Obama in his eight years of foreign policy blunders, including his failure to support the Iranian "Green Revolution," his siding with Muslim Brotherhood Islamist organizations over secular leaders and his creation of a power vacuum and an American reticence to be involved which aided in the development and growth of the vile ISIS.

Given the *Times'* historical record, we should perhaps not expect anything different. But recall that after the recent election, where the *Times* cast off any pretense of fairness in its advocacy for Hillary Clinton, perhaps the most flawed candidate ever, due to her "pay for play" with the Clinton Foundation, her record as secretary of state, her lies about the attack in Benghazi, her close relationship with a Saudi woman with a Muslim Brotherhood background, and her illegal dealings with emails and national security, the *Times* wrote a letter to their readers. Arthur Sulzberger Jr., publisher, and Dean Baquet, executive editor, wrote on November 13th:

> After such an erratic and unpredictable election there are inevitable questions: Did Donald Trump's sheer unconventionality lead us and other news outlets to under-estimate his support among American voters? What forces and strains in America drove this divisive election and outcome? Most important, how will a president who remains a largely enigmatic figure actually govern when he takes office?
>
> As we reflect on this week's momentous result, and the months of reporting and polling that preceded it, we aim to rededicate ourselves to the fundamental mission of *Times* journalism. That is to report America and the world honestly, without fear or favor, striving always to understand and reflect all political perspectives and life experiences in the stories that we bring to you. It is also to hold power to account, impartially and unflinchingly. You can rely on The New York Times to bring the same fairness, the same level of scrutiny, the same independence to our coverage of the new president and his team.

Do you believe the *Times'* promise to "report America and the world honestly, without fear or favor, striving always to understand and reflect all political perspectives and life experiences in the stories that we bring to you. It is also to hold power to account, impartially and unflinchingly?

As the *New York Times* pushes the story that Trump's national security diligence will promote anti-Americanism by Islamists and perhaps all Muslims, they quoted on the front page an Iraqi lawmaker, Mouwafak al-Rubaie, (who we are supposed to believe tells the truth), as follows: "I think this is going to alienate the whole Muslim world."

Come on now. The most Muslim-friendly president in American history, Barack Obama, who often stretched the truth and had his own "alternate facts" about the history of Muslims in America and even their total numbers, in fact alienated the Muslim world. Did Obama's appeasement of Iran's nuclear ambitions turn Iran into a friendly country? Did Obama's tolerance of terrorism, his misnaming it as "workplace violence" or "lone-wolf" violence reduce the violent jihad and attempts to spread illiberal Sharia law and Islamist supremacism throughout the non-Muslim world? Or did the Islamists and such groups as the "Palestinians" feel less blowback for their violence because of Obama? The word is "appeasement" but that word does not appear in the lexicon or world-view of the *Times*.

The *Times* too often portrays the Muslim world as one unified people, which we know is false; there are many different Muslim countries, there are Arab Muslims and non-Arab Muslims, there are Shiite Muslims and there are Sunni Muslims and they often don't get along. Responsible journalists would give a lot more coverage to reformist Muslims who eschew the easy game of blaming America and Israel for the backwardness and lack of human rights in the Muslim world. These reformists are our hope for a non-violent future where Islam purges itself of violent supremacism and seeks to promote liberal values, overriding accepted theology where necessary.

The vile Georgetown University Islamist, Nathan Lean, (director of research for *the Pluralism, Diversity and Islamophobia project* at Georgetown University's Prince Alwaleed bin Talal Center for Muslim-Christian Understanding) actually called for a "public uprising" to overthrow Trump. It seems to me that when the apologists for Islamism start to join the radicals and call for violence, that pretty much validates all of our concerns that they are submitting to radical Islam or Islamism.

The great American-Israeli commentator, Caroline Glick, in her essay of February 6, 2017, *The Evolving Threat of Jihad in the West*, notes that to the American and European left-liberals, the very act of mentioning bad behavior carried out by a specific group (like Muslims) in itself is seen to be bigoted. Ms. Glick argues correctly that it is not bigoted to point out the bigotry of others to confront and challenge it. This message should be heard by the Trumpophobes.

Former secretary of labor under Bill Clinton, Robert Reich, has been spending large amounts of time writing about how to "resist" the Trump White House. On a Facebook posting of February 1, 2017 (facebook.com/RBReich/posts/1457837370895521), Reich says it is noteworthy that "the resistance is a growing inside federal departments, coming from federal workers charged with implementing Trump's agenda." He praises the 180 federal employees who have signed up for a workshop, where experts will offer advice on workers' rights and how they can express civil disobedience. After listing another 8 ways federal civil servants (who are charged with implementing the president's policies) are actually resisting them, he says: "Let us pause to appreciate and applaud our federal workforce." It is as if in Reich's mind, Trump is a Hitler-like figure and therefore it is moral to tell civil servants to resist. Reich, a retired professor who taught at University of California (Berkley) and at Harvard, fancies himself the leader of this "resistance" movement. On his website *robertreich.org*, one can read his "The First 100 Day Resistance Agenda" and other material that this well-to-do leftist intellectual, dwelling in the la-la land of Berkley, recommends doing to resist the lawfully chosen president, and written before the president was even sworn in. A phobia indeed.

As reported by Britain's *DailyMail.com*, a famous American comedian, Sarah Silverman, actually tweeted, "Wake up and join the resistance, once the military is with us, the fascists get overthrown." Am I the only one who worries that people like her would be prime candidates to support an alliance between Islamists and Leftists to overthrow the president and put in power someone the Islamists and the Leftists like? Is Hollywood filled with people like her? How many people if given the choice between submitting to the rule of Trump compared to the rule of the Muslim Brotherhood would choose the Muslim Brotherhood (or some more moderate-sounding front organization)? I hazard the guess that Ms. Silverman knows or cares little about the checks and balances built into the American democracy – by Congress, the judiciary, and as Charles Krauthammer noted in his column on March 3, 2017, by the increasing willingness of the courts to grant standing to states to challenge federal actions by lawsuit.

Trumophobes feel that "resistance" is their tactic, but it is an ill-defined term. When Trump gave his first address to Congress, activists gathered in Lafayette Park near the White House ahead of the speech to hold a "resistance address," discussing how to defend human rights and civil liberties in a time of "moral crisis." See: *commondreams.org* -February 28, 2017.

"The Trump administration does not represent the values of most Americans," said Wenonah Hauter, executive director of Food & Water Watch, one of the groups organizing the rally. "We're here to remind him that not only are his policies unpopular, they are also destructive to the fabric of this nation and our planet. That's why the state of the resistance is stronger than ever—and will continue to grow."

Larry Cohen, a former union leader with wide experience in organizing workers, became Bernie Sanders' liaison to organized labor in the 2016 campaign. Rather than accepting defeat, Cohen has been working with Sanders on an anti-Democratic Establishment organization, pompously named *Our Revolution*, which aims, similarly to what the Tea Party tried to do on the right, to siphon off left-wing support from the Democrats and try to attract working class people who in 2016 voted for Trump. Of course causing a division in the Democratic Party, if successful, will drive it further to the left. One would think that is a good recipe for defeat in 2020, especially if Trump retires, due to age or health or lack of support in the Republican party; or in the event he gets fed up with the constant fights with media and others that will sap his strength on the big issues, or constant scrutiny turns up some impeachable conduct.

The Democrats' flirtation with the left was shown after Tom Perez, former labor secretary under Obama, was elected chair of the Democratic National Committee. He was seen as the "establishment" Democratic Party choice, and he won out over the anti-establishment Bernie Sanders-supported anti-Israel, convert to Islam, Keith Ellison. To try to heal this deepening split, Perez decided to create a new position, deputy chair, and the assembled party members unanimously agreed to Ellison's appointment. But the assembly quickly showed the strength of the establishment Democrats, the insiders who kept Obama in power, when one of the key issues on Sanders' platform, removing the use of lobbyist funds and its influence in politics, was defeated. By the time these Democrats finish fighting with each other, their Trumpophobia may be on the "back burner."

Trumpophobia is also evident among European politicians. In part they fear success by Trump will encourage the spread of populist nationalism in their own countries, resulting in a loss of power for them. It is sad that right after Trump's pause on certain immigration, German's foreign minister, whose country is struggling against Islamist crimes including terrorism and sexual assaults, had the nerve to lecture Trump that "loving your neighbor forms part of America's Christian tradition." Perhaps he should instead ask the multitude of German women who were sexually assaulted by male Muslim refugees, if they are prepared to "love" the new neighbors their country is allowing in. He should know, however, that loving this type of neighbor is masochism, not true love.

Are There "No-Go" Zones?

An area of the world where nationalism was predominant for so long, where imperialism and colonization were rampant, where world wars were fought, would seem to be a place that would protect its citizens from enemy forces taking part of their territory. But the nature of contemporary ideologies, as outlined in this book, have created a place that not only tells the State of Israel to give up sovereignty over land to be given to the enemy to launch rockets against its civilians, but would tolerate the same suicidal conduct for itself. It may not have reached that stage yet; as we shall see in this chapter, there is much debate about the very concept of "no-go" zones. However, looking at these issues from the concept of *sovereignty* might be useful within the context of an overall discussion of submission.

Most of us have seen videos of the Muslim youth rioting in the Paris suburbs (banlieus) with the burning of cars, damage to buildings and attempts to keep out the police. In areas of high Muslim youth unemployment, radicalization by Islamist imams, drug-dealing and rejection of French values, it seems reasonable to refer to "no-go" zones. Many articles and videos are there to show them in France, Sweden, Belgium and other places where immigration of Muslims have outpaced employment, education, and integration into society and culture. Notwithstanding this evidence, leftist writers and government officials in these countries minimize the problem and we see denialism stemming from political correctness, as an ideological screen through which all facts must pass.

Perhaps, the reactions to such a devastating blow to French political and cultural notions of equality and fraternity will naturally resist seeing the truth or at least acknowledging a major problem in the making. In this chapter we shall look at some of the evidence and some of the resistance to the evidence and contemplate how abandoning sovereignty, a little or a lot, manifests the ultimate submission to Islamist forces.

This book is being written before the May 2017 run-off election in France; we shall see what will happen in France should Marine Le Pen be elected.

Al Jazeera reported on April 20, 2017 that young people in this era of economic decline were being attracted to Le Pen.

Polling for the first round of the presidential election puts Le Pen at around a quarter of the vote, which would be enough to get her into the runoff, where she currently polls at around 40 percent.

Notably, says Al Jazeera, "the largest demographic for Le Pen's National Front support comes from "voters aged between 18 and 24, where Le Pen polls at 40 percent."

"That number stands in stark contrast to other European countries, including the UK, where the centre-left Labour party was the most popular among the age group at around 43 percent and the anti-immigration UKIP polled at just eight percent." It will be interesting to follow the phenomenon of France's anti-immigrant young in the next few years.

James Longman, writing for the *BBC* about France on February 18th, 2017, downplays the Islamist angle: "For the young men here, the state is the enemy."

He writes of a current allegation that police anally raped a black youth: "Police cars drive up and down the roads, through column after column of social housing. Groups of young men shout 'rapists' as they go by."

Local activist Franco, from the anti-negrophobia league, says the anger is justified.

"This violence is a system, and this keeps us in a place where we cannot progress. When there is no justice, we have to fight to have it."

Longman sees this as part of a bigger "cycle of violence" that "keeps on spinning. Youth vs police; black vs white; haves vs have nots. And communities left behind."

We must note that "cycle of violence" is an infamous politically correct term used by people who see all parties equally at fault in a type of cultural relativism, and has been used mostly by tolerists of Palestinian terror met by Israeli self-defense. So Mr. Longman's report does not help much to understand the violence and distrust.

A few days after the November 2015 Paris ISIS-sponsored terrorist attack that killed 130 including over 80 at a concert, *Time Magazine* ran a piece by Naina Bajekal that acknowledged the Islamist radicalization in the French suburbs, but also managed to blame France—not the Islamists:

> (T)he attacks on Friday that left 129 people dead have reverberated from the city's core to its periphery, where residents of the *banlieues*—or the suburbs—are also chilled by the warning by ISIS militants that the attacks are simply the "first of a storm."
>
> The fear of being terrorized also comes with a fear of being scapegoated. French Muslims have found themselves under an uncomfortable spotlight for the second time in just ten months, especially those in the long-neglected *banlieues* often portrayed as breeding grounds for radical Islam and homegrown terrorism.

Bajekal disputes the accuracy of that idea ("That picture isn't always accurate") but then confirms that "France has seen more of its citizens join ISIS and other jihadist groups than any other European country" and that "at least two of the eight attackers on Friday were French nationals who emerged from the *banlieues:* Omar Ismail Mostefai, who blew himself up at the Bataclan concert hall, grew up in the southern suburb of Courcouronnes while Samy Amimour, another attacker at the Bataclan, lived in the northeastern suburb of Drancy before he reportedly left for Syria two years ago." Yet the author still feels compelled to note that not all of the terrorists came from the banlieues, since "many of the 1500 foreign fighters who go to the Middle East to fight for ISIS came from middle-class, educated families."

In other words, France has a problem with radicalized Islamists in the banlieues *and also with* middle-class educated Islamists. Moderate Muslims who decry this radicalization speak out, according to the writer, sounding "the alarm that growing numbers of young Muslims in their communities are drifting towards radical groups who see the French state and its people as an enemy to be destroyed. 'We have told the police so many times about the dangers here and they have done nothing. I want to know why," says Jaafar Rebaa, vice-president of the Drancy Mosque, known for its famously moderate imam, Hassen Chalghoumi, who supports the country's ban on the burqa and speaks out against the dangers of extremism."

Rebaa, who moved to Paris from Tunisia thirty years ago, says that in the past five years he and other Muslim community leaders have alerted local authorities to the presence of numerous "basement mosques" in the neighborhood – underground prayer rooms where radical Salafists gather.

Rebaa, according to Bajekal, says they lure in disenfranchised youth by offering them not just luxuries like free meal vouchers but also a purpose, something many young people in the *banlieues* lack. "If these people had jobs or studies, they wouldn't get drawn in, they wouldn't get brainwashed," he says.

And so we see that governments must empower the moderates and enlist their help in countering, by deportation if necessary, the radical Islamists. In a liberal country, with strong laws protecting freedom of religion, this is a herculean task, but there are moderates who understand the problem and can be enlisted to help. If the government cannot differentiate between men like Rebaa and Chalghoumi and the Islamists, there is no hope to solve the problem of the "no go zones."

And it is a real problem: anthropologist Geoffrey Clarfield and political theorist Salim Mansur, in Canada's *National Post* on October, 11, 2016, have written an essay: "Europe's no-go zones: Inside the lawless ghettos that breed and harbour terrorists":

They suggest the reason why it seems that terrorists can suddenly appear to do their evil deeds:

> The answer to how these terrorists are able to appear all of a sudden, as if out of nowhere, and strike at the heart of Western civilization should now be clear. The reason apparently lone assassins suddenly materialize in prosperous European cities and are able to kill scores of people and wound hundreds is that they have a state within a state that gives them refuge, the no-go zone. There they do not need a passport. There they can store arms. There they can prepare their attack plans. From there they can quickly go out and wreak havoc. If they get lucky, their co-

conspirators can disappear back into the no-go zones, knowing they will be seen as heroes by their neighbours, their religious leaders and the growing number of alienated, drug-dealing youth gangs.

And they understand that, for the purpose of sovereignty over these areas, the Europeans must take back these ghettos:

Before the French, Belgian, German and British governments — including their police, courts, schools and housing authorities — offer resident Muslims in Europe the blessings of a secular society, they will have to take back the ghettos. They will have to disarm the militants, deport scores of preachers, pacify the gangs, cut off the drug supply and cut off funding from Saudi Arabia and Iran. And they will have to persuade key players in the ghetto to stand up to their violent neighbours and instead support the peaceful aims of the state.

Finally Clarfield and Mansur warn what will happen if the Europeans do not re-establish their sovereignty:

However, if the European ruling elites and the mainstream media have stopped believing in the liberté, égalité, fraternité (liberty, equality, fraternity) that was proclaimed on that fateful day of July 14, 1789, then the future of France and much of western Europe will be one of a growing series of terrorist nightmares. They will have lost the war against the jihadists, the authority of the state will wither, and the French and other European majorities will be treated like a conquered people in their own lands. The same fate awaits the British, if they do not soon take preventative action.

If someone would have told you 30 years ago that European nations would be voluntarily ceding areas of their sovereignty to anti-western, anti-Christian and anti-Semitic groups, who would block entry to police and reject the nation's constitution and justice system in favor of a different justice system based on different values, you would not have believed him.

In fact the issue of no-go zones in Europe is said, by some government officials or leftist writers, to be over-stated, while others warn it is a serious issue for law enforcement, ambulance and fire services, who are sometimes attacked as they try to do their jobs in Muslim ghettos.

The "politically correct" media perhaps do not like to report on the no-go zones because it is a very difficult issue, but there is a revealing video from Sweden's *DGS-TV* where host Paulina Neuding interviews Gordon Grattidge, president of the Sweden Ambulance Union:

The host notes that "the ambulance union has asked for military equipment in order to protect paramedics on emergency calls" and the union head confirms that "we've talked about tactical units … we would have special equipment to be able to go with police into dangerous situations."

However, the requests have not been successful. "We have not received any response to that request. But we work with lighter protection in form of body armour and helmets."

The host then asks if the situations where such armour is necessary are "the risk areas we have in Sweden … so-called 'no-go' zones." The union head confirms it, as delicately as possible: "I know it's a sensitive and controversial issue. But for us it's really a no-go because we have directives not to go into dangerous situations … We are supposed to get personal protection from the police when we enter a no-go zone."

The poor Swedes are so-shackled by political correctness this head of the ambulance driver's union, knows better than to refer to "Muslim ghettos." He refers to the no-go zones as "segregated areas" or areas where "the majority of people are immigrants." He pleads, "We see that this type of area is increasing in number … it is important that we have a high risk approach and that we get personal protection …"

The host asks, "Is it too dangerous to enter" and he responds,

> It is too dangerous to enter. We can be prevented from entering. We may be blocked from getting out. Vehicles may be sabotaged at the site. We can be exposed to physical violence. In seconds it can turn to attacks on our vehicles or against us personally.
>
> It can be stone-throwing and even worse. Hand grenades have been thrown at police so that is a great concern." The union head goes on to say it feels that they are intruders in these no-go zones and his drivers and paramedics "have been afflicted with post traumatic stress disorder … It can be a lot of people (attacking us), up to 20 to 30 persons is very common … about once a week a

driver feels threatened and has to back out … We know from experience that it's a dangerous area and we have to wait for police.

And what of being a police officer in Sweden today? Interviewed in *RT.com*, Swedish journalist, Ingrid Carlqvist, editor-in-chief of newspaper *International Dispatch*, considered right-wing on these issues, cites a report that Swedish police are failing to control up to 55 no-go zones. She states that 3 Swedish police officers quit their jobs every day. She alleges that the job is so horrible and it is made more dangerous by the head of the police restricting his forces from doing the necessary job. Carlqvist states that Sharia law is being implemented in these areas and many of the population there do not consider themselves to be living in Sweden.

David Chazan, writing for Britain's *The Telegraph* on December 18, 2017, reports that there are female no-go zones in Paris, where women are not welcome and this is confirmed in videos. As often happens, the French government declined to get involved. Axelle Lemaire, the minister of state for digital affairs, said the footage appeared to show an "intolerable" and "illegal" case of "discrimination against women." But she hastened to add that it was not a question of religion and France's Muslim communities should not be blamed.

On the other hand, liberal writers like David Graham writing for the *Atlantic* magazines, deny there is such a thing as no-go zones and that it is a "myth." He says the myth is made possible because firstly, there are some Islamic courts allowed which deal with family matters but to him that is no more dangerous than Jewish religious courts; secondly the rise of some vigilante Sharia squads, which he claims are just ad-hoc groups, and thirdly, there are urban planning areas in France called "Zones Urbaines Sensibles," or "sensitive urban zones." These areas "are characterized by high unemployment, high rates of public housing, and low educational attainment." Says, Graham, "As it happens, many of these areas are populated largely by poor immigrants from the Muslim world, creating a neat but misleading correlation."

And a French news site (thelocal.fr/20170223/the-ten-real-no-go-zones-in-paris) put forth its own list of ten no-go zones satirically outlining ten areas of bad traffic, tourist spots, metro lines, etc. which it said were the only no-go zones of concern.

Then from *Bloomberg*, Carol Matlack, writing on January 14, 2015, *Debunking the Myth of Muslim-Only Zones in Major European Cities*, argued that "stories about big Western cities surrendering neighborhoods to control of Islamist extremists are "shocking—and totally false."

Yet, in the wake of the 2015 Paris attacks, the Molenbeek municipality in Brussels was described by the *Independent's* Leo Cendrowicz, in his article on visiting Molenbeek (home of two of the gunmen in the Paris attack), as a no-go Muslim area, where gang violence, Islamic radicalism had fed on Molenbeek's marginalization, despair and festering resentment of authority. In 2015 Belgium's home affairs minister said that the government did not "have control of the situation in Molenbeek" and that the terrorists' links to this district were a "gigantic problem."

Wherever notions of tolerance, compassion and empathy overtake good sense and the duty of governments to provide safety and security for residents, no-go zones will be created. And Israel has followed the same path, as Jews, many of whom, or their parents or grandparents, were refugees themselves, feel the compassion. As reported by Gilad Zwickau in *En.mida.org.il*, South Tel Aviv has been overwhelmed with predominantly African illegal refugees. He writes:

> The rapes, violence, intimidation, and the lost sense of security, intensify the feeling that South Tel Aviv is losing its Israeli character. This feeling is backed by a report published by the Knesset Research and Information Center (KRIC) last June which estimated that the illegal immigrant population in South Tel Aviv is greater than the Israeli population. This assessment was based on information received from different branches in the Tel Aviv municipality. It estimated that at the beginning of 2016, the illegal immigrant population in South Tel Aviv numbered between 48,000-60,000 people, whereas the Israeli population in that area is 39,150 according to 2014 statistics, with those numbers declining annually.
>
> While the demographics issue can be quantified, the personal sense of security cannot. In 2015, the police commissioned a survey of residents in South Tel Aviv. Although surveys are not always reliable, the results were jaw dropping. 62% of Israelis in South Tel Aviv are afraid to leave their homes at night, 40% don't feel safe in their homes, and 34% worry they will be a victim of assault,

whether it be physical or verbal threats. 20% of victims don't even report crimes due to lack of faith in the police. In 2012, at a time when the illegal immigration population was much smaller in number, the Tel Aviv police chief testified that illegal immigrants were involved in more than 60% of robberies and sexual assault cases in South Tel Aviv.

And so, Israel is not immune from this empathy built on tolerism, with the resulting crime and loss of morale. The power of the ideologies are so strong that the Israeli government, charged with creating a homeland where Jews would be secure and safe, has not wanted to deal with the African illegal migrant problem and the security problems it has brought.

About no-go zones, we can state two things for sure. The first is that while governmental laws, access for emergency personnel, and non-Muslims are not now prohibited in every so-called "no-go" zones, it is close-minded to deny that there are problems in these areas. It is close-minded to deny that there is an erosion of state sovereignty when a people of one religion, often unemployed and uneducated, and sometimes extremist in their interpretation of that religion, who have sometimes adopted Islamist positions, live in distinct areas into which police and others are unwelcome.

Secondly, we cannot deny that in the case of French Jews, non-Muslims are being attacked and are not welcome with any signs of dress or head covering that shows their Judaism. We cannot deny that the occupants of certain areas are in fact more allegiant to their culture and religion than to the state. One can say this at times in history for other groups than Muslims, but where we are dealing with Islamists, we must agree that no-go zones are real, less extensive perhaps than some claim, but also growing, and a place of danger occupied by Islamists and their radicals and their terrorists. We can also say that we are not seeing the assimilation to French values among second generation, European-born Muslims, that would equate with previous non-Muslim immigrations and neighborhoods. Now is the time to worry about loss of sovereignty, and blame radical Islamists for the problem, and work with non-radical Muslims, to whatever extent is possible, to eject the Islamists.

CHAPTER 26: EVIDENCE OF SUBMISSION

The Endgame

In *Tolerism*, we noted the increase in books about sexual submission and sado-masochism, and indications that sexual masochism has increased at the same time as cultural masochism.

This book has argued that, with the advent of an ideology that I call "tolerism," the West is continuing down an ideological path that could well result in "submission." We have discussed a number of ideologies that would seem to facilitate this ultimate submission. This is the endgame long sought by Islamists, and their intentions are now well known. However, even an unreformed Islam, which associates when convenient with Islamism and does not move to more explicitly accept western freedoms, will be a threat as it might be attractive to western liberal secularists who have tired of the freedoms of western culture. We shall explore more in this chapter. Ideological submission is an era of weakening support for, and understanding of, traditional Christianity and Judaism. I believe that we must actively support Muslim reformers, that is, those who want to moderate the illiberal components and make it reconcilable with a peaceful and respectful presence in the "free" world. We must immediately proceed to start working with some of the liberal Muslim organizations; we have no time to lose.

To start this chapter then, we must see that the issue for the West is the same as the central theme of Dostoyevsky's great novel, *The Brothers Karamazov*—namely the burden of freedom or autonomy. In this 1880 classic, a medieval cardinal from the Spanish Inquisition meets the second coming of Jesus. The aged cardinal goes on to level several accusations at Jesus, including the accusation that man cannot deal with the freedom bestowed upon him:

> Instead of taking over men's freedom, you increased it and forever burdened the kingdom of the human soul with all

its torments ... man had henceforth to decide for himself, with a free heart, what is good and what is evil, having only your image before him as a guide — but did it not occur to you that he would eventually reject and dispute even your image and your truth if he was oppressed by so terrible a burden as freedom of choice? ...

You want to go into the world, and you are going empty-handed, with some promise of freedom, which they in their simplicity and innate lawlessness cannot even comprehend, which they dread and fear — for nothing has ever been more insufferable for man and for human society than freedom! But do you see these stones in this bare, scorching desert? Turn them into bread and mankind will run after you like sheep, grateful and obedient, though eternally trembling lest you withdraw your hand and your loaves cease for them.

How can western liberated feminist women, often with advanced university degrees, make common cause with Islamists who persecute women, gays and minorities? Is there something about the freedom now offered by our culture that brings back to relevance Eric Fromm's important 1941 book, *Escape from Freedom*?

Without going into too much detail, Fromm argued that in the process of becoming freed from authority, we are often left with feelings of hopelessness that will not lessen until we use our 'freedom to' and develop some form of replacement of the old order. However, a common substitute for exercising "freedom to" or authenticity is to submit to an authoritarian system that replaces the old order with another of different external appearance but identical function for the individual: to eliminate uncertainty by prescribing what to think and how to act.

Are our universities now prescribing what to think? Here is a quote from University of Toronto's president Meric Gertler, from the winter 2017 issue of *U of T Magazine*, which I am sure he thinks is completely politically correct:

Some of the world's most powerful and progressive countries are turning inward, (with a) temptation to build walls ... In my travels on behalf of the university, I hear my international colleagues express concern. But they also express their admiration – for U. of T. and the wonderful experiment in diversity we call Toronto ... It is Canada's time to shine, as a beacon of inclusion and hope ...

Our universities accept uncritically the left-wing globalist arguments for inclusive diversity. If they will not deal with the issues raised in this book, and if they insist on terming all opposing arguments "racist," then our students are not learning to think, but to protest and propagandize on behalf of politically correct groupthink.

And so, tolerism is one response to the challenges of freedom, and full-fledged submission to the strongest authoritarian regimes of the day is another that we must prevent at all costs. Query whether Leftist/Islamist control of media and universities and school systems creates its own type of authoritarianism.

It is not as if we do not know about the Islamist plans for us. Two important examples of Islamist plans, which originally were secret, but which were discovered by the West, are firstly *the Manchester Manual*, and secondly, *The Project*.

In his book, *Enhanced Interrogation*, Dr. James Mitchell discusses *the Manchester Manual* as an important foundational document for Islamist terrorist groups. He argues that traditional rapport-building techniques typically used by law enforcement did not work with Islamic terrorist detainees because they were trained to resist using various methods laid out in *the Manchester Manual*. The manual was a computer file found by Manchester Metropolitan Police in 2000 in the home of Abu Anas al-Libi, a Libyan under indictment in the United States for his part in the 1998 U.S. embassy bombings. Al-Libi worked as a computer specialist for Al Qaeda. The 180-page document on how to wage war included instructions on how to withstand interrogation methods and falsely claim torture.

Secondly, as discussed earlier, we have the Muslim Brotherhood's 1982 manifesto titled *The Project*, authored by Sa'id Ramadan, the son-in-law of Hassan al-Banna, the founder of the Muslim Brotherhood.

The Project was distributed to Muslim Brotherhood members around the world who were ordered to strictly guard its content from outsiders. They did so until November of 2001 when a copy of *The Project* was discovered during a police raid of a senior Muslim Brotherhood financier's home in Switzerland.

The Project outlined the Muslim Brotherhood's 25 strategies, including the deception of taqiyya, to infiltrate and to eventually subjugate the rest of the world under Islam.

Anti-terrorism consultant Patrick Poole has been in the forefront of disclosing this document, in essays published in *Frontpagemag.com* in 2006 and 2008. He writes in 2008:

> What makes *The Project* so different from the standard "Death of America! Death to Israel!" and "Establish the global caliphate!" Islamist rhetoric is that it represents a flexible, multi-phased, long-term approach to the "cultural invasion" of the West. Calling for the utilization of various tactics, ranging from immigration, infiltration, surveillance, propaganda, protest, deception, political legitimacy and terrorism.
>
> Naïve Westerners continue to be used as pawns in clearly sketched-out plans to defeat the House of War (non-Muslim countries) and incorporate them into with the House of Islam. The method of conquest is an aggressive, but strategic and insidious assault using existing institutions; yet still, political correctness persists; many people are hesitant to speak about what is happening for fear of coming across as a conspiracy theorist, despite the clear documentation of this initiative.

On March 29, 2016, in an article in *American Thinker*, entitled, "On the Path of Submission to Islam", Dan Calic disclosed some fundamental goals of *The Project*:

> · Networking and coordinating among like-minded Islamist organizations
>
> · Avoiding open alliances with known terrorist organizations and individuals to maintain the appearance of moderation
>
> · Infiltrating and taking over existing Muslim organizations and redirecting their goals in line with Muslim Brotherhood goals
>
> · Using deception to mask the intended goals of Islamist actions, as long as it doesn't interfere with Sharia law
>
> · Establishing financial networks ... to fund the conversion of the West
>
> · Conducting surveillance, obtaining data ...
>
> · Monitoring Western media to warn Muslims of plots fomented against them

· Build networks of schools, hospitals and charitable organizations ... dedicated to Islamist ideals ...

· Using Western institutions until they can be converted into service of Islam

· Involving ideologically committed Muslims in democratically elected institutions on all levels in the West

· Supporting jihad movements across the Muslim world

· Inciting hatred by Muslims against Jews and rejecting any discussion of conciliation and coexistence with them

· Develop a comprehensive 100 year plan to advance Islamist ideology throughout the world

In his July 24, 2008 article in *FrontpageMag*, Poole reviews what can be learned from the book, *HAMAS: A History from Within* (Northhampton, Mass.: Oliver Branch, 2007), and authored by a well-known international Muslim Brotherhood operative and HAMAS insider, Azzam Tamimi, who heads the Institute of Islamic Political Thought HAMAS front organization in London.

Poole notes that "understanding the historic role of "The Project" as part of the global strategy of the Muslim Brotherhood is essential. Fortunately, Azzam Tamimi's account fills in several blanks that had gone unreported:

· Its adoption at the 1983 Amman Conference;

· Its actual title – the "global project for Palestine";

· Its origination by the Kuwaiti Ikhwan leadership (Tamimi also reports that they donated $70,000 in start-up money for the Palestinians to buy arms and to send leaders to Jordan for military training);

· Its strategic role in defining how the Muslim Brotherhood would focus its efforts and resources to Palestine to make that a key issue in advancing their global Islamic supremacist agenda;

· Its ideological importance representing the shift in methodology to a more revolutionary approach and the embrace of Sayyid Qutb's vanguardist vision by the organization globally.

Tamimi's account provides new details about "The Project," and his status as a high-ranking international Muslim

Brotherhood figure adds considerable weight to authenticate much of what had already been reported. An examination of that strategic plan, as well as the many exhibits that came from the Holy Land Foundation terrorism finance trial (in 2007) gives us a glimpse at the Muslim Brotherhood's global playbook and how far they have come in achieving their long-term goals of infiltrating the West and establishing a global Islamic state ruled by Islamic law. What we find by looking at those measures and from seemingly daily reports is that their relentless coordinated campaign for Islamic global dominance has met with astounding success.

The Muslim Brotherhood and its affiliated organizations are sophisticated in their advance of Islamism. Judith Bergman writing for *Gatestone* on March 30, 2017 (gatestoneinstitute.org/10132/ muslim-brotherhood-social-justice) warns us to get ready for the next wave of propaganda, women's marches and deceitful public relations. She notes that according to a report by the Middle East Media Research Institute (MEMRI) the Muslim Brotherhood has launched a heavy lobbying effort in the United States to, as she puts it, "charm decision-makers in the Trump administration and Congress" to give up on the Muslim Brotherhood Terrorist Designation Act of 2017, re-introduced on January 9, 2017, by Senator Ted Cruz. They have hired American law firms and PR firms and are recasting the Islamic 'narrative' as 'social justice'.

Bergman, a writer and lawyer, writes that the Muslim Brotherhood, is set to take advantage of American ideological confusion by framing itself as a force for "social justice." The problem is that its motto is, "Allah is our objective; the Prophet is our leader; the Quran is our law; Jihad is our way; dying in the way of Allah is our highest hope."

First they duped Americans that Islam under the control of Islamists, is a "religion of peace." Now they figure that they will be successful in portraying themselves as a non-violent, pluralistic social justice movement. However, nothing has changed from the 1995 statement by its spiritual leader Yusuf al-Qaradawi who said, "We will conquer Europe. We will conquer America! Not through sword, but through Da'wa" (proselytization).

A fascinating book explaining in detail how America has failed to process the threat posed by Islamism, and has engaged in massive self-deception in its thinking on this topic is Bill Siegel's *The Control Factor: Our Struggle to See the True Threat* (Hamilton Books div. of Rowman & Littlefield, 2012).

Siegel, in his explanation of denial (which I have posited becomes an ideology of denialism), explores faulty ways of thinking. He contrasts a horror film, where the audience knows the suspense will be over in a couple of hours, to the horror of the Islamist threat: "(I)t is extremely difficult for the American mind to remain in such a state of insecurity, danger and terror that our Islamic Enemy poses. Instead, our minds are geared to eliminate as efficiently as possible any horrifying experience and re-establish the sense (or illusion) that control exists or is obtainable." Siegel terms our psychological mechanisms that try to eradicate our loss of control the "Control Factor." He argues that this artificial and delusional sense that we are in fact in control where we clearly are not must be understood, in all its aspects, in order for America and the West to "marshall the collective will, creativity and solidarity to formulate an acceptable path to victory."

Siegel analyzes in his chapter 5, the paths of denial in American thinking, by organizing them as all starting with the letter "D": Denial, Distraction and Deflection, Deletion, Detachment, Displacement, Discoloration, Delusion, Distortion and Demonization. It is well worth reading.

I concentrate on four aspects of the paths of denial that he and I both recognize are increasing the threat, and which I go so far as to argue that they are leading to submission to the enemy. And so I call it a "D"feat, and organize these four ideologies based on four Ds— denial, delusion, decline and depression.

We have discussed the ideology of denialism with its delusions in this book. We shall shortly look at how certain authors, particularly in France, have accepted the ideology of decline.

Thoughts of Decline are unfortunately increasing as a pervasive sense that our "civilization" is in decline, or that, in the "clash of civilizations," a concept made famous by political scientist Samuel P. Huntington, our civilization may in fact lose. "The Clash of Civilizations" is a hypothesis that people's cultural and religious identities will be the primary source of conflict in the post-Cold War world.

We sense that decline is all around us:

- Decline in our nations' financial health as huge deficits and government debt give the feeling that we are leaving our problems to our children and grandchildren
- Decline of the active participation in Christian and Jewish religions by the liberal, college-educated secularists
- Decline of affordable housing for our younger generations, combined with heavy debt loads from college loans, leaving them the first generation lately to be doing financially worse than their parents
- Decline in our manufacturing sector the solutions for which were so much a part of Trump's election
- Decline in the birthrate in Western European countries, Canada and the United States, at the same time as birthrates in poor Islamic countries stay high (although they too start to fall after a generation of living in the West)
- Decline in the livability of our cities as long commutes, expensive housing, and dangerous inner cities continue to make once great cities unsustainable
- Decline of the environment
- Decline in respect for our "traditional values"
- Decline in the morality of international institutions like the United Nations, once filled with hope, and now dominated by Islamic countries appeased by European states in decline
- Decline in our safety in public places caused by Islamist terrorism
- Decline in the number of people who can cope with our anxious age without resorting to one or more addictions: alcohol, illegal drugs, legal prescriptions, sexual addictions including pornography, addictions to work or play
- Decline in the quality of our schools and universities
- Decline in interest or study of your country's history or world history
- Decline in reading books compared to reading short texts and messages on social media

We sense a certain depression in the West, in part from the Declines just mentioned. Depression is caused primarily, say psychologists, from turning anger inward and from catastrophic thinking in response to anxiety producing challenges. This can be reversed and we shall conclude this book with the steps that must be taken. But first let us look at the depth of the problem. Only when we understand the ideological quagmire, and face it squarely, will we be able to fight it.

There are now a number of fine books on appeasement and Islamism, including Bruce Bawer's *Surrender: Appeasing Islam, Sacrificing Freedoms*. Stephen Pollard in his excellent review of this book for the *New York Times*, July 24, 2009, says in Europe, terror is real, but "a more insidious problem has now taken hold: many liberals and others on the European left are making common cause with radical Islam and then brazenly and bizarrely denying both the existence of that alliance and in fact the existence of any Islamist threat whatever." And so we are seeing denialism and submission together.

Christopher Caldwell points out in his prescient 2009 book, *Reflections on the Revolution in Europe*, that Europe has engaged in self-shaming for so long that it reviles everything about its own culture, idolizing minority culture instead, as a kind of *mea culpa* for their colonial sins against the Third World. In this book, we have similarly explored the guilt-basis of Europe for its readiness for submission.

A study of French culture will help us understand that in fact there is a serious chance of submission to either Islamism or even the reformed Islam that we have up to this stage of the book, advocated as a restraint on Islamist violence and illiberal components. The French intellectuals, having led their country into tolerism, lately have been taking the lead in recognizing, if not promoting, the likely submission of the French in the face of a more moderate Islam, after the populists help defeat the Islamist infiltration of European society.

As to the French, let us take a look at two recent books and how they reflect submission. Are the French intellectuals, from a tradition of secularist liberties in a country that is, outside of Sweden, the most tolerant of Islamism, just ahead in recognizing the likely endgame of our cultural history? We need to think about what is most likely to happen as the leftist-Islamist versus the nationalist-populist struggle plays out.

A very important political/cultural novel is Michel Houellebecq's *Submission*, set in 2022. Here is a summary of the plot taken from a review by Michael Delahunty appearing in *The Federalist* on December 23, 2015:

Submission is set in France in 2022, during a presidential election. The traditional parties of Right and Left—Gaullists and Socialists—have lost the first round so are out of the final runoff. The two remaining parties are the nativist, anti-immigrant National Front and the Muslim Brotherhood. The two traditional parties throw their weight behind the Muslims, who win. Whether this scenario is likely or not, this premise gives rise to a fascinating story about the protagonist, Francois. As a character, says Delahunty, "Francois is meant to be a 'decadent' of the contemporary type. There is nothing larger than himself that he serves, purports to serve, or wishes to serve; but he knows that his self is a naught."

Francois, who is in his mid-40s, is of course non-religious. He is unmarried, childless, and estranged from his (divorced) parents. He drifts from one meaningless affair to another with his women students, all of them 20 or more years younger than he. Says Delahunty: "Francois' life is mean, grubby, loveless, and despairing. He is the epitome of the secularized Western intellectual, except in one respect. Francois, though a conventional man of the Left, is too lucid or disillusioned to be politically correct."

The turning point for Francois comes with the electoral victory of the Muslim Brotherhood, in alliance with the traditional Right and Left parties. The Brotherhood is led by a clever, capable, and intelligent man, Mohammed Ben Abbes who wants to create a Muslim-dominated European Union, centered on the Mediterranean Sea, with Tunisia, Algeria, Libya, and eventually Egypt and Turkey as members.

The Muslim Brotherhood runs on a platform of improving education and social services, and increasing the birthrate, thus bringing the focus back to the family.

They see secularism, not Catholicism, as the enemy, and propose that Islam can help bring France back to its greatness. Rather than seeing France as Dar al-Kufr (the realm of infidels) like the Islamists do, the party wants to bring France into Dar al-Islam (the realm where Muslim law rules). After the elections, the party implements a soft version of Islamic law, the effects of which are not too dramatic—at first.

The French do not fight; those who won't convert leave their jobs with a nice pension provided by the Saudis. The populists fade away, as the mood of the country changes to quiet acquiescence. Not so different than the French submission to the Nazis.

The only Ministry the Muslim Brotherhood insists on is the Education Ministry – which they get, because the Socialists would rather have the Muslims control French education than allow the National Front to win.

Ben Abbes loathes violent Islamic radicals. When he comes to power, the threat of civil war in France disappears as does violence in the inner cities. Employment (for men) soars as women are encouraged to exit the work force and stay home and have babies.

Francois is purged from his university job because he is not a Muslim. But his new masters give him a golden handshake, so he doesn't mind. His life is pointless. He decides to take a trip outside of Paris and winds up in a village called Martel. It is named for the medieval French hero who defeated the Muslims.

He begins to feel religious stirrings and contemplates adherence to Catholicism. He tries a monastery for a couple of days but leaves: he decides that Catholicism is played out, just like France. He cannot recover its "vanished universe."

The new Muslim leadership of his university wants Francois back. But first, he must convert to Islam. They offer him a chance to edit some books in a prestigious series and he agrees. He speaks to the new university president, Rediger, a convert to Islam who had also rejected Catholicism.

With none too subtle coincidence, Rediger lives opulently in the mansion that once belonged to the author of the pornographic novel, *The Story of O*, a sado-masochistic story about submission.

Rediger makes a plausible intellectual defense of Islam. He also knows Francois' price for conversion. It will be a bigger salary— enough to support the three wives the Brotherhood will give him. One of Rediger's wives is an older woman: she is a superb cook. Another is a 15-year-old in a Hello Kitty T-shirt. Despite being a

Muslim, Rediger serves superb wine. Francois takes the offer and becomes a Muslim.

And so his conversion facilitates, notes Delahunty, "the bourgeois comforts most Westerners took for granted until the 1970s—a wife, children, good meals, regularity."

Of course, the critics of the book object to what it says about feminism: The Muslim women, even those in polygamous marriages, are presented as happy because they have submitted to a greater will (the man's). To me, it doesn't seem so preposterous because of the current feminist attraction to Islamist organizations. When the Muslim Brotherhood takes over, Houellebecq has the women leave their jobs; their dresses begin to cover and conceal their bodies.

The leftist critics also object, argues Delahunty, that "Francois is motivated above all by very bourgeois longings for ease, comfort, and stability. Francois in the end sells out for a good price: tenure, not too much teaching, no doctoral students, three wives of various ages, a good salary. What left-wing academic would turn down that deal?"

Doesn't it make sense to us that an Academy that has already sold out to political correctness and the quid pro quos of Saudi Arabian financial gifts and anti-Israel nonsense, would also be likely to sell out to a moderate form of Islam? Doesn't it make sense in this world where political policy damns our children and grandchildren to astronomical housing costs, huge government debt, and large student loans, that those who would submit to moderate Islam would readily give up the Education Ministry, as long as they could maintain their salaries, benefits and right to imbibe fine wine?

Just as Islamic conversion laws make little real demands on converts, Francois' conversion makes negligible demands on him. It merely represents, says Delahunty "a kind of return to bourgeois normality. His new Islamic faith does not require Francois to abjure any of the 'good things of life' that a consumerist culture offers. His 'conversion' is simply a matter of signing an employment contract."

But if the Islam to which Francois submits seems domesticated and tame, argues Delahunty, why should secularized critics find fault with that? Isn't that undemanding, "reformed" type of Islam precisely what our progressives dream about?

Houellebecq's literary masterpiece is to both portray Islam as non-threatening to intellectual secularist elites and accurately as allowing polygamy and desirous of spreading around the world by whatever means it takes. This element of the book is the truly scary part.

How can Muslims or European leftists object to a book that portrays Islam as superior to both Christianity and secularism? How can the leftists object to polygamy when sexual license have brought into respectability all kinds of sexual relationships previously taboo? Isn't Islam more realistic than Christianity in its depiction of the lusts of ordinary men compared to Christian goals of transcendence of urges, in its holiest men, the priests?

Of course, one should question this idealized portrait of Islam as practiced by the convert Francois. But the book is hugely frightening because it shows just how easy it would be for the average intellectual to ignore the evil parts and acquiesce in a religion that exactly meets his existentialist angst and cultural poverty.

Concludes Delahunty:

> [Islam] answers the human need for submission to something higher. It understands that liberty cannot be a goal in itself, that human beings require hierarchy and direction. Instead of allowing us to pursue our passions without limit—that way lies loneliness and despair—it grasps that they must be socialized. The novel shows us what 'decadence' means in our time. For the many decadents among us, that message comes too close to home.

And my reaction is: This is one writer's brilliant diagnosis of the possible submission that I warn about in this book. It is also scary how easily the secularists in the novel give up control of the education system to the Muslim Brotherhood. In fact, it is clear to me, that the West has in fact already given up control of its education system to tolerists and Islamists who are promoting Islam in our public schools.

In our world of Christmas without Christ, Halloween that has a hollow hallow, and Thanksgiving without a knowledge of Who we are thanking, we are increasingly worshiping a *traditionalism* without real knowledge of our traditions. And so, Catholic writer, John Médaille, has pointed out:

> When tradition becomes an ideology, it turns out ANY
> tradition will do the required ideological job. I am not now
> nor have ever been a Traditional-ist; I am a Roman-rite
> Catholic, embedded in a certain tradition, one that avoids
> the "ism" by always being open to self-criticism, by being
> semper reformanda.

This is a fascinating insight into our God-less traditionalism and
how it can be linked to submission. Our social media age has no
room for self-criticism; it's easier to criticize your "Facebook friends"
by dissing them and "un-friending" them. Without self-criticism, how
shall we ever understand our ideologies?

I was recently doing some reading about the Great Depression. If
we ever end up with a large economic catastrophe, how well will that
be handled by secular hedonists? What will happen when they seek
more transcendent meaning in their spiritually and financially
impoverished worlds? It occurred to me that in our hedonistic world
with a shaky grasp of how our traditions should be *religious* and not
just *customary*, how easy will it be to exchange one set of traditions for
another? In the Twitter world we have created for our children, has
religious tradition fallen to mere traditionalism, where any tradition
will do?

In Catholic writer, Susannah Black's review of *Submission*,
(providencemag.com/2016/06/ook-review-houellebecq-submission-
surprising-darkness/), she sees how the life of Francois is based on
his rejection of Catholic theology and practice:

> He is a miniature of French society—the welfare state
> whose denizens are so pampered that they can't be
> bothered to have children and have no connection to their
> parents. He is the Last Man, the thing of Straussian
> nightmares, the barely-there listless observer.
>
> And Islam offers itself to him as a rescue from this; and
> a very good rescue it seems to be: tempting precisely
> because its diagnosis is so accurate, and its solutions so
> nearly spot on.
>
> But it's a rescue that can only appeal because François—
> and by implication France—has chosen against Catholicism.
> It's only by that choice that he is empty enough to make
> Islam a fairly easy yes. The culture of the *fin-de-siecle* isn't
> strong enough to stand against it; neither is the old
> bourgeois order which the Decadents had rejected; neither

is the eighteenth century radical atheistic Republicanism which the nineteenth century had attempted to assimilate into its Third Republic cozy life; neither is the modern EU-inflected *laïcité*, with its perpetual peace hovering just around the corner as soon as we can convince the religious crazies to get with the program. Islam, with its acknowledgement of the transcendent, and its social cohesion, is a far stronger thing than these others.

It is essential to know just who the Muslim Brotherhood and its affiliated organizations, including the Muslim Students Association, really are. Those of us bored and tired with lives of decadent secularism, must realize that the "Other" may think differently. Failure to recognize that it is a lie when tolerists say "we are all the same" is very dangerous; know thy enemy.

Submission is a warning that rapid cultural change and the insecurity of our left-liberals must be managed very carefully. The rise of the populist-nationalists in reaction to tolerism and its related ideologies may be so threatening to the tolerist, secularist, masochistic, globalist, elites that the result could be very worrisome.

As M.J. Oprea, also writing in the *Federalist*, December 19, 2015, has put it: "When you believe in nothing, Islam becomes something." Houellebecq has given us a lot to contemplate.

Many French intellectuals now understand that the traditional French licentiousness, its "wine, women and song" morality, leaves France open to a charge of "decadence," and, like *Submission*, French decadence may facilitate submission as an escape. And so we have another important book to discuss – Michel Onfray's *Decadence: The Life and Death of the Judeo-Christian Tradition*, which as of the writing of this book has not yet been translated into English.

Onfray, a philosopher, has a background as an atheist, hedonist and anarchist. As such, he has an interesting perspective on the failure of his own ideologies and the success of Islamism. Is he too extreme when he compares the West and Islam?

"We have nihilism, they have fervor; we are exhausted, they have a great health; we have the past for us; they have the future for them," he writes. Moreover, "Judeo-Christianity ruled for two millennia: an honorable period for a civilization. The boat now sinks; we can only sink with elegance."

Of course, there is something particularly French about this self-flagellation. For the opposite approach, a defense of the Judeo-Christian morality, see Diane Weber Bederman's *Back to the Ethic: Reclaiming Western Values.*

Rachel Donadio, writing in the *New York Times* (February 3, 2017) interviews Onfray and also canvasses some recent books all about France's "decline," which she notes has spawned the word "déclinisme," or "declinism" in France. She goes so far as to refer to France's "booming decline industry, a spate of books and articles (with a handful of TV shows) that explore the country's (and the West's) failings and France's obsession with those failings."

Donadio mentions other recent books on the subject of France's decline. *The Returned*, a best seller by the journalist David Thomson, is an investigative report about French jihadists who've returned home from Syria. *A Submissive France: Voices of Defiance* compiles interviews on France's troubled banlieues, or suburbs, overseen by the historian Georges Bensoussan. *Chronicles of French Denial*, by the right-leaning economist and historian Nicolas Baverez, is about how France continued its economic decline under President François Hollande.

"To put it in Manichaean terms: Anything positive doesn't sell, and anything negative sells, as if there were a sort of masochism on the part of some readers," said the historian Robert Frank, the author of the 2014 book *The Fear of Decline: France from 1914 to 2014.*

The French Suicide by the conservative journalist Éric Zemmour, has sold 510,000 copies since it appeared in 2014; it argues that immigration and feminism have contributed to French decline. The philosopher Alain Finkielkraut's *The Unhappy Identity*, about French multiculturalism and its discontents, was much discussed in 2013, while *The Time Has Come to Tell What I Have Seen*, a 2015 political memoir by the politician and writer Philippe de Villiers that dwells on decay in France has been a best seller.

Donadio also writes of *An Imaginary Racism* by the left-leaning philosopher Pascal Bruckner, who was recently cleared of charges of inciting hate speech. He argues that fear of being labeled Islamophobic is leading people to self-censor their speech. In November, 2016, Professor Gilles Kepel published *The Fracture*, which explores how the radicalization of some young Muslims is tearing apart French society.

Donadio quotes Professor Sudhir Hazareesingh, a professor at Oxford University and the author of *How the French Think:* "The thing that's very striking now is how pervasive those ideas are. One of the things characteristic of the present moment is this idea that decline and decadence are not just the preserve of the extreme right."

And so, finally, the left opens its mind to the likely effects of its destructive mentality of tolerating Islamist evil – as opposed to tolerating their fellow citizens who want to preserve their nation, their people, their traditions and their free way of life. The question for France, as well as the rest of what is sometimes termed *Eurabia,* is whether the decadence, decline and submission are too far along to avoid the feared Islamist takeover; and whether they are allowed to discuss the topic without charges of "Islamophobia." One fears that France is the leader of this depressive group and that countries like America, Canada, Australia, and perhaps Britain and some Eastern European countries, can summon the courage, in Ofray's parlance, to look forward, not back, and to restore fervor for freedom, not nihilism.

"Yes, the French speak about 'déclinisme' and are fascinated by decadence, but the most popular political figure in France today is the only one that speaks of hope," said the political scientist Dominique Moïsi, author of *The Geopolitics of Emotion: How Cultures of Fear, Humiliation, and Hope Are Reshaping the World.*

He was referring to Emmanuel Macron, the former economy minister in the current Socialist government who founded his own insurgent party and has been gaining momentum. We might also look at Donald Trump who was elected on a promise to "Make America Great Again." Perhaps humans that have been exposed to liberty will ultimately choose hope over submission.

By the time you read this we shall have seen whether the hard-right National Front and the center-right Republican Party have been able to capitalize for the April 2017 elections on sentiments of decline exacerbated by economic malaise and terrorist attacks. My hope is that, instead of just focusing on declinism, the French and others will start to analyze the ideological components of the pathway to submission, as we have done here, and realize that a Europe that survived two major world wars in the 20th century can rise again as liberal democracies in the 21st.

The United States and Canada must pay attention, because the intellectual "virus" that has afflicted France and the rest of Europe has already started spreading, as we have seen. I do not think that America is immune from the French declinism, especially in view of the unprecedented political acrimony after the Trump election. We have no real choice I think; we must choose hope and freedom over submission and we must deplore the mediocre ideologies that have brought us to this point.

We need to think a lot more about submission, what it means, when it happens, and how we can follow Israel's example in coming together with patriotism and a strong will that the Islamists with their terrorists will NOT win.

Where we in the West see compromise, Islamists see surrender, or submission. Ask the Israelis what they accomplished with the Oslo process, or giving up Gaza or helping the Palestinian economy. Every act of compromise was seen as partial submission, which requires more submission.

There is a violent fighting sport called Mixed Martial Arts, or the UFC – which stands for "ultimate fighting championship," being the best known MMA organization.

There are three ways to win: knock out your opponent or have him so hurt that the referee calls the match, win on points after punishing your appointment over the full course of the fight, or have the opponent "tap out" or signal that he has given up as his leg or arm are painfully twisted or after some kind of choke hold. The latter is termed a "submission." While knocking out someone with a giant swing, as in boxing, must be very satisfying to these warriors, read what one MMA veteran had to say on what he likes best and why:

UFC lightweight veteran Jim Miller, interviewed in *bloodyelbow.com*, explained the finer points of why a submission finish is the best.

> I'm a little bit of a psychopath in that I fight because I want to, like, destroy people. I want to completely beat the crap out of them. The thing is, I want to fight the best and do

that. Making someone choose that the fight is over—putting them in a position and having them decide, "Yep, no more ..." in my opinion, that is pretty much the top.

Here's a grown man that trained for eight weeks, stepped into a cage with me, then decided that he didn't want to be in there with me any longer. When you knock somebody out or get the TKO, it's not up to them to keep fighting or not. It's up to somebody else. When they decide that they no longer want it and tap, that's a rush for me.

In other words, nothing satisfies this fighter more than breaking the other man's will. A knockout means the other fighter just can't get to his feet before the count of ten; but a submission is the surrendering act of acknowledging your opponent has bettered you and put you in extreme pain or in a position where you cannot breath, rather than having judges decide on points. The tap-out is when the beaten fighter indicates his submission in floor grappling by tapping the opponent or the floor with the hand, or verbally submitting to the opponent.

With a knockout or a points victory, your opponent just stands there at the end of the fight while the referee raises your hand in victory. The opponent can shake your hand or not. But with a submission, your opponent has to publicly indicate through the tap-out that you are his better. Remember that—when we contemplate why Islamists want us to do certain things or not do certain things; it is all about submission.

Here are some indicia of *submission* in western political culture:

· Multiculturalism and its foundation in cultural relativism
· Bill Siegel's *Control Factor* where we delude ourselves into thinking that we can control certain threats that we actually cannot, and so we are willfully blind to the threat from Islamism
· Passing laws/motions that especially target Islamophobia rather than bias/hate against other religions/races
· "no-go" areas some of which are subject to Sharia law rather than the country's legal system
· Allowing Muslim prayers in public schools and other public space
· Christian Churches, for example The Presbyterian Church U.S.A., allowing Muslim prayers

- Non-Muslim Politicians praying in mosques
- Political mis-statements overemphasizing Islamic contributions to western society or numbers of Muslims
- The United Nations especially its Human Rights Council
- Declining birthrate in the West
- Decline in interest/study of your country's history
- The attempt to allow a super-mosque on the 9/11 site
- Allowing Saudi funding of American university programs
- Lawfare – Islamist-funded lawsuits
- Rate of conversions to Islam (including prison conversions)
- Demoralization of our young adults who in many cities cannot afford to buy housing
- Public statements that the West is evil, stupid, corrupt or in serious decline
- The now 500 "sanctuary cities" in the United States, virtually all Democratic, which are pledged not to cooperate with the Department of Homeland Security in its efforts to secure borders, identify terrorists, and deport criminal aliens.

CHAPTER 27: AVOIDING SUBMISSION

Social Resilience and Post-postmodernism

Submission as a response to terrorism and Islamism is not an inevitable response. To understand this, and to see how societies can be so ordered to make submission less likely, it is useful to review the literature on how Israelis have dealt with the huge amount of terrorism directed against their civilians. The Israelis have also had to deal with European countries that are appeasing Islamism criticizing and counseling Israel to create an Islamist terror state in its heartland after the experiment in giving up Gaza turned out so poorly.

Professor Dov Waxman of the City University of New York, in a 2011 essay entitled "Living with terror, not Living in Terror: The Impact of Chronic Terrorism on Israeli Society" in Perspectives on Terrorism (www.terrorismanalysts.com/pt/index.php/pot/about/view/living-with-terror/html), re-viewed the literature and brought together psychological, sociological, economic and political factors into a most enlightening study:

> Given the many effects that Palestinian terrorism had on Israeli society during this period, one might conclude that it was highly effective. This is true in so far as it exacted a heavy toll on Israelis. But the purpose of terrorism is not just to kill people, inflict material damage, or frighten an audience. ...

Terrorism, says Waxman, seeks to alter the social and political dynamics of the societies it targets and through indiscriminate attacks, attempts to change the political agenda of the targeted population:

> ... One of the key objectives of terrorism, then, is to demoralize the targeted society—to induce a widespread sense of helplessness and hopelessness and feeling of despair among members of the society. If the targeted society does not become demoralized, terrorism fails in this respect.

This is the key, according to Waxman.

> By this criterion, Palestinian terrorism during the second
> Intifada was ineffective because it did not succeed in
> demoralizing the Israeli-Jewish public. While Israelis were
> certainly fearful of terrorist attacks, they did become
> despondent and dispirited. Rather, Israelis demonstrated
> resolve and steadfastness in the face of relentless
> terrorism. Indeed, any visitor to Israel during the second
> Intifada could not help but be struck by the seemingly
> nonchalant manner with which Israelis lived with the
> constant threat of terrorism. Instead of panic and public
> hysteria, there was stoicism and fortitude. Israelis did not
> allow the threat of terrorism to dominate their lives.
> Although they experienced high levels of stress and fear,
> they went on with their lives.

I was in Israel during the height of the second intifada, during late 2001 and early 2002, writing my novel about Israel, entitled *The Second Catastrophe: A Novel about a Book and its Author*. I personally witnessed the behavior that Waxman writes about.

> When one considers the huge toll in Israeli lives that
> Palestinian terrorism during the second Intifada took—from
> September 2000 until May 2004, 1030 people had been
> killed, and 5788 injured in more than 13,000 terrorist
> attacks, which means that approximately 0.1 percent of
> Israel's population was injured or killed (the same
> percentage in the United States would equate to a
> staggering 295,000 people being injured or killed) ... the
> ability of Israeli society to cope with this terrorism is quite
> remarkable. ... How did Israelis cope with ongoing terrorism
> despite suffering enormously from it?

One coping mechanism is:

> ... acclimatization to chronic terrorism. In other words,
> Israeli society basically became accustomed to terrorism
> and adapted accordingly. The threat of chronic terrorism
> simply became part of normal life in Israel during the
> second Intifada. ... The only time that daily life in Israel was
> seriously disrupted by terrorism was during the first few
> months of 2002 when suicide bombings were taking place
> in Israeli towns and cities every few days—there were five
> attacks within just ten days in March 2002 killing a total of
> 51 Israelis. During this period of unrelenting terrorist
> attacks, people avoided crowded places and stopped going

out to cafes and restaurants. They didn't take buses or go shopping in malls. They stayed indoors. Palestinian terrorism was succeeding in terrorizing Israelis and disrupting their normal lives. However, this was short-lived. When the volume of terrorist attacks declined, life in Israel returned to normal.

The other coping mechanism: "(M)ost importantly, social resilience got stronger. Resilience is a characteristic of both individuals and societies."

Waxman quotes Nehemia Friedland in *The Elusive Concept of Social Resilience* (*The Concept of Social Resilience*, Samuel Neaman Institute for Advanced Studies in Science and Technology, Working Paper, December 2005). She writes that like individual resilience, social resilience involves the "ability to withstand adversity and cope effectively with change."

In a paper in 2013 by Markus Keck and Patrick Sakdapolrak, they define social resilience as being comprised of three dimensions:

· 1. *Coping capacities*–the ability of social actors to cope with and overcome all kinds of adversities;

· 2. *Adaptive capacities*–their ability to learn from past experiences and adjust themselves to future challenges in their everyday lives;

· 3. *Transformative capacities*–their ability to craft sets of institutions that foster individual welfare and sustainable societal robustness towards future crises.

(academia.edu/3110553/What_is_Social_Resilience_Lessons_Learned_and_Ways_Forward)

Thus, with regards to terrorism, Waxman states, social resilience prevents terrorism from seriously disrupting the normal functioning of a society. It means that a targeted population is able to cope with the threat of terrorism and not be intimidated or demoralized by it.

I believe that the concept of "social resilience" is a key to overcoming demoralization and submission, especially if we can learn the coping, adaptive and transformative capacities identified by Markus Keck and Patrick Sakdapolrak. We have little choice: if we react to major terrorist attacks by appeasement, by striving to be nice to all Muslims, or by adopting a cultural Stockholm syndrome, or a guilt which turns into masochism or depression, this will cause us to lose the war declared against us.

> The concept of social resilience, therefore, helps explain why Israeli society was not demoralized by repeated terrorist attacks, despite the serious affects these attacks had on Israelis. Israeli-Jewish society demonstrated a high level of social resilience during the second Intifada. One factor that contributes to social resilience is social cohesion. Israeli-Jewish society is still very cohesive, notwithstanding its serious political, cultural, and social divisions. There is a strong sense of social solidarity among Israeli Jews. Although this sense of solidarity has declined over the years, it rises during times of external conflict (as mentioned earlier, this occurred during the second Intifada). Hence, war and terrorism bolster social cohesion in Israel, which helps it to cope with these violent episodes. Social trust is another factor behind social resilience. In Israel's case, the high level of trust that Israeli Jews have in the country's army and security services boosts their social resilience. During the second Intifada, the Israeli-Jewish public had confidence in the Israeli military and believed that quick and effective actions were being taken against Palestinian militant groups that were carrying out terrorist attacks (at least during the tenure of the Sharon government). In this respect, Israel's counter-terror actions helped prevent Israeli society from becoming demoralized. Finally, Israelis Jews are very patriotic—this is most apparent in their high level of willingness to perform military service—which also contributes to their social resilience.

Query whether a compulsory military draft in America would aid in social cohesion and patriotism and enable the country's youth to have a better sense of purpose and responsibility. One can suggest that the drafted could specialize in national security work, and those with a talent for computers, could be trained in intelligence and find skills that would later be transferable to the private sector. One can also suggest that if fewer soldiers are being bogged down in Middle Eastern Muslim against Muslim wars, and more were seen to be directly protecting the home front including airports, train stations, malls, concerts, etc., the attitude of Americans to their military would improve. These are the sorts of questions that must be asked in these times, when there really is a war against the West.

I think we have to study how the West can best become inured to prolonged terrorism. Research indicates that the more resilient a society is, the less it will be demoralized by terrorism. Research on strengthening social resilience is one way to defeat terrorism as a winning strategy. Right now, America, with its terrible split between pro-Trump and anti-Trump mentalities, and its lack of respect between Left and Right with its eroding middle ground, is losing social resilience.

And a nation with good social resilience will resist the self-defeating strategies of appeasement and dysfunctionality.

States Waxman:

> Although terrorist attacks do succeed in causing mass fear and anxiety, they do not necessarily undermine a society's morale and willpower. Terrorism tests a society's unity and resolve. Israeli society essentially passed that test in the second Intifada due to its social resilience. As such, it offers a useful example that other societies faced with the threat of terrorism can potentially learn from.

This is a War. Either we submit to Islamism or Islamism submits to us. Those within Islam will also have to decide whether submission to Allah means no submission to western liberties. We cannot share our sovereignty with those Muslims who continue to submit to the Islamists.

In March 2017 we witnessed a future where Islamist states with considerable diaspora in Western countries seek to influence the diaspora Muslims who are allowed to cast votes for elections or referenda back home. The *Associated Press* reported on March 22, that Turkish President Recep Tayyip Erdogan ramped up his anti-European rhetoric warning that the safety of Western citizens could be in peril if European nations persist in what he described as arrogant conduct.

Erdogan's remarks came amid tension over Dutch and German restrictions on Turkish officials who tried to campaign for diaspora votes ahead of an April 16 referendum on expanding the powers of the Turkish presidency.

European countries are therefore now getting resistance from Islamist states when they try to assert their sovereignty over Muslim citizens. Erdogan's threatening statements were, in my opinion, scandalous:

"Turkey is not a country that can be pushed and shoved, whose honour can be toyed with, whose ministers can be ousted, whose citizens can be dragged on the ground," Erdogan said. "These developments are being watched in all corners of the world," he said. **"If you continue this way, tomorrow no European, no Westerner anywhere in the world will be able to step onto the streets safely, with peace of mind."** [my emphasis]"

Erdogan was also quoted by Russell Goldman of the *New York Times* on March 17, 2017 as telling Turkish Muslims in Europe: "Go live in better neighborhoods. Drive the best cars. Live in the best houses. Make not three, but five children. Because you are the future of Europe. That will be the best response to the injustices against you."

Turkey is a NATO member country with significant numbers of Western residents and visitors. However Erdogan, whether or not he was trying to campaign for nationalist Islamist votes, actually went to the extent of saying the European Union was provoking "a struggle between the cross and crescent," casting the tension as a dispute between the West and Islam.

I suggest that this is a new and larger danger than what we have seen before. It is a significant increase in Islamist attempts to hurt western governments' sovereignty over their Muslim citizens, and if it continues, will result in major conflict. Europe must stand up to the Islamists; otherwise continued Muslim immigration will in fact create "Eurabia" with threats both from non-state terrorist organizations and, as with Erdogan, Islamist states. It is perhaps time to eject Turkey from NATO. Turkey has turned itself from a secular Muslim state into an Islamist state, and it is no surprise to see the beginnings of its participation in the Islamist war against the West. There must be clearly-drawn lines in the sand with respect to Islamist states' actions and words to Western Muslims.

We must persuade the women, the blacks, and the leftists who think Trump is the enemy that it is the Islamists who are the enemy. A country with the divisions in its body politic resulting from the 2016 American election will have a hard time resisting the submission that the Islamists want. The best thing Americans can do is to put aside their conflicts and show a resolve to win the war. Americans can still wage fierce political campaigns, but in the end, they must stop taking steps meant to damage the morale of the country.

To me, one of the major issues faced by our intellectuals is their attempt to posit grand intellectual movements crossing political theory, art, literature and even architecture. For students of philosophy, there seems a never ending supply of commentary about modernism, postmodernism and now *post-postmodernism*.

As a real estate developer specializing in the renovation of unused heritage institutional buildings into affordable rental housing for low income working people and unused factories into affordable retail/commercial, cultural and artisanal space, I view myself as a post-postmodern developer; that is, I seek to re-use and save heritage buildings with classic architecture as opposed to constructing postmodern towers of glass and steel. Moreover, my aim in each project is "double bottom line" in that each project must have one bottom line of making money (although we are satisfied to make less than single bottom line developers) and another bottom line of affordability and sustainability as social justice or cultural enhancement. Since the philosophical theorists seem to find the intellectual movements to cross disciplines and areas, can we say that we are advocates, in our study of ideologies, of a reaction to postmodernism or what might be called a post-postmodernism?

In my real estate development career, I have sought to reintroduce, to the extent I am able, values into esthetics.

That is not always well received. For example, the baby-boomers who have ridden Vancouver's property boom to riches, did not react well to my critique of social justice and values, entitled *Exploring Vancouverism: The Political Culture of Canada's Lotus Land*. (However, their children loved it.)

There seems to be a recognition that postmodernism, especially that part contaminated by moral relativism, is on the wane. Intellectuals are in the early stages of deciding what it is that has replaced it and what to call it. We are not here interested in the complete discussion of the intellectuals, but it is interesting to see how our analysis fits in the wider debate.

A good summary is found in the work of theologian Kyle Roberts (patheos.com/blogs/unsystematictheology/2016/07/we-are-witnes-

sing-the-end-of-postmodernism-and-the-beginning-of-post-postmo-
dernism/)

Modernism, Roberts summarizes, involved the quest for universals,
for trans-cultural knowledge, for "absolute truth." Often utopian in
orientation, it was also often elitist and racist (and socialist) in its
visions of what utopia looks like. Modernists were optimistic about
conquering the world and its problems and believed they were
(however slowly but surely) progressing toward the positive climax of
history.

Roberts argues that with WWI and WWII, all this utopianism
ended and the positive (and naive) assumptions about human nature
were one casualty. Bombs and concentration camps revealed that the
world was not getting better, but much worse.

Modernity, says Roberts had been based on an optimism for
humanity's direction and goal, absolute Truth over localized,
standpoints on truth; the pragmatics and supposed neutrality of
technology over suspicion about its uses; individual rationality over
authority (like that of religion and metaphysics), and the elimination
of mysticism in favor of science and reason.

Then, from the post-war years up to recent times,
"Postmodernism was the age of skepticism, of deconstruction, of
epistemic humility (how can we *know* anything, really?), and of the
heightening of awareness of those society has left on the margins.
Technology was no longer seen as neutral and its use in the service of
global capitalism was deeply noticed."

Roberts cites Jean-Francois Lyotard's *The Postmodern Condition*
(1979) as understanding that this was the end of a unifying,
underlying "grand-story," or narrative that would justify knowledge,
behavior, and action. Postmodernity was "incredulity toward the
meta-narrative," and this incredulity, or radical skepticism, would
effect the emergence of discrete, distinct communities each with a
shared "language game," a way of seeing the world which only *that
community* could access.

In theory a postmodernism (of our intellectuals and other
cultural actors) was not dangerous because these communities,
were still largely governed by a sense of humility. They had *their*
truth, *their* morality, *their* values, *their* nation, *their* politics, *their*

god. But who was to say that *theirs* was better than *yours*? Or that *yours* was better than *theirs*? Let us live our lives, believe and practice our religion, and have our morality: you can have yours. Let's agree to disagree.

The postmodern world was inherently susceptible, then, to a moral relativism. Even worse (if there is such a thing), the intellectuals assumed that they were representative of all good people everywhere, and did not understand the brewing storm soon to hit of a militant and supremacist radical Islam, which utilized the postmodern expectation of humility as a cover for its outer-directed jihad and movement to create a world-wide caliphate.

Roberts is representative of philosophers, including Christian theologians, who understand that sometime around 2016, political correctness and the universality of Globalism began to be seriously challenged. The problem is so many have let postmodernism lead to, or reflect, a cultural relativism that they can only see an opposition to postmodernism as an "intensified nationalism, an angry tribalism/localism, and an open disregard for the well-being of anyone outside "my" group, or my language-game."

Thus, someone like Roberts, can say that he has:

> long thought of postmodernism as, at its core, a *deep toleration for difference and otherness*

and that:

> this toleration of otherness is turning into an intensified, angry *rejection of difference and otherness* and the attempt to overcome the problem of difference, not by rational argument or toleration, but by the sheer exertion of power, by the politics of fear, and by a polemics steeped in rhetoric but devoid of substance ... Post-postmodernism is tribalism to the extreme and with gloves off.

And so for Roberts, *post*-postmodernism does not reflect the epistemic humility which he sees in postmodernism, but rather a hardened certainty. He contends that, "In the post-postmodern mood, there may be a recognition that we don't have the Absolute Truth, *but that doesn't make any difference, because we don't care.*" (Query whether Trump as a post-postmodern actually learned that Power is the goal from a postmodern like Barack Obama.) Has fear of certainty replaced fear of evil?

This is where we differ: Roberts sees postmodern toleration as a good. I see postmodern toleration as so extreme that it has morphed into an ideology, a way of seeing the world, an excess of toleration towards those who are illiberal and intolerant, in the name of epistemic humility. Accordingly, my optimism is for a post-postmodern world to reject the various ideologies that I have identified as springing out of tolerism and postmodernism. I hope to see post-postmodernism learn the real lesson of Auschwitz that post-modernism failed to understand. Auschwitz does not stand for bringing about a humble tolerance of differences, but for courage in the face of evil and steadfastness in understanding when our enemy is so evil that it necessitates us doing everything possible and even taking up arms as a last resort to stop the evil.

Postmodern competitions for victimhood have taken us to a sometimes silly result. Remember that Michelle Obama, whose life consisted of being helped by affirmative action, who attended Princeton, then Harvard Law School, and got a very highly paid large law firm position and then a very high paying public sector job, was still so influenced by Black Victimhood that she actually stated during her husband's first election campaign, "For the first time in my adult life, I am really proud of my country because it feels like hope is finally making a comeback."

A post-postmodern will understand that the worst Islamophobia comes at the hands of other Muslims. How can anyone looking at contemporary Syria, Iraq, Afghanistan or Yemen, fail to understand that? A post-postmodern will understand that we have every right, and duty, to defeat Islamism not only for our benefit, but for the sake of everyday Muslims who would benefit from freedom. A post-postmodern would go back to the time in American history before postmodernism and be unafraid in discussions with the postmodern to quote the statement by Barry Goldwater in his acceptance speech as the 1963 Republican candidate for president: "I would remind you that extremism in the defense of liberty is no vice! And let me remind you also that moderation in the pursuit of justice is no virtue!"

The sooner we understand the ideologies that lead us from tolerism to submission to the enemy, and the sooner that we can have a moral replacement to postmodernism, and the sooner we follow the Israeli example of resistance, patriotism and social cohesion as a way to build social resilience, the sooner we can reverse our losses and start winning this war. In fact, studies show that the terrorism against Israel has been spectacularly unsuccessful with respect to breaking the resolve of the Israelis. But terrorism against the West has been spectacularly successful, such as the Madrid rail bombings that changed the result of the Spanish elections, or 9/11 which bizarrely increased Islamophilia rather than Islamophobia. We need to show the terrorists that they will be the losers when it comes to terrorism.

How to create the social resilience necessary to strengthen our citizens for the struggle ahead is surely a difficult question. But I am certain that unless we understand, and overcome, the negative ideologies, starting with tolerism, discussed in this book, we shall have little chance of ultimate victory.

Social resilience and social cohesion cannot emanate from the ideologies of denialism, inclusive diversity, cultural relativism, Trumpophobia, empathy, undeserved respect, pacifism, resistance, declinism, postmodernism, and Islamistphilia. Our media, especially, must be educated on the nature of these ideologies, which so often infuse the writing in their pages, without an understanding of the context thereby created. There can be no fair press, or free press, when a press is captured by one or a few ideologies, and bans and boycotts competing ideologies. There can be no good education in our schools and universities without a study and appreciation of the role of ideologies in our post-postmodern world.

The first step is reversing the Obama era's refusal to face and name the enemy. The second step is understanding that this is a war, but if we stick together and develop social resilience, we can win this war. The third step is to understand what ideologies are damaging our ability to win the war. The fourth step is to differentiate on the one hand, between the Islamists and their supporters, and on the other hand, those Muslims willing to reform their religion's compatibility with our justice system and our liberal democracy as a precondition to joining the center of our societies rather than the margins. The final step is to teach our children (after teaching the teachers) that we are the good guys, that the world has bad guys, and that we cannot tolerate a descent into submission to the bad guys.

POSTSCRIPT: WAR AND REPRESSION

The Wilsonian Problem of Civil Liberties During War

In this postscript we attempt to start a discussion, firstly about "propaganda" and, secondly, on the proper course of action, as it relates to civil liberties and due process, should the West ever find itself in an active war against Islamism and its state sponsors (although that war may well have been started already). What is the historical record during wartime, and what type of actions will we in the liberal West, decide to undertake?

There is a fine line between politics and propaganda, especially when the media supports the propaganda, for one reason or another. Whether it was the pro-war and anti-enemy "aliens" media propaganda during the United States entry into World War 1 under Woodrow Wilson, or the pro-Islamic propaganda by the media under Obama, it is natural for media to cross the line between responsible journalism and outright propaganda: "Natural" but not "proper."

There is also a fine line between truth and lies, as we note from Barack Obama's remarks in December 2016 when he bragged that "in the last eight years, no foreign terrorist organization has successfully executed an attack on our homeland that was directed from overseas."

Carlos Garcia at *Theblaze.com* stated that:

> Clearly there have been terrorist attacks on the American homeland that could be considered as ordered by the Islamic State, just not directly coordinated. The San Bernardino, California, terror attack might not have been directly ordered by ISIS, but the attackers specifically pledged allegiance to the terror group, and their tactics were those encouraged and propagated by ISIS. Obama specifically said that the Orlando, Florida, terror attack was not "directed" by ISIS — it's almost as if he was preparing

the narrative on each attack just so that he could make this claim.

What if an organization, with the support and encouragement of its government, or that government itself, incites its people to hate America, to take violent steps against America and other western countries, in pursuit of jihad and a world-wide caliphate and Sharia law? Is that not a War against America, its civil liberties and its values? I think Obama was being disingenuous. There is an Islamist War against the West, Obama's denialism, notwithstanding.

In the face of such threats, assuming they constitute a war, where do we draw the line between fighting against the Islamists, on the one side, and, on the other, protecting the civil liberties of Muslims living peacefully in the West—and not inciting for Sharia law, jihad, a separatist caliphate and against western values and laws?

Obviously, a study of America during World Wars 1 and 2 causes us much concern for how we might handle a coordinated response or war against the Islamists. I think the time for this discussion is now, not the day after the next 9/11. Accordingly, in this Postscript, I attempt to summarize the legal and cultural attempts to deal with "enemy aliens" and others deemed "disloyal" during these crucial wars. We must study the facts, difficult as they may be, because with the growth of Islamism, and the Islamic State, and the increasing military strength of Iran (as a consequence of Obama's sad agreement allowing the Iranians to perfect the nuclear bomb), we must be ready the next time a war is started, to determine how we can fairly, and with *due process*, deal with those who are actually enemies and actually pose a threat. If we are frozen by indecision and confused about how a liberal democracy can defend itself, with due process, and without undue repression, the Islamists may find democracy's Achilles' heel.

Woodrow Wilson during 1914 to the spring of 1917 steered Americans into a supposedly neutral position in the War between Germany and the Austro-Hungarian Empire on the one side, and Britain, France and Russia, on the other. In fact, the United States economy was heavily involved in manufacturing product for the British war effort and eventually the attacks on the American merchant marine by German submarines and the long stalemate of a brutal war by two sides dug into trenches without making progress, drew America into the War.

Wilson hoped that, by becoming decisive in the winning of the War, America could help frame a peace, according to Wilson's 14 point plan, which included his plan for a "League of Nations" to help avoid such future barbarian conflicts by creating a framework for diplomacy.

Unfortunately, Wilson could not even sell the concept to his own Congress. Moreover, the British and French need to extract some revenge on Germany for the deaths of so many of their young men, imposed such draconian terms on Germany, including reparations, that the seeds for the development of the Nazi party seemed to have been planted.

On April 6, 1917, President Woodrow Wilson told Congress, that his declaration of war was meant to embark upon a crusade to "make the world safe for democracy." His noble intentions, however, were soon followed by new laws on the homefront meant to quell all opposition to the War and protect the country from the "sedition" of German immigrants and any others who were perceived to be disloyal. This included not just German-Americans, but socialists, pacifists, and even the leadership of the Industrial Workers of the World, who opposed this intervention. Congress enacted laws to curtail the constitutionally guaranteed freedoms of speech and press, at the same time as the government embarked on a concerted propaganda campaign to "sell" a war to its citizens.

According to *World War I Propaganda and Civil Liberties, 1917-1918* (ic.galegroup) the administration decided that in order to mobilize the citizenry behind a War that did not involve a direct attack on the nation by the enemy, a massive campaign of propaganda was needed. Wilson established the Committee on Public Information (CPI), under the leadership of George Creel. The Committee's job was to convince wavering citizens that the war was a righteous one and to educate all Americans about American war aims. With the help of over 100,000 artists, writers, actors and scholars, the war against the evil "Huns" was sold to the American people, and unlike later wars, some of the wealthiest and most educated young men were the first to enlist. Censorship of the press was not necessary as it voluntarily complied with the government's wishes, and while the CPI was never given powers of censorship, the illusion that it had the power of such was enough to bring the media into compliance.

Eventually in the early summer of 1917, the *Espionage Act* was passed, giving the government authority to limit the rights of speech and the press. The attack on civil liberties in wartime began to grow.

Title I, Section 3, of the *Espionage Act* made it a crime to make false reports which would aid the enemy, incite rebellion among the armed forces, or obstruct recruiting or the draft. Then, another law, in May, 1918, the *Sedition Act* provided penalties of up to ten thousand dollars and twenty years imprisonment for the willful writing, utterance, or publication of material abusing the government, showing contempt for the Constitution, inciting others to resist the government, supporting the enemy, or hindering production of war matériel. Under this law, it was unnecessary to prove that the language in question had affected anyone or had produced injurious consequences. In addition, the Postmaster General was empowered to deny use of the mails to anyone who, in his opinion, used them to violate the act.

There also grew up some "populist" super-patriotic volunteer organizations dedicated to spreading propaganda and to discovering alleged traitors, saboteurs, and slackers. The super-patriotic volunteers, encouraged by the Creel Committee's propaganda, produced a wave of war hysteria which harmed thousands of innocent citizens. This hysteria helped to create conditions leading to such postwar emotional outbursts as the Red Scare and the race riots of 1919-1920. Sadly, the black Americans who, by serving their country so nobly in the fields of France, should have returned to a newfound respect, found an illiberal America as racist as ever.

Then, in World War 2, the United States again was late in entering the War, and it took the attack on Pearl Harbor by the Japanese to wake up the Americans. With the benefit of hindsight, we wish that Americans had acted earlier to stop a Nazi regime, allied with Japanese and Italians and others, and pledging to kill all Jews and many others, in an era where weapons development would soon make War an existential threat to the entire world. Again, America was faced with the concern of "enemy aliens."

An excellent resource about the forced removal of Japanese Americans for purposes of confinement in War Relocation Authority (WRA) camps is the internet site, *encyclopedia.densho.org/*.

According to *History.com:*

> Two months after the Japanese bombing of Pearl Harbor, U.S. President Franklin D. Roosevelt signed Executive Order 9066 ordering all Japanese-Americans to evacuate the West Coast. This resulted in the relocation of approximately 120,000 people, many of whom were American citizens, to one of 10 internment camps located across the country. Traditional family structure was upended within the camp, as American-born children were solely allowed to hold positions of authority. Some Japanese-American citizens of were allowed to return to the West Coast beginning in 1945, and the last camp closed in March 1946. In 1988, Congress awarded restitution payments to each survivor of the camps.

The writers of *History.com* argue that:

> The relocation of Japanese-Americans into internment camps during World War II was one of the most flagrant violations of civil liberties in American history. According to the census of 1940, 127,000 persons of Japanese ancestry lived in the United States, the majority on the West Coast. One-third had been born in Japan, and in some states could not own land, be naturalized as citizens, or vote. After Japan bombed Pearl Harbor in December 1941, rumors spread, fueled by race prejudice, of a plot among Japanese-Americans to sabotage the war effort. In early 1942, the Roosevelt administration was pressured to remove persons of Japanese ancestry from the West Coast by farmers seeking to eliminate Japanese competition, a public fearing sabotage, politicians hoping to gain by standing against an unpopular group, and military authorities.
>
> On February 19, 1942, Roosevelt signed Executive Order 9066, which forced all Japanese-Americans, regardless of loyalty or citizenship, to evacuate the West Coast. Many were forced to sell their property at a severe loss before departure. Social problems beset the internees: older Issei (immigrants) were deprived of their traditional respect when their children, the Nisei (American-born), were alone permitted authority positions within the camps. 5,589 Nisei renounced their American citizenship, although a federal judge later ruled that renunciations made behind barbed

wire were void. Some 3,600 Japanese-Americans entered the armed forces from the camps, as did 22,000 others who lived in Hawaii or outside the relocation zone. The famous all-Japanese 442nd Regimental Combat Team won numerous decorations for its deeds in Italy and Germany.

The Supreme Court upheld the legality of the relocation order in *Hirabayashi* v. *United States* and *Korematsu* v. *United States*. Early in 1945, Japanese-American citizens of undisputed loyalty were allowed to return to the West Coast, but not until March 1946 was the last camp closed. A 1948 law provided for reimbursement for property losses by those interned. In 1988, Congress awarded restitution payments of twenty thousand dollars to each survivor of the camps; it is estimated that about 73,000 persons will eventually receive this compensation for the violation of their liberties.

Also detained were approximately 11,500 people of German ancestry and three thousand people of Italian ancestry, many of whom were United States citizens. These detainees were housed in Justice Department and army camps scattered across the country.

Wikipedia has summarized the detentions as follows:

At the time of WWII, the United States had a large population of ethnic Germans. Among residents of the USA in 1940, more than 1.2 million persons had been born in Germany, 5 million had two native-German parents, and 6 million had one native-German parent. Many more had distant German ancestry. During WWII, the United States detained at least 11,000 ethnic Germans, overwhelmingly German nationals. The government examined the cases of German nationals individually, and detained relatively few in internment camps run by the Department of Justice, as related to its responsibilities under the Alien and Sedition Acts. To a much lesser extent, some ethnic German US citizens were classified as suspect after due process and also detained. Similarly, a small proportion of Italian nationals and Italian Americans were interned in relation to their total population in the US. The United States had allowed immigrants from both Germany and Italy to become naturalized citizens, which many had done by then.

In the early 21st century, Congress considered legislation to study treatment of European Americans during WWII, but it did not pass the House of Representatives. Activists and historians have identified certain injustices against these groups.

Britain and Canada both detained Germans but many of those detained were actually German Jews.

British Prime Minister Winston Churchill "was worried there could be spies among the Jews, and he asked Canada and Australia to house them as internees," according to a report in the *Toronto Star*, cited in a story by Michael Kaminer in the August 8, 2013 internet edition of *Forward.com*.

Kaminer writes that

> Canada's immigration minister at the time, Frederick Charles Blair, also believed "an international Jewish conspiracy was trying to skirt Canadian immigration policies by sneaking the refugees into the country," according to JTA. And anti-Semitic attitudes among Canada's Protestant elite had hardened in the run-up to World War II.

Kaminer writes of one camp holding 700 Jews in rural New Brunswick in Canada.

Canada's treatment of Japanese Canadians living in the western province of British Columbia, was also scandalous. According to the *Canadian Encyclopedia* (thecanadianencyclopedia.ca/en/article/Jap-anese-internment-banished-and-beyond-tears-feature/):

> Beginning in early 1942, the Canadian government detained and dispossessed the vast majority of people of Japanese descent living in British Columbia. They were interned for the rest of the Second World War, during which time their homes and businesses were sold by the government in order to pay for their detention.
>
> Just over 90 per cent of Japanese Canadians — some 21,000 people — were uprooted during the war. The majority were Canadian citizens by birth.

As to Britain and its detention of Germans, a study was done by *BBC*. (bbc.co.uk/history/ww2peopleswar/timeline/factfiles/nonflash/a6651858.shtml):

> At the outbreak of war there were around 80,000 potential enemy aliens in Britain who, it was feared, could be spies, or willing to assist Britain's enemies in the event of an invasion. All Germans and Austrians over the age of 16 were called before special tribunals and were divided into one of three groups:
> · 'A'-high security risks, numbering just under 600, who were immediately interned;

· 'B'-'doubtful cases', numbering around 6,500, who were supervised and subject to restrictions;

· 'C'-'no security risk', numbering around 64,000, who were left at liberty. More than 55,000 of category 'C' were recognised as refugees from Nazi oppression. The vast majority of these were Jewish.

The situation began to change in the spring of 1940. The failure of the Norwegian campaign led to an outbreak of spy fever and agitation against enemy aliens. More and more Germans and Austrians were rounded up. Italians were also included, even though Britain was not at war with Italy until June. When Italy and Britain did go to war, there were at least 19,000 Italians in Britain, and Churchill ordered they all be rounded up. This was despite the fact that most of them had lived in Britain for decades.

Thousands of Germans, Austrians and Italians were sent to camps set up at racecourses and incomplete housing estates, such as Huyton outside Liverpool. The majority were interned on the Isle of Man, where internment camps had also been set up in World War One. Facilities were basic, but it was boredom that was the greatest enemy. Internees organised educational and artistic projects, including lectures, concerts and camp newspapers. At first married women were not allowed into the camps to see their husbands, but by August 1940 visits were permitted, and a family camp was established in late 1941.

That many of the "enemy aliens" were Jewish refugees and therefore hardly likely to be sympathetic to the Nazis, was a complication no one bothered to try and unravel—they were still treated as German and Austrian nationals. In one Isle of Man camp over 80 per cent of the internees were Jewish refugees.

The purpose of our survey of the American, British and Canadian treatment of those they perceived to be, by birth or otherwise, sympathetic to the enemy, is meant to open up to discussion a topic which has been relegated to the past, but is most important to review, in the event of a future war.

We have, in this book, sought to differentiate the Islamists as true enemies of our Western values and freedoms. We have concluded that Muslims who do not support violent jihad, imposition of Sharia law, and a world-wide caliphate, and support Western values and freedoms, even when they conflict with historical Muslim values, should be welcomed and supported in their quest for peaceful abode in our western nations. But, as to those who give active support to the Islamists, allow them to dominate their mosques, organizations and schools, they must be warned that a choice has to be made. They must take the responsibility to reform their religion to ostracize the radicals, the Islamists, and cleanse their mosques, schools and political and cultural organizations of the people who have made themselves into the enemy of the West.

The Islamists should be treated as the enemies they are: deportation, detention and such, after due process, should be their future. We must be careful to give them the due process, and the benefit of law that they never give to any of their victims, be they of other religions or even Muslims who are the most common victims of the Islamists, as we see in such places as Syria.

It is an enormous challenge to defeat the Islamists without harming the civil liberties of the average Muslim. And yet, in return for partaking of life in the economically and culturally rich Western nations, the average Muslim must take sides and must repudiate the values of the Islamists and embrace the values of the West, even as they worship their God. Indeed, this may require some reforms in the realm of religion, which we normally do not seek; however, when the Muslim religion has become a tool of fanatic anti-liberal and violent organization(s), it is up to the members of that religion to rid themselves of the fanatics. If they don't do it, they will leave it up to outsiders to do.

There are difficult decisions to be made. For example, is the Muslim Students' Association an associate of the Muslim Brotherhood, financed by Muslim Brotherhood people in Qatar? Should we therefore try to help moderate Muslims replace the MSA with a different university organization pledged to accept Western values, and pledged not to participate in threatening talk at universities aimed towards Jews who support the peaceful existence of the historical Jewish homeland, Israel? Should we object to Saudi Wahabist financing of new mosques in the West, and the staffing of them by imams, schooled entirely in Saudi Arabia or Egypt without any understanding of western values?

The questions here raised, in the context of understanding our historical record, are very difficult to answer. We do not want to make the mistakes that Woodrow Wilson made. We do however want to keep our democratic freedoms; we cannot control what Muslims choose to do in their majority Muslim nations. We must not lose control of what people do in our liberal democracy, especially those who have come here for a life impossible to lead in their nations of origin.

In this chapter, we have reviewed the all-too-often tendency to respond to war with repression. Studying and debating what should be our proper responses, and how much money and effort we should spend to provide due process to anyone we deprive of our liberties, are extremely important. I welcome the debate that should follow.

So many have worked hard for our liberal democracies; many died for our liberal democracies. It is now up to us to design a framework to allow us to pass on to the next generation the liberties given to us by the previous generation. We must not submit to any other; accordingly, this book is meant to open up the dialogue on the problems herein described and how we can go about ensuring the victory of liberal values, with Muslims in a partnership for this end, rather than fall victim to submission to the evil Islamists, and the ideologies that are conducing to that submission.

SOME DEFINITIONS

IDEOLOGY: *Merriam-Webster* defines it as:

a : a systematic body of concepts especially about human life or culture

b : a manner or the content of thinking characteristic of an individual, group, or culture

c : the integrated assertions, theories and aims that constitute a sociopolitical program

Ideology in its most powerful form is hidden from the view of the person who submits to it. Once it can be clearly perceived it effectively loses its power of social control; obversely, to believe oneself to be non-ideological is actually equivalent to being driven primarily by ideology.

No matter which orthodoxy we may live under, Slovenian philosopher Slavoj Žižek explains, we usually enjoy our ideology, and that is part of its function. Paradoxically, it hurts to step outside of it and examine it critically; by default we tend to resist seeing the world from any angle other than the one fed to us. (*How ideology seduces us – and how we can (try to) escape it* by Yosef Brody quoting Slovenian psychoanalytic philosopher Slavoj Žižek Wednesday, November 28, *Truth-out.org*)

SUBMISSION: the action or fact of accepting or yielding to a superior force or to the will or authority of another person or to the Divine.

TOLERISM: Tolerism is my term for an excessive tolerance, in fact a leniency, for the intolerant and unsupportable views that threaten our very freedoms. It has become an ideology for those who hold tolerance to be a higher virtue than justice and human rights. Tolerism is the skill in consuming massive quantities of political correctness, and moral and cultural relativism, without displaying the obvious signs of the drunken leniency toward, and even taking pleasure in, the slow ascendancy of Islamist values of terrorism, breach of human rights, and attempted reversals of the wonderful liberties and advances made in western societies, where church and state have been successfully separated, and an enormous degree of freedom reigns.

Made in the USA
San Bernardino, CA
17 February 2018